Wheelwrights an
Picturesque De
Manufactures &

William Harding House (No. 23 Walton Road, Walton). This former farmhouse was for many years the Harding family residence. It was rebuilt in 1728-30, but some of the interior beams are of earlier date. It is now part of Park School.

Apprenticing in a Market Town

The Story of William Harding's
Charity, Aylesbury, 1719-2000

Best wishes & thinking you,

Mike Griffin

Betty Foster   *Roger Evans.*

Penni Thorne

Bill Chapple,   *Anne Brookes*

L. Shelihn

Apprenticing in a Market Town

*The Story of William Harding's
Charity, Aylesbury, 1719-2000*

Hugh Hanley

Phillimore

2005

Published by
PHILLIMORE & CO. LTD
Shopwyke Manor Barn, Chichester, West Sussex, England

© Hugh Hanley, 2005

ISBN 1 86077 324 9

Printed and bound in Great Britain by
ANTONY ROWE LTD
Chippenham, Wiltshire

Contents

List of Illustrations

Colour Plates (between pages 52/3)

Acknowledgements

I am indebted to Roger Bettridge for reading the draft text and thus saving me from many typographical and other errors; he is not responsible for any that remain. Dr John Broad of London Metropolitan University kindly read earlier versions of chapters 3-8 and made a number of helpful comments and suggestions. John R. Millburn, Alan Dell, Barbara Willis and Clifford Webb generously shared information about individuals. Dr David Thorpe compiled additional statistics of Buckinghamshire apprentices in the 1891 census for my benefit. My thanks to them and to the many others who helped in various ways, including Susanne Spinks of Parrott & Coales, John Vince, Jim McKay and, not least, the staffs of the Centre for Buckinghamshire Studies and the County Museum.

The Trustees of William Harding's Charity wish to thank the following individuals and institutions for providing copies of photographs and other illustrations and for granting permission to reproduce them: Michael Farley (colour plates IV-VII and nos 4-10, 14, 17, 18, 29, 30, 33, 34, 37, 38); Bernard Hall (frontispiece and no. 39); Buckinghamshire County Museum (I, III); *Bucks Herald* (II, IX); Queens Park Centre (VIII); Buckinghamshire Archaeological Society (13 and cover illustration); Centre for Buckinghamshire Studies (1, 3, 11, 12, 15, 16, 19, 23, 24, 25-8, 31, 32, 35); The National Archives (2); John Vince (20 and endpapers); Alan Dell (21); Philip Roche (36); Nick Carter and The Aylesbury Society (40); and Parrott & Coales (22).

Foreword

In the year 2004 the *Bucks Herald* called on its readership to nominate 'Aylesbury's most famous citizen' and nobody nominated William Harding. Not surprising really, as nobody knew him personally, but no one has had a greater influence on education in Aylesbury than Mr Harding.

The Trustees of the William Harding Charity decided to commission Hugh Hanley to write this history of the Man and the Charity. We are most grateful to Mr Hanley for all the hours of research and study that he has devoted to the production of this most interesting account of William Harding's life and the success of the Charity.

Harding's Charity has been administered for many years by Messrs Parrott & Coales, Solicitors, and now is under the watchful eye of Mr John Leggett, the senior partner. He is ably assisted by Mrs Sue Spinks and Mrs Doudja Godleman. I do not know when Parrott & Coales first took on this role, but no doubt the book will tell me.

Fortunately, the Harding farmhouse on the edge of Walton Pond in Aylesbury survived a German landmine in the 1939-45 war. It also survived the bulldozers when it was decided to 'modernise' Aylesbury. The house is now used to accommodate the Sixth Form Centre of the Park School.

In an article in the *Times Educational Supplement* written by Harvey McGavin, Ruth Cutler, Park School's Headteacher in 2003, is quoted as saying, 'William Harding must have been a nice guy because he left a good buzz behind.' I get the same feeling when we hold Trustee meetings; the same 'good buzz' is present. A similar enthusiasm must have led our previous Trustees to make the wise investments in property of yesteryear which will provide funding for future projects as the 'New Aylesbury' expands in the years to come.

I still think that William Harding was Aylesbury's most famous citizen. When you have read this book, the question will be, 'Do you agree?'

MIKE GRIFFIN

PART ONE

THE FOUNDER AND HIS FAMILY

I

Founder's Kin
The Families of Harding and Jennings

1. The Hardings of Walton

William Harding's Charity, today easily the best known of Aylesbury's ancient charitable foundations, was founded under the terms of the will of an obscure yeoman of that name, who lived in what was then the hamlet of Walton and died in the year 1719. No personal papers have been traced, and the title deeds and legal documents relating to the family properties with which William endowed his Charity are missing from its records. Fortunately, however, a brief itemised receipt list of the deeds (including some documents dated post-1719) compiled in 1739, when they were released to one of the Charity's trustees and apparently never returned, is entered in the Charity's earliest record book.[1] Once arranged in chronological order, the entries in the list provide sufficient clues to enable us to trace William Harding's antecedents back as far as the late 16th century, which, as we shall see, is when the Hardings first settled in Walton. With the help of the list, too, some of the original documents have been identified in 'artificial' collections of miscellaneous deeds preserved by antiquarians and dealers.

The surname Harding is one of the commoner names indigenous to Buckinghamshire and is particularly associated with the southern, or Chiltern, part of the county, where it is resonant of religious nonconformity. The Hardings of Amersham and Chesham are known to have been active as Lollard heretics at least as far back as the 1460s. Thomas Harding of Chesham, who was burnt at the stake in 1532, has a place in Foxe's celebrated *Book of Martyrs*, first published in 1559, one of the most important propaganda works of the Protestant Reformation. The association with nonconformity continued after the Reformation, for, in the 17th century, many of the Hardings are known to have been Baptists.[2]

The first Harding entry in the Aylesbury parish register is dated 1592, more than a quarter of a century after the commencement of the register, but this is misleading, because references in surviving local community records show that – as in Amersham – the connection actually goes back to late medieval times, if not earlier. In the published 1522 muster roll for Buckinghamshire – which, in theory, covers all adult males – three Hardings are listed under Aylesbury,

3

The family of William Harding of Walton from 1562

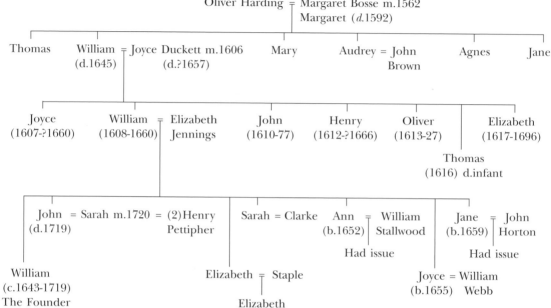

two under Bierton and one under Stoke Mandeville; Walton, however, which is separately assessed, has no Hardings listed.[3]

Few court rolls dating earlier than 1700 survive for the manor of Aylesbury, or, more accurately, Aylesbury with Bierton, for it extended into part of the adjoining parish (though not into Walton), but those that do exist contain some references to the Harding family and their property. In October 1548, for example, it is certified that William Harding has settled two virgates of land in Bierton, for which he pays an annual rent of 38 shillings to the lord of the manor, on Isabel, his wife, for her life and after her death on Robert Harding, his younger son, and his heirs.[4]

A virgate, or yardland, was the traditional family holding of a better-off peasant in medieval times, equivalent to 30 acres or less. In Aylesbury itself fragmentation over the years had made such units obsolete, but they survived in the more rural Bierton portion of the manor, as elsewhere. That William Harding was in a position to settle two such holdings on a younger son is evidence that the family was prosperous. Such differentiation in the size of landholdings had been apparent since the 14th century, and was given renewed impetus after 1520 by rising population, severe inflation and widespread economic expansion. The situation was particularly favourable to freeholders and those manorial tenants who, as in the manor of Aylesbury with Bierton, enjoyed fixed customary rents and freedom from arbitrary entry fines (sums payable to the lord on admission to a manorial holding). William is possibly the same William Harding who is listed under Bierton in the 1522 muster roll, where he is assessed at £1 6s. 8d. on goods.

No more court rolls are extant until 1557. In a court held in August of that year Henry Webb, one of the tenants, certified the surrender, made to himself 'out of court' by Thomas Harding, of a virgate of land called Rysons, in the fields of Bierton and Aylesbury, for which an annual rent of 14s. was payable to the lord. This land was to be held by Webb to the use of (in trust for) Oliver Harding. In a court held in November of the same year the death of Thomas Harding of Bierton was reported; he had died since the last court, which had been held in connection with another of his holdings, a freehold virgate in Bierton and Hulcott, for which a 'relief' or entry fine of 6s. 8d. was payable to the lord. The first of these two entries is particularly significant because Oliver Harding was the great-grandfather of William Harding, the founder of the Charity.[5]

Oliver Harding appears again as a juror in an action in a manorial court held in January 1558 to which Henry Webb was a party,[6] and once more in December 1560, when he was amerced (fined) 4d. for defaulting on his obligation to attend the court. After this there are no more court rolls, only a few manorial rentals. In a half-yearly rental for the manor of Aylesbury dated 1569, Oliver Harding is entered under Bierton as paying a rent of 7s. (presumably for Rysons) together with John Harding, who paid 8s. 4d., and 'the heirs of William Harding', paying 19s. 2d.; unfortunately, no details are given, but the rent payable for Oliver Harding's holding is the same as that due for Rysons. Some thirty years later, in c.1602, however, a manorial survey of Aylesbury shows Oliver Harding's only landholding in the manor to be a freehold piece of meadow called Spicers Hams, with an annual rent of six shillings, which was still in the family's possession in 1627,[7] after which nothing more is heard of it.

Meanwhile, Oliver Harding had married Margery Bosse at Bierton on 5 June 1562. The Bosse family of Bierton were minor gentry who acquired armorial status in this period. Their most distinguished representative was Oliver's contemporary, John Bosse, esquire, a leading local lawyer and justice of the peace and 'of the quorum' for the county. Bosse had purchased the small manor of Burleys in Stoke Mandeville in 1539, and he was named as one of the aldermen in Aylesbury's first, abortive, borough charter, which was granted by Queen Mary in 1554.[8] In terms of social status the alliance was a distinct step up for Oliver and it would have brought a useful dowry as well. We know that Oliver was still resident in Bierton at this time, because the baptism of Elizabeth, daughter of Oliver Harding, is entered in the register in April 1563, and later evidence indicates that either or both of the children named Audrey Harding and Thomas Harding, who were baptised in the following year and for whom no parentage is given, could have been – and probably were – his.

Between 1570 and c.1602, then, it seems that Oliver Harding had disposed of all his property in Bierton and had also become a parishioner of Aylesbury, for in 1592 the burial of Margaret, wife of Olaver [*sic*] Harding, is entered in the Aylesbury parish register; she was presumably his second wife. A few years later, too, Oliver Harding had the distinction of being one of nine 'men of good credit and conscience in the towns of Aylesbury and Hartwell', named as new 'feoffees', or trustees, of Bedford's Charity. He was confirmed as such in the local Act of Parliament passed for the Charity's re-formation in 1597. Founded by the will of John Bedford, who died in 1494, the charity's objects were the upkeep of the parish highways and the relief of the poor by means of an annual dole. As administrators of Aylesbury's wealthiest charitable trust, the nine 'incorporated surveyors of the highways' (their official title under the Act) enjoyed great patronage and prestige locally. This was augmented by the power vacuum created when the borough corporation, established under the 1554 charter, lapsed in the face of hostility from the Pakingtons, lords of the manor.[9]

How – and precisely when – had this transformation come about? The answer is provided by a conveyance, dated June 1582, from a certain 'Mr Fountain' of 'a house &c. in Walton' to Oliver Harding, followed by a further conveyance in March 1586 from Richard Fountain of a messuage (a house with outbuildings and land) and 110 acres of land in Walton fields, a substantial yeoman holding equivalent to three yardlands, and so considerably larger than Oliver's Bierton inheritance. This property was within the manor of Walton, which was completely separate from the manor of Aylesbury. It was to form the core of the Harding family patrimony from this time forward. It was not Oliver's only acquisition at this time, for in June 1578 he had purchased 25 acres of manorial demesne land in the parish of Aylesbury from John (later Sir John) Pakington (1549-1625), a courtier with an extravagant lifestyle to finance. This land was not in Walton, and it may have included the Spicers Hams previously mentioned; Oliver seems to have disposed of some or all of it by *c.*1602.

The Fountain family, from whom the principal purchases were made, were effectively lords of the manor of Walton by virtue of a lease for 90 years from the prebendary of Heydour-cum-Walton, to whose prebendal stall in the cathedral church of Lincoln it was attached. The lease, originally made to one Christopher Dighton in 1566, had been assigned three years later to John Fountain of Walton, gentleman. This John Fountain, who died in 1596, had been a feoffee of Bedford's Charity, as was his son and heir, Thomas, later of Hulcott. It is not known precisely where Richard Fountain, the vendor in 1586, fits into the family tree. Another Thomas Fountain, possibly nephew of Thomas Fountain of Hulcott, was to be MP for Wendover in the Long Parliament.[10]

At this time Walton was a hamlet situated within the parish of Aylesbury but outside the limits of the borough as defined in the 1554 charter. It occupied around a thousand acres of heavy clay soil and had its own open-field system which, unlike Aylesbury's, included extensive common meadows and pastures. Most of the latter adjoined the brook, which formed the boundary in the flood plain to the north-west of the hamlet. The village itself, though located only a few minutes walk away from Aylesbury market place, was a separate community.

Most of the houses were grouped around the green, mentioned in a deed of 1571, near the junction of the Wendover road and Akeman Street (the present A41), which, prior to the construction of the present High Street in 1826, performed a circuit through Walton to enter the town via Walton Street. In a survey of the diocese of Lincoln made in 1563 the number of families in Walton is given as 22, compared to 119 in the rest of Aylesbury.[11]

Oliver Harding died, still a widower, in May 1605, by which date he is likely to have been well over sixty. He had thus considerably exceeded the average life expectancy, which at this period was around forty years at birth; many of his descendants were to be equally long-lived. In his will, made on 16 March 1605,[12] he describes himself as of Walton, 'yeoman'. Bequests are made to two sons, Thomas, described as 'my eldest son', and William, and four surviving daughters, Agnes, Jane, Mary and Audrey. Only one of these, Audrey, described as the wife of the testator's son-in-law John Browne, is indicated as being married or having children.

Thomas is left only three acres of meadow ground at Dunsham (in the manor of Aylesbury), a well head there and three acres of open field arable in Walton. William, unusually for a younger son, receives the residue of all the testator's lands and goods not otherwise bequeathed and, even more surprisingly, is named as executor, with the obligation of bringing up and maintaining his sister Jane until her marriage. Agnes is to have £6 13s. 4d. at marriage and Jane £20; Jane is also to have two beasts (cows). Mary receives only a silver spoon. Silver spoons also go to John Browne and his wife and to Samuel Browne, the testator's godson, while John Browne's children are to have twelve pence apiece.

Charitable bequests are limited to 10s. to the poor of Aylesbury and Walton, 5s. for repairing Aylesbury church and – appropriately for a Bedford's feoffee – the same sum for repairing and maintaining the highways about Aylesbury and Walton. These latter bequests are preceded by the customary profession of faith couched in a conventional Protestant formula. William North the elder and Thomas Meryden are named as overseers of the will; both surnames are found in Walton later in the century.

It seems clear that Oliver had made his younger son William his principal heir and this impression is confirmed by a surviving deed of July 1604 relating to a house in Walton and lands in Walton fields.[13] By it Oliver conveys the reversion of all the property in Walton which he 'lately' purchased from John Fountain, gentleman, deceased, to John Browne and William North, of Stoke Mandeville, yeomen, in trust for William, reserving to his own use only 'his little cottage now in the occupation of Roger Samner, labourer', and six and a half acres of arable land. The consideration for the conveyance is stated to be 'the great good will natural love and fatherly affection' which he bears towards William Harding, his second son, and 'for the dutiful service and obedience of him the said William Harding unto the said Oliver Harding'. The inescapable implication is that his elder son Thomas had not shown himself equally dutiful.

Thomas's name does not reappear in the parish register after this, though he purchased two acres in Walton in 1609 and three and a half acres at Dunsham in 1623. William, on the other hand, married in February 1606, less than a year after his father's death, his bride being a certain Joyce Duckett, whose origins are obscure. The parish register shows seven children, five sons and two daughters, of William Harding, all born between 1607 and 1617. Two of the sons, Oliver and Thomas, died in infancy, leaving five surviving children, namely Joyce (baptised 1607), William (1608), John (1610) Henry (1612) and Elizabeth (1617). Remarkably, the evidence suggests that only one of these, William, the heir and the founder's grandfather, was to marry and have children.

William Harding did not replace his father as a feoffee of Bedford's Charity, but it is possible that he may have become one later, for the 1739 list of deeds includes a lease of lands in Walton made by William Harding and 'the Feoffees' in 1638. Previously to this, in 1625, he was one of the three assessors named in a surviving tax return for Walton which only 22 people were sufficiently affluent to be liable to pay. Sixteen of these were assessed on their lands, of whom Jeffrey Bampton paid 16s., Henry Bampton and William Bampton paid 8s. each and the rest a uniform 4s. apiece. William was one of the six assessed on their goods, being liable for 8s., which was the lowest in this category. The other five were Thomas Fountain, gent., £1 12s., Francis Frewen, £1 6s. 8d., William Jourden, 16s., Thomas Meryden, 10s. 8d., and Henry Barnaby, 10s. 8d.[14]

Some fifteen years later, in 1642, on the eve of the Civil War, a return for Aylesbury-with-Walton of all those who had made voluntary donations for the relief of the distressed Irish Protestants includes William Harding 'senior', paying 5s., a relatively generous amount, and William Harding 'junior', paying 1s. (only two parishioners gave as much as £1 and seven others gave 10s.). Three other Hardings are listed, all called John, who gave 1s., 6d., and 2d. respectively. One of these is likely to have been William Harding's second son of that name.[15]

During the Civil War the inhabitants of Walton escaped the close confinement suffered by their fellow parishioners living in the town of Aylesbury behind the fortifications hastily erected by Parliament in 1643 to protect the garrison established there. Conversely, however, Walton was more exposed to the danger of attacks from the Royalist forces based at Oxford and Brill, and it could not escape the quartering of – in this case Parliamentary – soldiers in large numbers, a universal grievance. One can only guess at the hardships and fear suffered by local people and the disruption caused to agriculture by the constant skirmishing and foraging of the opposed forces, not to mention the large number of men impressed as soldiers.

In 1646, when fighting was at an end, claims were entered in the name of William Harding for work done on the Aylesbury fortifications and for the free quartering of troops on him, his total bill for the latter being £27, the second largest for any individual in the village.[16] By this time William senior had died, aged well over 60, his burial being recorded in the parish register on 3 August 1645. Unlike his father Oliver, William had not succeeded in adding to the family property. His widow, Joyce, survived until 1657.

The so-called parliamentary survey of the manor of Walton made around 1650, following the abolition of prebendaries and other such church dignitaries, gives the fullest picture we have of the manor and its tenants prior to the late 18th century.[17] The manor house, the two-acre site of which immediately adjoined the green and Walton Street, had been 'pulled downe in the ... late Warrs', leaving only a little cottage and two sizeable barns, each of eight bays, made of timber and tile. Altogether, the manorial demesne (the lord's home farm) consisted of 63 acres of enclosed pasture and meadow, including the close of meadow called Old Court Close (13 acres) adjoining the site of the manor house and the streamside meadow called Great Cholling Mead (12 acres), having an estimated annual value of £45 6s. 8d., together with 164 acres of arable valued at £41, making a grand total of 227 acres. Some 22 acres of the arable is stated to be dispersed in the open fields called Friars Pits, Bedgrove and Dean Fields; the remainder was enclosed in seven large named 'parcels' of, for the most part, 12 to 30 acres in size. There was also a water mill and its land, worth £30 yearly, meadow land, in Walton Suck Mead and in other common meadows, and profits of court and other perquisites.

1 *Excerpt from conveyance dated July 1604 by Oliver Harding (d.1605) of his property in Walton in trust for his younger son William. Oliver Harding was the first member of his family to settle in Walton.*

The manor was unusual in having only freehold tenants, paying small annual fixed quitrents, or 'rents of assize', totalling £11 5s. 8d. Altogether 41 tenancies are listed, comprising 42 holdings, of which 31 include dwellings (nine more than the 22 families estimated for Walton in 1563). They comprise 13 messuages and land, 11 tenements and land, 7 cottages (2 with land) and 11 with land only.

Rents vary greatly in amount. The highest were paid for the 'messuage' holdings, which were substantial dwellings, and mostly ranged between 9s. 4d. and 30s. (£1 10s.), but in one case was only 3s. 6d. The 30s. was paid by Thomas Friar, the solitary 'gentleman', for Rook Farm, which is the only named property. It had once belonged to the Lees of Quarrendon, notable enclosers.[18] Thomas Barnaby paid 26s. 8d. for his messuage holding and William Harding (the founder's father, possibly resident in Stoke Mandeville at this time) paid 18s. 6d. Jeffrey 'Bainton' (Bampton) held three such messuage holdings with a total rent of £2 7s. 8d.; his sub-tenants are not named. None of the other tenants paid more than 12s. 4d. 'Tenements' properties' rents varied from as low as 3d. to 9s. Cottages paid 5d. to 8d. apiece, with one exception (2s. 4d. for a cottage and land).

The reserved rent formerly due to the prebendary was £20, which was a fraction of what the estate was worth. The lessee's (the lease is stated to have been assigned to William Mead by Alice Fountain in June 1650) only other obligation had been to entertain the prebendary and his retinue of not above six persons and six horses twice yearly for six days and nights, in the event of his coming to view the manor or to preach.

The overall impression is very much of a small peasant community with a non-resident, leaseholder lord, inhabited by one gentleman, three or four yeomen (substantial freeholders who worked their own lands and ranked next to gentlemen in the social hierarchy), some twenty husbandmen, or smallholders, and a relative handful of cottagers, or labourers, most of whom had some land of their own. All or most of the villagers would have enjoyed extensive rights of commons in addition to their holdings. But the manorial survey on its own does not quite give the whole picture. There was, or had been, at least one other cottage on the village green held of the tiny sub-manor of Bawds Fee, and there may have been others.[19] Bawds Fee had belonged to the Pakingtons, lords of the manor of Aylesbury, who still held over 160 acres of land on the north-west side of the hamlet of Walton, inherited from their predecessors the Baldwins, part of which was later known as Broughton Pastures. Much of this land had been enclosed for pasture – not without violent resistance – by the Pakingtons as engrossing landlords in the 16th century,[20] and leased to successive tenant farmers at commercial rents. The Pakingtons were active Royalists and in 1650 their estates lay under sequestration as a punishment for their 'delinquency', but in the long run it was with such large tenant farmers that the future of agriculture would lie.

On his death in 1645, William Harding's heir was his eldest son of the same name, the founder's father; he is the William named in the c.1650 manorial rental, although he was apparently not actually resident in Walton at the time. Later evidence indicates that he had married and set up house during his father's lifetime, but the Aylesbury parish register records only the births of three daughters, Ann, Joyce and Jane, born in 1652, 1656 and 1659 respectively, two of whom were still living in 1719. Neither his marriage nor the baptisms of any of his other known children can be traced.

The disruption caused by the war and its aftermath and the chaotic state of religious observance during the Commonwealth could be to blame for these omissions, but there is a simpler explanation. This is that, at the relevant dates, William was living in the adjoining parish of Stoke Mandeville, where the relevant parish register is missing. We know for certain that he was living there in 1649 after his father's death.[21] Again, we know from the 1739 list of deeds that in March 1646 William Harding conveyed a house in Walton to a certain John Eggleton and – more significantly – that in July 1648 he sold 'all his household goods in Stoke' (Mandeville) to Henry Harding, who is presumably his brother of that name.

Fortunately William's will, unlike his father's, survives, and it tells us that he left a wife named Elizabeth, two surviving sons, William (the founder) and John, and two daughters, Elizabeth and Sarah, in addition to the three listed in the Aylesbury register, all of whom were still under age in 1660. Since four of the children were evidently born before 1652, William, the eldest, is likely to have been born around 1643. In addition, an incidental reference in a property deed of 1671 in the Lee of Hartwell MSS tells us that his wife's maiden name was Jennings.[22]

This last piece of information ties in with several widely spaced transactions involving persons named Jennings in the 1739 list, beginning in 1649, the details of which are unknown. The Jennings family were small landowners who had been resident in the Hartwell area since medieval times and, more recently, at Stoke Mandeville also. They were related to the Hartwell branch of the Hampden family, predecessors of the Lees as lords of the manor there, from whom they borrowed the given names of Alexander and Michael, which they favoured. Francis Jennings (d.1619), of Hartwell, is one of the trustees of Bedford's Charity named in the 1597 Act of Parliament, together with Oliver Harding and Thomas Fountain.[23]

The Jennings presence at Stoke Mandeville is documented in the 1642 list of contributors for Ireland, previously cited, which records three persons of that name: 'Mr' Alexander Jennings (£1), Thomas (5s.) and Michael (1s.). Also listed are a William Harding paying 6d., and a John Harding.[24] It thus appears that William Harding's move to Stoke was closely connected with his marriage. It remains unclear why, having inherited the Walton farm in 1645, he continued to live at Stoke for at least a further four years before returning to his native parish, but access to the family homestead may well have been complicated by the customary right to reside there enjoyed by his widowed mother Joyce Harding.

Between 1649 and 1656 William Harding purchased pieces of open field land in Walton totalling nine acres and one 'land' (a half-acre arable strip) from five different owners, the largest purchase being six acres from Thomas Jennings in 1656 (the others were from Richard Whitchurch, John Hatgood, Jeffrey Bampton and John Pratt). During the same period he was also involved in a series of four family transactions. The first of these was a conveyance dated 26 May 1649, from William to Mrs Elizabeth Harding, of 37½ acres in Walton field. It raises the question of who Mrs Harding was, since a man could not convey land to his wife.

The answer is supplied by the original deed and accompanying bond, which fortunately survive.[25] They make it clear that the Elizabeth Harding in question was in fact William's unmarried sister, then aged thirty-one. Though framed in the form of a conveyance, as was usual, it is in fact a mortgage between William Harding of Stoke Mandeville, yeoman, and Elizabeth Harding of Walton, spinster, and it bears Elizabeth's neatly written signature (William's, equally neat, is on the bond). Thus the 'Mrs' of the list is a courtesy title only, meaning 'Mistress'. One surmises that Elizabeth was living with her mother and that the money lent may have been a legacy from her father by way of a marriage portion. Unlike married women, whose property belonged to their husbands, spinsters and widows enjoyed the freedom both to own property in their own right and to dispose of it by will or otherwise as they thought fit.

The notional sale price (the amount of the loan) was £160, a very substantial sum, and the transaction was to be voided if William should pay Elizabeth the sum of £172 16s. on 27 May 1650 'at the now dwelling place of Joyce Harding, widow, in Walton'. Joyce was their mother, with whom Elizabeth was presumably sharing the house in Walton and who died in 1657. The amount of the repayment represents a rate of interest of a little over 8 per cent, which was the maximum allowed by legislation passed in 1624. The land so mortgaged is stated to be arable land dispersed in the fields of Walton and forming part of 110 acres of arable, meadow and pasture belonging to the 'messuage or farm' there, 'heretofore purchased of one John Fountaine of Walton gent by one Oliver Harding of Stoke Mandeville [sic], yeoman and grandfather of William Harding'. There is thus no doubt as to William's identity.

The deed incorporates a terrier, or detailed description, of each separate piece of land as it lay in the open fields. The parcels range in size from two acres to five acres, indicating that a significant amount of consolidation of the arable strips had taken place over the years as a result of exchanges between owners of adjoining strips. It was a process which facilitated limited experimentation with cropping and the creation of temporary grass 'leys', demonstrating a degree of flexibility in the open field system. Presumably William used some of the money advanced by his sister to finance the land purchases mentioned above, but the mortgage was apparently still in being over 10 years later, by which time the aggregate interest paid would have amounted to more than the principal.

One of the other three family transactions mentioned above is an agreement, dated 14 June 1649, between William Harding and Richard Jennings of London, William's brother-in-law. No hint of its purpose is given but it is reasonable to surmise that it related to William's wife's inheritance. Richard can be identified as the Richard Jennings described as 'grocer of London' in a 1653 document relating to lands in Stoke Mandeville.[26] In June 1650 William Harding executed a conveyance and lease of a messuage, house and 100 acres in Walton field to John and Henry Harding, evidently his two brothers. In context, this must be a family settlement of some kind rather than an outright transfer of property, with John and Henry acting as trustees, and possibly also as lessees, of all or part of the property. The last in the series of such transactions listed (again without specific details) is a deed, dated October 1656, by which William Harding settles a jointure on Elizabeth his wife. A jointure was in effect the settlement of an annuity on a wife in case she should outlive her husband. It usually formed part of a pre-nuptial settlement, constituting a kind of *quid pro quo* for the bride's dowry or marriage portion, but in this case the evidence is against any second marriage for which a marriage settlement might have been made; it could reflect a decline in William's health, dissension between him and his wife, or both.

William Harding, the founder's father, died in May 1660 and was buried on the 22nd of that month, a few days before the restoration of Charles II; he was almost 52 years old. His will, dated 8 May 1660, contains clear indications that he and Elizabeth were not on good terms, even allowing for his physical state (he is described as 'sick in body'). Her name is mentioned only once, without endearments, to the effect that 'Elizabeth my now wife' shall make use of the household goods 'only equal with my executor so long as she shall keep herself a widow'. Even more tellingly, for it was contrary to the normal practice, she is passed over as executrix in favour of the testator's elder son, William, the founder, despite the fact that, as it later transpires, the latter was still legally too young to undertake this responsibility when probate was granted the following November.[27]

Under the terms of the will, William's second son, John, was to receive £110 when he had reached the age of 21, and his five sisters – listed in descending order of age as Elizabeth, Sarah, Ann, Joyce and Jane (the latter just over one year old) – were to have £50 apiece at the same age (sufficient to set up house in a modest way), a total of £360, which would have to come out of the estate. In case the executor should refuse to pay the legacies when due, provision was made for the sale of the testator's 40 acres [*sic*] of arable, ley and meadow in Walton fields, or some part of it, for this purpose. Provision is also made for repaying the debt due to the testator's sister, Elizabeth Harding of Walton, spinster, on a mortgage of 'several lands' in Walton fields, doubtless referring to the 1649 conveyance noted above, or possibly a subsequent one. She is, at harvest time next, to have free view of the testator's best corn and to choose 20 acres of his best corn now growing in Walton fields, being wheat, barley, beans and rye, in order to discharge the mortgage. Any surplus after valuation is to be returned to the executor.

The only household items specifically bequeathed are the bed in the parlour, the table in the hall (the principal living room) and the court cupboard, all of which are reserved to William the executor. The other goods in the house are to be divided, half to go to the executor and the other half to be divided equally among the other children, except horses, cows and sheep. The residue is to go to the executor. The overseers of the will are named as the testator's 'loving brother', John Harding of Walton, and Richard Whitchurch the elder, also of Walton, who are each to have 2s. 6d. for their pains with which to buy gloves; no other friends or relations are remembered. The witnesses are John Woster, who signs with a mark, and Thomas Moncke.

In the event probate was granted to the testator's brother, John Harding, as legal guardian (*curatore*) for the heir William during his minority, which, apparently, had several years to run.

2. *The Jennings family of Stoke Mandeville*

Elizabeth Harding, the founder's mother, played a much bigger part in his life, and in the lives of all her children, than their father, if only because she lived to a ripe old age, so it is it is fortunate that sufficient information has come to light to enable us to form an impression of her family background. It confirms that, socially and economically, the Jennings were 'a cut above' the Hardings and are probably best described as minor gentry. Elizabeth's father, Alexander Jennings, the founder's maternal grandfather, was born at Hartwell in 1585, the son of Thomas Jennings and his wife Maria, daughter of Thomas Hampden, of the junior, Hartwell, branch of that ancient landowning family.[28]

Alexander lost his father at an early age and his mother remarried, her second husband being Isaac Sheppard of Bishopstone in the parish of Stone, gentleman. In 1604 Alexander, then aged about 19, married one Anne Brooks, of whom little is known despite the existence of a marriage settlement. Her parentage is not revealed in this document, so she may have been an orphan and possibly under age. After eight years of marriage their first surviving son, also called Alexander, was baptised at Hartwell in 1612. Other children are known to have followed but no record of their baptisms has been traced. Various deeds in the Lee family archives show that between 1612 and 1616 Alexander Jennings, gentleman, was actually living at Moreton, a hamlet in the parish of Dinton, moving later (by 1618) to Bishopstone.[29]

The connection with Stoke Mandeville dates back at least as far as 1617, when Alexander, now aged 41, purchased the small manor of Burleys there (to which was annexed the manor of Stonors and some land) from Thomas Bosse, a distant relation of the Hardings, and his wife. Alexander evidently settled in Stoke about this time, and nothing more is heard about his other property either in Bishopstone or elsewhere. Like Oliver Harding in 1586, he had found himself a new centre of operations in middle life. No details of his estate have been traced, but in the 1625 subsidy previously mentioned Alexander Jennings, gentleman, was assessed at £1 4s. on his lands in Stoke Mandeville. This was the largest single assessment recorded, though Edmund Brudenell, lord of the manor, and his son of the same name paid £1 8s. between them. The following

The maternal descent of William Harding from the Jennings family of Stoke Mandeville from 1584

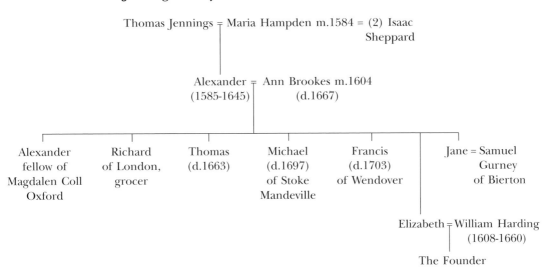

year, too, Alexander was considered rich enough to be numbered among the few hundred Buckinghamshire inhabitants to merit the doubtful honour of a Privy Council letter requesting a 'voluntary' loan of £10, an expedient made necessary by Parliament's refusal to grant another subsidy to Charles I. On this occasion he is described in the list of recipients as 'yeoman'. He appears to have paid up.[30]

Ten years later, on 1 June 1636, Alexander Jennings made his will. Its contents and, still more, the circumstances surrounding its creation, show him to have been a man of unusually strong principles and independence of mind, for there can be little doubt that it was made in anticipation of his imminent arrest by order of the Privy Council for refusing to pay his assessment for the Ship Money tax. Three weeks or so after it was made he was committed to the custody of the Council's messenger, a certain William Butts. Alexander had made up his mind that, this time around, he was not going to submit to any extra-parliamentary exaction.[31]

First levied in October 1634, without the authority of Parliament, and renewed in following years, the Ship Money tax and the resistance to it are forever associated with the name of John Hampden, Alexander's kinsman and near neighbour. As is well known, it was Hampden's refusal to pay the £1 assessed on his property in Stoke Mandeville (the land in question was actually located at Prestwood, then a detached portion of Stoke parish) which sparked off the chain of events which inflamed popular feeling nationally and helped to create the climate for civil war between King and Parliament. Hampden's example was followed by many of humbler status, including 30 of his neighbours in Great

Kimble, but unlike Alexander, not many were prepared to carry their defiance to the point of sacrificing their liberty.[32]

In July, together with two fellow prisoners, George Goodson of Weston Turville and Joshua Halsey of Chesham, he petitioned to be released on grounds of hardship. Butts, the messenger, by now growing anxious about the legality of his position and the payment of his fees, attached his own comments:

> I had a warrant from the Board in the latter part of June last for one Alexander Jennings for refusing to pay the ship-money and about the 2nd of July I brought the said Jennings to Oatlands where he was heard before His Majesty and the Board and then refusing to pay I had commandment from the Lords ... to keep him in my custody which I have done ever since ... Now I do understand by the said Jennings that on Sunday next he intends to petition the Lords again ... and is not willing neither to pay the ship-money nor my fees ... his example will be prejudicial to His Majesty all the kingdom over for the shipping business. Mr Jennings questions me by what warrant I do detain him ... Sir he runs every week to the carriers and receives letters and news from the country. My opinion is if there be no stricter warrant for restraining of him than as yet I have he will never pay His Majesty nor me.[33]

Butts had evidently taken the measure of the man. Jennings was now removed to the harsher environment of the Fleet prison in London. In January 1637, having spent 19 weeks in the custody of the messenger and 12 in the Fleet, Alexander again petitioned the Council for relief so that he could attend to his affairs and remove himself from 'the contagion in the city', but apparently without agreeing to pay the tax or fees. It is not known precisely when he was eventually released or whether Butts' prediction was proved correct. There was, however, a high-level sequel to the affair, for when Lord Chief Justice Bramston was impeached by the House of Commons in 1641, one of the articles of impeachment was that he had refused to discharge Jennings in 1637 on a writ of habeas corpus.[34]

Alexander's will is in itself remarkable, among other things, for its brevity. He begins by appointing his wife and his eldest son Alexander as his executors with instructions to sell all his lands and his 'lease', none of which are specified, in order to pay his debts and legacies. Each of his children, except Alexander, is to receive £250 at the age of 24, rather than at 21, as was customary. However, their names are not stated, nor are we told how many of them there were, and no distinction is made between male and female children. In case Alexander should refuse to join in selling the property, or, alternatively, to give his mother security that she will have a third part of the lands for her lifetime, then he is to have £500 and be replaced as executor by Alexander's next eldest son (not named), who is to carry out the sale. The executors are further instructed to 'keepe my Children which are not Apprentices at fifteen yeares and to keepe them at Schoole the meane tyme And to provide my Daughters services till they come to the age of fower and twentie yeares'.

In making equal, or at least similar, provision for all his children and in its apparent indifference to preserving the integrity of the estate, Alexander's will runs clean contrary to the typical family strategy of his fellow landholders. Surprisingly, too, although the will was drawn up to meet a particular crisis situation it was never revised or updated in order to take account of altered circumstances, such as the marriage of his daughter Elizabeth. By 1636 his eldest son, then aged around 24, was already launched on an academic career, having matriculated (as a 'pleb') at Magdalen College, Oxford, in 1633 and been awarded a fellowship there in 1635.[35] In fact it seems that altogether there were five sons, Alexander, Richard, Thomas, Michael and Francis, and two daughters, Elizabeth and Jane. This means that their portions amounted in aggregate to £2,000, if Alexander's £500 is included. It is fairly certain that Richard, who became a London draper, must have served an apprenticeship but it is not clear whether any of the other sons did so.

It is tempting to speculate that Alexander, senior, may have been among the 3,000 or more Buckinghamshire 'freeholders and gentlemen' who rode down to London in January 1642 in support of John Hampden, their knight of the shire and Member of Parliament. Certainly he fits the political stereotype of the independent, incorruptible, small landowner of later Whig legend. The following year, with civil war only months away, his contribution of £1 for the Irish Protestants was third highest in the list for Stoke Mandeville after those of the lord of the manor, Edmund Brudenell (£2 10s.) and Elizabeth Brudenell (£1 2s.), while his son Thomas's contribution of 5s. was next highest.[36]

Three years later, in October 1644, as satisfaction for a debt of £500, Alexander executed a conveyance to Thomas Dover of Aylesbury, gentleman, with whom he had had many earlier transactions, of the whole of his personal estate, including his moveable goods and 'chattels, household stuff and utensils of household of what kind or property whatsoever they be which I now have remaining or being at Stoke Mandeville'. Though in the form of an outright sale, it can reasonably be surmised that it was intended as security for the debt. Possibly the money was the amount promised to his eldest son in the event of his renouncing the executorship; certainly when Alexander's will was proved the following May the executors were Anne Jennings, the widow, and her son Richard. Alexander died, aged 60, in 1645, the same year as the founder's other grandfather, William Harding.[37]

Later evidence indicates that the Stoke estate was not sold. Instead Anne retained her third share until her death in August 1667 and the rest was divided among her four younger sons. The combined income and poll tax assessed in September 1660 lists, under Stoke Mandeville, 'Mistress Anne Jennings', holding land with the annual value of £27 4s. and taxed at 10s. 6d., Richard Jennings (whose name is struck through) and Thomas Jennings, gentlemen, each with land valued at £12, and Michael Jennings, whose holding is valued at exactly twice that amount, though all three men are taxed at 4s. 10d. This suggests that that the total annual value of the estate had been over £70 and that the division was the result of a family arrangement, under which Francis disposed of his interest to one or more of his three brothers for cash. There is apparent confirmation of this in a later reference in Thomas Jennings' will to a property deed of 3 December 1653, made between Richard on the one part and Thomas, Michael and Francis on the other.[38]

Something of the later history of the estate can be traced in surviving tax assessments for the years 1665 and 1673 and occasional later clues. In 1665 only 'Mistress Jennings', taxed at £1 3s. 6d., and Michael, at £2 1s. 6d., are listed. In 1673 Anne has been replaced by her son Richard, who had presumably inherited on her death in 1668, taxed at 8s., while Michael is taxed at twice that amount. The lordship of the manor of Burleys also descended to Michael Jennings. Whatever the reason, Michael, who died in 1696, seems to have been the last of the family to reside at Stoke Mandeville and there are no Jennings entries in the first Stoke Mandeville parish register, which begins in 1699. The Jennings estate was no more. Nevertheless, as we shall see, a portion of it seems to have become attached to the Harding family holding via the founder's mother, Elizabeth Harding.[39]

William Harding (c.1643-1719)

A Buckinghamshire Yeoman

William Harding, the founder, was a youth of not more than 17 when his father died, with several years yet to pass before he legally came into his inheritance. Too young to have any but the haziest recollections of the upheavals of the Civil War period, he had, it seems, spent his earliest years in Stoke Mandeville before moving, with his parents, younger brother John and two sisters Elizabeth and Sarah, to the family farmstead in Walton around 1649-50. Here, according to the parish register, two more sisters, Ann and Joyce, were born in 1652 and 1656 respectively, and a third, Jane, in 1659. They were aged seven, four and one year when their father died. In fact it is not unlikely that the newly widowed Elizabeth was left with five children under 14 to care for on her own.

As a child growing up in Stoke and Walton, William would have received at least a basic grounding in the 'three Rs', to which we can safely add a fourth – for this was an age obsessed by religion. He was probably first introduced to letters at his mother's knee, since Elizabeth, unlike many country girls, had received a formal education, her father having left instructions in his will that all his children should go to school until the age of fifteen. William may also have gone to school locally, perhaps attending the free grammar school in Aylesbury. All we know for certain is that, unlike his brother John, he could write. He appended his signature to his last will, for example, and there is evidence in the first Charity record book that he was in the habit of making memoranda of financial transactions in a pocket almanac.

Judging by the rather summary inventory[1] made many years later, after William's own death in 1719, and from other clues, the family home in Walton was not untypical of the houses of other substantial farmers in the Aylesbury area. It was a traditional timber-framed building with a thatched roof that had to be renewed every ten years or so. The principal ground floor rooms were the hall, the parlour and the kitchen. The hall was the centre of the household. It had a fireplace and was simply furnished with a long table, joined stools and one wooden chair. 'The furniture belonging to the table in the hall' had been left to William in his father's will, as well as a 'court cupboard' (a kind of sideboard) not separately mentioned in the inventory. The parlour also functioned as a bedroom and contained a feather bed and a flock bed and bedding, presumably the same 'bed in the parlour' which William also inherited. The kitchen was equipped with a furnace, a jack (a mechanical turnspit) and unspecified utensils of pewter and brass, the whole worth just under £20 in 1719, or more than six times the value of the contents of the hall. Five other service rooms comprised a 'milk house', containing a barrel, milk bowls and a powdering tub for pickling meat; a 'drink house', with six hogsheads and barrels; a 'further house', with more barrels and other items; a cheese chamber containing cheese, shelves and trestles; and a malt chamber with malt mill (a hand mill for grinding malt before brewing) and boards.

Upstairs were three bedchambers described respectively as the 'chamber over the hall', the 'middle chamber' and the 'best chamber'. The first of these contained a single feather bed, a coffer (a box or strong box) and 'two old trunks, &c.', valued at £2 in total. The second was more comfortably furnished with two feather beds, a quilt, blankets and curtains, valued at £5. The best chamber, besides a feather bed, quilt and blankets, had such luxuries as a looking glass and a fireplace with a brass fire hearth-shovel, but the valuation of £25 10s. also included a silver tankard and 14 spoons.

In the absence of any deeds or surveys the extent of William's landed inheritance can only be guessed at, but earlier and later evidence suggests it probably amounted to well over 100 acres of mostly open field land and that it was relatively unencumbered. The acres in question are likely to have been customary acres and so rather less than statutory acres. In his will William senior had made detailed provision for the speedy repayment of the money borrowed from his sister. No other debts are recorded, but a general release, dated March 1662, to William from Robert Edmonds, a prosperous Aylesbury tenant farmer and a near neighbour (see below), would seem to indicate that money had been due in this quarter too, and that it was speedily paid off by the executor. There remained the legacies to the younger children amounting to £360 in total, a considerable sum but the less burdensome because it was payable in well-spaced instalments over an extended period.

In the surviving assessment for Aylesbury-with-Walton for the combined income and poll tax raised in September 1660 in order to pay off the armed forces, William Harding, though, as we have seen, still under age, was assessed at 13s., implying that he was assessed on his property, while his mother, 'Widow Harding', not having any property, paid the flat rate of 1s. per head.[2] The two entries follow each other and clearly relate to the same household; the other members of the household were evidently too young to be liable for the tax. Listed together, and apparently forming a single separate household, are William's bachelor uncles, John and Henry, and his spinster aunt, Elizabeth Harding, who were assessed at 3s., 2s. and 1s. respectively. William's other Harding aunt, Joyce (born 1607), is not included in the assessment, but the burial of a Joyce Harding is recorded in the parish register in December of the same year. The Hardings did not have any servants.

It is clear from the assessments that uncle John and uncle Henry were both landholders by this date, although neither had been listed among the tenants of the manor of Walton in the survey of *c.*1650. Younger sons of yeomen could not normally expect to receive a share of the family holding, but the more fortunate were sometimes able to acquire holdings of their own, helped in some cases by small family legacies. From 1657, the year of his mother's death, when he was in his late forties, John was making small purchases of arable land in Walton from a variety of owners, beginning with a single acre from his brother William. By 1660 these totalled 14 acres, the largest being 11 acres purchased from a certain John Parsons. Three more purchases were to follow between 1663 and 1666, comprising one of five acres from William Bampton and two purchases amounting to 15 acres from John Hartwell, bringing the grand total to 34 acres, a not insignificant holding, but it had taken some nine years to accumulate.

The original deed for the five acres purchased from Bampton in 1663 shows that the purchase price was £60 and that the property had previously belonged to Henry Bampton, the vendor's brother, a coachman living in Middlesex.[3] When, in 1677, John died aged 69 and, according to the parish register, still a bachelor, some or all of his property may have descended to one or both of his two nephews, and thus joined the main estate, which would explain the inclusion of the purchase deeds in the 1739 list. How Henry acquired his land, and how much there was, is not known. His absence from tax returns after 1665 makes it likely that he is the Henry Harding whose burial is recorded at Bierton – where he also held some land – in 1666.

2 *Part of the probate inventory of William Harding's goods taken 10 December 1719 by two of his neighbours. It lists and values the goods and chattels in his house, room by room, enabling us to form an idea of his circumstances and way of life.*

The restoration of the monarchy brought many changes at local level, not least the re-establishment of the Church of England and the return of the ecclesiastical courts, both much diminished in authority. Among those fined in the episcopal visitation of 1664 for failing to pay their church rate the previous year was the young William Harding, who neglected to put in an appearance. A note in the margin states that he was still a minor (*in minore etate*), which seems to confirm that he cannot have been born earlier than about 1643. William's uncle and guardian, John Harding, was fined for the same offence.[4]

Whether from prudence or conviction, the family chose to conform to the established church, in the long run at least. Many others did not and suffered a degree of persecution from the secular authorities that varied in intensity according to local and national circumstances in the years between 1660 and the passing of the Toleration Act of 1689. The hamlet of Walton was something of a hotbed of religious dissent in the 1660s, for of five illegal conventicles reported in the parish of Aylesbury in 1669 three were located there.[5]

The ecclesiastical court records contain another intriguing entry at this time concerning 'Harding spinster', cited for having been delivered of a bastard child in Walton between May and July 1664. The entry continues 'Mr Arth[ur] Claver tells me that this business is depending before the official of the Jurisdiction & she is his wives kinswoman'.[6] The spinster in question was almost certainly one or other of William's sisters, of whom Elizabeth, the eldest, was then probably about eighteen. The outcome of the charge, for which the punishment was public penance, is not known. Claver, whose connection with the Hardings has not been verified, was registrar of the archdeaconry court and thus in a position to hush the matter up. Unsurprisingly, there is no relevant baptism entered in the parish register.

William Harding's name reappears in other surviving assessments for more conventional taxes levied during the 1660s. In the first of these, dated 1665, the entry reads 'Thomas Bigg for William Hardings land', £1 15s. 5d., indicating that he was not farming his own land at this time. But three years later, in 1668, when he would probably have been about 25 years old, he was paying a similar amount (£1 16s. 8d.) in his own name, while in 1673, when the tax was at a lower rate, he paid 9s. 8d. and also acted as one of the assessors. Clearly he was by now well launched on his farming career. In comparative terms his holding was one of the larger ones. In 1668, for example, he appears to have been one of only five men in Walton who were assessed at over £1, the others being Joseph Bampton (£2 6s. 4d.), Henry Babham, gentleman (£2 2s.), who also paid tax in Stoke Mandeville, Thomas Barnaby senior (£1 18s. 6d.) and Thomas Barnaby junior (£1 15s.). To these should be added Robert Edmonds, who was assessed at the very large sum of £6 12s. 'for Broughton grounds', a property which formed part of the Pakington estate.[7]

As a widow with a young family, Elizabeth Harding, the founder's mother, is likely to have remained in close touch with her mother and at least some of her siblings, including, one imagines, her sister Jane, who had married Samuel Gurney, a yeoman, then of Bishopstone, and who later (*c.*1670) settled at Bierton. Elizabeth clearly had a particularly close relationship with her unmarried brother Thomas Jennings. In April 1663 Thomas, who was still living at Stoke Mandeville, fell sick, and he died later the same year. In his will, proved in October 1664, he left all his lands in Stoke which had belonged to his father, as well as those which had come to him by virtue of a deed of 1653 to which he and his brothers Richard, Michael and Francis were parties, to his 'beloved' sister Elizabeth.[8]

Elizabeth was also appointed residuary legatee of her brother Thomas's personal estate. Unlike her late husband, Thomas Jennings had sufficient confidence in his sister's abilities to make her his sole executor, even though this involved her in a complicated series of transactions concerning money owed to the testator by his 'cousin' Samuel Richardson of Islington, gentleman. In his will Thomas also remembers his mother and his sister, Jane Gurney, and appoints as overseers of the will his 'beloved friends' William Harrington, Doctor of Laws, and his brother Francis.

This bequest is the origin of the three acres of arable land in the fields of Stoke Mandeville, sold by Elizabeth (described as 'of Walton, widow') to William Foard in 1671 for £30, or £10 an acre. The original deed for this transaction (which is not included in the 1739 list) indemnifies the purchaser against claims arising through her four brothers. It bears her signature, neatly written without capital letters. There may well have been other sales and there would also have been some income from land, for in the 1673 assessment for Stoke Mandeville 'Widow Harding' is assessed at 3s. 8d. Although it is not specified in her will, it would seem that the bulk of her brother's property (amounting on later evidence to in the region of 30 acres of arable land) remained in her possession and was inherited by her son William.[9]

Relations with the Jennings family were not all smooth. In 1663 Elizabeth, in her capacity of administrator and beneficiary of Thomas's will, began a Chancery action against Richard, Michael and Francis over the personal estate of their father, Alexander Jennings. From the record of this case it appears that there had been earlier disputes over the estate, said to be worth £100 a year and upwards, in the 1640s between Alexander Jennings, the eldest son, and Richard, the next oldest, ending in an arbitration which had been confirmed by Chancery. Following this, Richard and his three younger brothers, all three then residing at Stoke Mandeville, by the deed of 1653 previously mentioned, had agreed to divide the real estate equally among themselves, subject to the widow's third share. Later Richard had sold his portion. Elizabeth's case was that Thomas had not received his full share of the personal estate, comprising leases, goods and chattels of considerable value.[10]

During the 1660s and 1670s William Harding's younger siblings were growing up and provision had to be made for their futures. Since about a third of the population was under the age of 15, children were an important factor in the labour market.[11] For many younger sons (including, in this period, many from the landed gentry) one alternative to farming or labouring was apprenticeship to a trade, a course which involved the payment of a premium which could range from as little as £5 to over £100, depending on the nature of the trade and on future prospects. One of Elizabeth Harding's own brothers had been set up in business as a London merchant in this way while the eldest had gone to university.

But in the majority of cases children of labourers and younger sons of small farmers, cottagers and to a lesser extent yeomen, began their independent working lives in their early teens by hiring themselves out (traditionally at the local 'statute' hiring fair) for an annual wage as living-in farm servants, or 'servants in husbandry'. Thereafter they tended to move from farm to farm within a locality until they married and settled down, usually keeping in close touch with their families and occasionally returning home between hirings.

It was a system which went back to late medieval times and lasted well into the 19th century. A Buckinghamshire man, Joseph Mayett (1783-1839) of Quainton, has left a uniquely vivid and detailed record of his 12 different hirings in the Aylesbury area (interspersed with periods spent at home) between the ages of 13 and twenty. Almost a century earlier William Clerk, a native of Aylesbury, was leading a very similar existence – including a stint at Walton – receiving wages of £3 10s. to £3 15s. a year in addition to his keep. In the existing circumstances, however, young John Harding may well have stayed at home to help his brother in running the family farm, though, as we have seen, he eventually became a farmer in his own right.[12]

Girls, too, had a place in the labour market. In the Jennings household the daughters seem to have been expected to remain at home until marriage, but in most farming families only the eldest daughter was likely to be so privileged. Younger daughters were occasionally apprenticed but the choice of trades was extremely limited and most of those not left to look after ageing parents seem to have gone into farm service like their brothers, specialising in 'female' tasks such as milkmaiding. Others found employment as a living-in domestic servants. The logic of the system was that it gave young people the opportunity to accumulate resources to enable them to marry and set up households of their own, and encouraged them to postpone marriage until the joint resources of a couple were sufficient. Overall, it is estimated that around forty per cent of all children were servants of one sort or another for some part of their lives.[13]

The Harding girls were fortunate in that they could look forward to ready-made nest eggs at 21 and thus had no need to postpone marriage beyond that, but they would still have been required to leave home at an early age. That Sarah Harding's possessions at her death (on the evidence of her mother's will) included her 'trunk' suggests that she, at any rate, had been in service.

Although William himself remained a lifelong bachelor and his brother John nearly so, all his five sisters eventually married and, with one exception, are known to have had children. Elizabeth, who seems to have been the eldest, married Thomas Staple at Stoke Mandeville in February 1667. If we assume that she was at least 21, then she must have been born not later than 1646. Jane, the youngest, married John Horton of Chearsley by licence at Oving in

August 1681, a few months after her 21st birthday, which was four years under the average age of marriage for women at this period. In contrast Sarah, who was born before 1651, must have been over 30 when she married Francis Clarke at Ellesborough in March 1682. The marriages of the other two have not been traced but Joyce is known to have married William Webb of Aylesbury, a blacksmith, and Ann's husband was William Stallwood.[14]

By 1670 William was sufficiently well established in the community for him to be appointed to represent Walton as one of the three churchwardens for the parish of Aylesbury for that year. This was an important responsibility for someone still in his twenties and, even though the choice was restricted to Walton, he seems to have been on a par with his two colleagues in office as a member of the parish elite. He served again in 1681, by which time the office had become so politicised that he was involved in a clearly vexatious action in the ecclesiastical court, which was appealed to the archbishop's Court of Arches. He served for the third and last time in 1712. William also acted as an overseer of the poor in 1678, 1699 and 1706, and was constable for the manor of Walton at least once, in 1687. As a parish officer his duties would have included the placing out of poor 'parish' children as apprentices. At Easter 1711 William Harding of Walton was one of two men nominated to be chief, or high, constables for the Aylesbury hundreds but for some unknown reason was not sworn.[15]

In his politics William was – as befitted a yeoman freeholder – a strong Whig. The Whigs were the political heirs of the Roundheads of 1642: they stood for the Protestant succession against the Tories (both names date from the late 1670s), for whom loyalty to the Stuart monarchy and to the claims of the Church of England came first. As a resident of Walton he was not entitled to vote in parliamentary elections for the borough of Aylesbury, but the long series of printed poll books for county elections which begin in 1701 show him, and his brother John, consistently voting for the Whig candidates. It is possible – even likely – that he was passed over as high constable in 1711 for political reasons since the Tories were in the ascendant locally at this time.

Such chicanery was commonplace at the time, for the two parties were so closely matched in Aylesbury that each would stop at nothing to gain an advantage over the other. In 1701 what began as a minor dispute over a disqualified vote in an election for the borough of Aylesbury spiralled into a constitutional crisis in relations between the Lords and Commons that convulsed the whole nation, a dispute known to history as the great case of 'Ashby versus White'. Between 1694 and 1715 Aylesbury borough elections were so numerous – and so tumultuous – that the inhabitants must have been in an almost constant state of political excitement. Violence was by no means uncommon on these occasions, sometimes directed at the chief actors. At an election held in May 1705 a large crowd of onlookers is said to have witnessed some of their number 'throw stones and brickbats at the gentlemen, and threaten them with sticks, and incite the crowd by shouting "Knock them on the Head; beat the Rogues' Brains out"'.[16] County elections were also held in the town, when thousands of freeholders from all over Buckinghamshire took part and voting was often prolonged over several days.

All this was to change with the accession of the Hanoverian monarchy in 1714, which placed the Whigs firmly in the saddle both locally and nationally, though of course Whig-Tory animosity did not disappear overnight. At Aylesbury the Tories fought a rearguard action focused on retaining control of the grammar school trust and succeeded in delaying its re-foundation for a number of years. But, deprived of official support, they entered upon a gradual decline and a period of greater political stability began. Henceforth Aylesbury borough elections were dominated exclusively by Whigs of various hues and the principal qualification for success was to be 'a moneyed man'.[17]

Politics was not the only source of excitement locally at this time. The corruption and licence in high places associated with the Restoration era did not go unnoticed in the provinces. One scandal which must have had a particular interest for the inhabitants of Walton was the long-running case of Hide v. Emerton.[18] In 1660 Mary Whitchurch, one of the three or more daughters of John Whitchurch of Walton, who in terms of landholding seems to have been little more than a smallholder (though his son Richard had somehow acquired sufficient wealth to purchase the manor of Chalfont St Peter in 1650),[19] married Sir Thomas Hide, baronet, of Aldbury in Hertfordshire, a village less than ten miles to the east of Aylesbury. He was 66 and a bachelor; his bride was thirty-two. How this unlikely match had come about is uncertain, but it was said that Mary's older sister Sarah (born in 1623) had been first Sir Thomas's servant and then his mistress before being married off to his bailiff. Moreover, Samuel Pepys considered Mary 'yet handsome' when he met her in 1667. Sir Thomas himself died in 1665, leaving a daughter Bridget, born in 1662.

Within weeks his widow, who inherited all his personal estate, had married Robert (soon to be Sir Robert) Vyner, an immensely wealthy London goldsmith, who was banker to Charles I. Both she and her daughter appear in Michael Wright's intimate group portrait of the Vyner family in 1673, which now hangs in the National Gallery. In October 1674, when little Bridget Hide, now heiress to the Hide estates, was 12 years of age, her aunt, Sarah Emerton, Lady Vyner's elder sister, connived at a clandestine marriage between the child and her cousin John, Sarah's son. Lady Vyner afterwards learnt of the marriage but died in January 1675 without having told her husband. There followed protracted litigation in the civil and ecclesiastical courts before the marriage was finally set aside in 1683 (the verdict was allegedly procured by bribery), by which time Bridget Hide had already been married to Peregrine Osborne (1658-1729), son of Vyner's friend and ally Thomas, Earl of Danby, who had been the king's chief minister in the 1670s and who, after many twists of fortune, was to re-emerge as a Tory leader in the early 1690s. Danby became 1st Duke of Leeds in 1694, to which title Peregrine succeeded in 1712. By such curious twists of fortune did the granddaughter of a Walton farmer become the wife of a duke.

Information about William Harding's farming activities is largely confined to what can be deduced from the probate inventory of his possessions previously cited, made immediately after his death in 1719, and from related executorship accounts. By this date the farm appears to have grown to some 150 acres in extent, including outlying portions in Bierton and Stoke Mandeville, making it a large farm in local terms. The broad picture is one of traditional mixed arable farming, the principal crop being wheat, with barley and beans also prominent. The inventory, made within a month or so of harvest, values the 'crop and stock of corn' stored in the barn, ricks and hovels, 'threshed and unthreshed', at £175 15s. The livestock, comprising 10 horses, mares and colts, 13 cows and bullocks, 185 sheep, four hogs and four pigs, is valued together at £108 8s. In addition, the stock of wool, with the hay rick and firewood, was worth £67. Farm equipment is not included in the valuation. The sheep flock was large by local standards. It was wholly, or largely, grazed on the common, for in addition to his own entitlement William had purchased a total of 65 sheep's commons from six of his neighbours at 4d. each.

Grain was sold on a weekly basis, presumably through the local market (in one instance its destination is given as Banbury) but barley was also sold to individual customers in the form of malt, as were wool and surplus sheep. At his death William was still owed a total of £73 2s. for 78 sheep and 48 lambs sold the same year to Thomas Parker. Threshing of grain continued throughout the winter months, keeping three to four men, of whom at least one was employed as a day-labourer, constantly employed, earning up to 4s. a week at piece rates of 3d. a bushel for wheat.

Between 1678 and 1701 the 1739 list of deeds includes a series of eight financial and property transactions involving a 'Mrs Elizabeth Harding', who is clearly identifiable as William's mother. The first of the documents is a conveyance to Elizabeth Harding of Walton, widow, in April 1678 of land at Dunsham in Aylesbury field which, as the surviving original deed confirms, refers to two and a half acres of meadow there.[20] It was doubtless acquired as an investment, since meadow land was valuable property which had the advantage of being easy to let on an annual basis. The other deeds, beginning in 1680, all appear to be either mortgages or bonds for sums lent out at interest. Not all the sums lent are stated, but those that are amount to over £250, an impressive sum. They include £80 and interest due from the executors of a Mr Guy of Wycombe on lands in Walton and a bond from Robert Lea of Great Kimble for £73.

William's mother was not William's only female relative to engage in financial dealing on her own account. On 23 July 1690 his elderly maiden aunt Elizabeth Harding (she was born in 1617), described as 'of Walton in the parish of Aylesbury, spinster', sold three and three-quarter acres of meadow ground called Jailors Platt situated near Haydon Hill in Aylesbury for the very large sum of £100. Her signature on the deed is little more than a scrawl and her first name is misspelt 'Elihabeh'. How and when she had acquired the property is not shown. She may well have engaged in a succession of moneylending transactions since the mortgage which she advanced to her brother in 1649.[21]

Sadly, money proved to be aunt Elizabeth's undoing, as is revealed by the records of the court of Quarter Sessions. At the court beginning 17 July 1690 Thomas Gray, 'gentleman', of St Andrews Holborn, London, was committed to jail to find sureties to appear at the next assizes to answer a charge of stealing £80 from Elizabeth Harding of Walton, spinster; Elizabeth herself was bound in the sum of £40 to appear and prosecute. Then in January 1691 John Leaver of Aylesbury, described elsewhere as a pinmaker, was indicted for defrauding Elizabeth Harding of 45s. 'under pretence of being the servant of the Duke of Ormond'.[22] The outcome of both cases is unknown, but Leaver's recognisance (surety) was discharged in July 1695. The following February the parish register records the burial of 'Elizabeth Harding spinster who was killed in her own howes [sic] a fowle murder'. An elderly single woman living alone and known to have money was all too vulnerable. She was 78 years old.

William's continuing links with his Jennings kindred are shown by two wills. The first is that of his uncle, Michael Jennings of Stoke Mandeville, made in October 1696 and proved the following April, in which he is named as residuary heir, jointly with Samuel Gurney, and also as one of the three overseers and trustees for the bringing up at school of the testator's under-age son Alexander, born in 1681; the others were Samuel Gurney and John Tockfield. In an evident reference to the Jennings manor of Burleys, the overseers are instructed to keep court once in three years, and for their trouble, to retain the quitrents. Gurney, who lived at Bierton, was William's uncle by marriage, having married his mother's sister, Jane Jennings. The quitrents, which are unlikely to have been of much value, are all that William is likely to have received, apart from a memorial ring bearing the initials M.J., the date of donor's burial and the sobering legend 'Think on death'.[23]

William fared better in the second of the two wills, made by another (presumed) uncle, Francis Jennings of Wendover, and proved in 1703. After making a number of bequests totalling some £80 in which the poor of Wendover, Stoke Mandeville and Walton were remembered, Francis left the residue of his goods and chattels to 'my cozen William Harding of Walton'.[24]

The death in September 1701 of William's mother Elizabeth, still resident in Walton and doubtless still sharing the family farmhouse with her sons, was a significant event in his life and the lives of all her children; although she must, on the youngest estimate, have been in her late seventies, and may well have been over eighty, her will, made in June 1699, indicates that she retained a close and loving relationship with her children and grandchildren. The motivation underlying her moneylending activities over so many years is now revealed in the shape of bequests to her immediate family totalling some £300. They demonstrate sound judgement and careful thought for the best interests of all concerned.[25]

Joyce Webb, the elder of her two surviving daughters, who appears not to have had any children, or at any rate any that survived, is left the interest on £60 at five per cent per annum, producing a useful annuity of £3. If her blacksmith husband should predecease her, she would be free to reclaim the principal sum, but if she herself should die first, the money would be shared equally by Elizabeth's nine under-age grandchildren (five girls and four boys), the offspring of her daughters Sarah Clarke and Ann Stallwood (both deceased) and Jane Horton. Jane, her youngest child, receives 20s. only, but Jane's five children get a total of £120 – £30 to each of the two eldest and £20 apiece to the others without distinction of sex. These sums are payable at the age of 21, but in the meantime the children are to receive the annual interest on their shares.

The two orphan children of Sarah Clarke, who had recently died, get £30 apiece on the same terms, and the two children of Ann Stallwood receive £30 and £20 respectively. Elizabeth Stable, or Staple, presumably the grown-up daughter of Elizabeth Staple, receives £5 and some linen. In the event of default by the person in whose hands the money is placed at interest, the resulting loss is to be shared by all the beneficiaries in proportion to the size of the legacy in each case. In her capacity of administrator of Sarah's goods, Elizabeth disposes of her and her late husband's personal effects for the benefit of their children and appoints her brother-in-law Samuel Gurney of Bierton and her son-in-law William Webb of Aylesbury as trustees for their 'bringing up and education'.

The testator's 'loving sons', William and John, are not forgotten. John receives £50 and William 'all my meadow ground lying and being in Aylesbury field', doubtless the meadow at Dunsham, purchased in 1678. Such of Elizabeth's goods as are not disposed of in her lifetime are to be equally divided among her two sons and the children of her daughters Sarah, Ann and Jane.

Three sons-in-law, John Horton, William Stallwood and William Webb, are left token sums of 10s. apiece for the customary mourning gloves; the fourth, Thomas Staple, receives only a shilling. The poor of Aylesbury town get 40s. and the poor of Walton 20s. William and John are named as joint executors of the will, which is witnessed by Benjamin and Hannah Deearing [*sic*] and Matthias Dagnall.

Apart from her brother-in-law Samuel Gurney, Elizabeth's will makes no reference to her Jennings family connections, nor are there any bequests to neighbours and friends. Probably she had outlived those to whom she had been close in both categories. More typical in some ways of widows' wills is that of her neighbour, Anne Whitchurch of Walton, who died the same month as Elizabeth. It distributes small sums totalling over £65 among 26 named individuals – besides others not named – residing in Walton, Wing, Mentmore (where she was buried) and elsewhere. They include a daughter, three grand-daughters and no fewer than 11 'cousins', nine of them female, as well as people apparently not related. Besides cash, or in place of it, some receive gifts of clothing ('my damask Gowne', 'one lined petticoat', 'my crepe gown', 'one apron and two Quoifs') or articles of furniture ('my great joyne[d] box and close stool', my bedstead and beding thereunto belonging').[26]

William was now approaching the age of 60 and was still a bachelor. If the continued presence of his mother had influenced his decision not to marry,

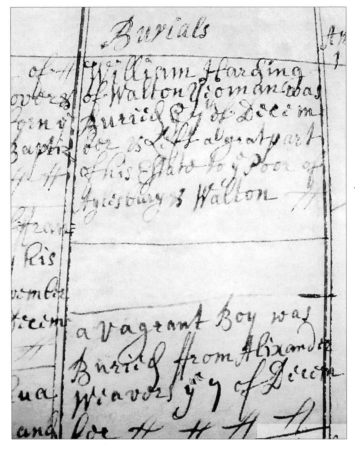

3 *Entry of the burial of William Harding on 7 December 1719 in the Aylesbury parish register. A note states that he 'Left a great part of his Estate to ye Poor of Aylesbury & Walton'.*

that obstacle had been removed, but he evidently judged it too late to change his way of life, for the evidence indicates that he continued in his bachelor state. There is, however, evidence from around this time of a close business (and presumably personal) relationship with his only brother John.

In 1705 William purchased an acre of land and three leys (arable converted to temporary pasture) in Walton field from Thomas Kemp and, the following year, land called Bierton Closes from Thomas Plamplin of Birmingham. The original of the latter document tells us that they comprised two closes of meadow on the south-east side of the main Aylesbury road, containing together 10 acres, and were part of ground formerly called New Pasture. This acquisition, being enclosed land not subject to common rights, would have added flexibility to his farming operations by enabling him to increase his number of livestock. It was not without encumbrances, however, as a small annual payment due to the Bierton Feoffees' charity had to be shared with the adjoining owner Samuel Gurney. The price paid was £300, or £30 an acre. This property was let after William's death at £22 a year.[27]

No other land purchases are recorded after 1706, but the accounts kept by his executors after his death show that at this period (and possibly earlier)

William, too, was lending out considerable sums of money on the security of personal bonds and mortgages, and that some of the loans were in the joint names of William and his brother. There are no fewer than 18 loans in William's name only, dated between 1697 and early 1719 and totalling just under £650. They range in size from £10, to Mr Loddington, the vicar of Aylesbury, to £100, on mortgage to Thomas Piddington of Whitchurch for lands in Bierton. In addition, nine notes of hand dated between 1703 and 1717, for sums due to William totalling £111 12s., are listed. The joint loans, for which dates are not given, are 13 in number and amount to over £450.

Nor is this likely to have been the whole story, for loans repaid before 1719 would not have been worth recording and one entry refers to an 'additional' mortgage to one client although only one is listed. In many cases the abode of the borrower is given. All lived within a 10-mile radius extending from Swanbourne on the north to Wendover on the south, with the greatest number located in Walton and Aylesbury. No doubt many, if not most, of the borrowers were friends and business acquaintances of the Hardings. Some were relations. William and Joyce Webb had a mortgage of £50 on their house in Walton Street and William Webb and William Stallwood owed £5 (in two loans) and £6 on notes.

Some individuals can be readily identified in addition to those already mentioned. Thomas Ligo of Stoke Mandeville, gentleman, who owed £25 on bond, was presumably the justice of the peace of that name; Clement Hunt of Upton was a prominent Baptist leader; John Goldsworth and Henry Bailey were Aylesbury tradesmen; Samuel Harrison, clerk, was rector of Oving; Thomas Edmonds, who owed £100 on mortgages, was one of a dynasty of Aylesbury tenant farmers and yeomen. In the absence of banks, lending surplus cash in this way was not uncommon and could even be more profitable than investment in land in the generally depressed state of farming of the late 17th century, largely the result of a virtually static level of population. But even William's extensive lending hardly compares with that of his neighbour, Christopher Webb of Bedgrove, who was owed over £3,000 'upon bonds bills and mortgages' at his death in 1681.[28]

William's brother John also made at least one loan on his own account. A stray deed dated June 1713 records that in January 1708 he had advanced £85 to Henry Freer of Little Gaddesden, Hertfordshire, on a mortgage of a cottage and four acres of enclosed meadow in Walton, then in Freer's own occupation. This mortgage is now assigned to a new lender, William Webb of Dunstable, Bedfordshire, a carrier. The interest due to John Harding works out at less than two per cent but 'other good and valuable considerations' are also cited for the transfer. John attests this document with an illiterate's mark.[29]

William's last loan, on security of a mortgage, was dated 3 April 1719, a few weeks before the burial of his brother John Harding, 'yeoman', is recorded in the parish register on 13 May. On 5 August he made his will; four months later he too was dead. Dated 7 December, the burial entry reads 'William Harding of Walton yeoman ... left a great part of his estate to ye poor of Aylesbury and Walton'.[30]

PART TWO

THE CHARITY

III

The Endowment

Managing the Estate, 1719-1754

1. The Will

Since William Harding's will, proved at London on 19 February 1720,[1] was the original governing instrument of the charity which bears his name, it comes as a surprise that a large part of it is devoted to a sister-in-law, Sarah Harding, widow of his deceased brother John. This is because no hint of her existence has been found before this date. The marriage does not appear in the Aylesbury parish register and there is no mention of Sarah in Elizabeth Harding's will of 1699. Since from later evidence it is obvious that there must have been a great discrepancy in the ages of the couple, the possibility arises that the marriage – like that of Bridget Hide – was clandestine, i.e. one celebrated, usually by licence but in contravention of canon law, in a parish where neither party was a parishioner.

Prior to the Marriage Act of 1753 some clergymen were able and willing to supplement their (often inadequate) incomes by facilitating such concealment. The vicar of Aylesbury was one such, and the vicar of neighbouring Hartwell another. For obvious reasons many parishioners of Aylesbury who wished to marry without publicity favoured Hartwell. Thus the marriage by licence at Hartwell on 19 June 1715 of John Harding and Sarah Gurman, of which no further details are recorded, could well be the one we are seeking.[2] But the registered copy of the licence seems not to have survived and the bride cannot be traced, so there can be no certainty. It is clear, however, that wherever the marriage took place, there were no children living in 1719.

John himself made no will and no grant of administration has been found, but it appears that William inherited his landed property. Judging by their joint financial ventures, the brothers had been close, at least in their business operations, for some considerable time. References in William's accounts, copied by his executors, indicate that since at least 1710 some of their livestock had been sold jointly, the proceeds presumably being divided. Indeed the evidence is compatible with William and John – and Sarah – having shared the family homestead.

Under the terms of William's will Sarah Harding receives a life interest in the following properties: a messuage in Walton in the occupation of John

4 *The first page of William Harding's will, as entered in the earliest minute book of the Charity.*

Search and the close of pasture in which it stands called Hardings Elms close; the messuage in Walton in which the testator now dwells (but not the land belonging to it), to be kept in repair by his trustees; 20 acres of land dispersed in the common fields of Walton, formerly the lands of the testator's brother John Harding; two acres of land in Walton and one acre in Walton Suck Mead, all purchased by John Harding.

In addition, Sarah is to receive all William's household goods, comprising plate, linen, pewter, brass, beds and bedding and all the furniture of the house whatsoever; all the testator's crops of corn by him sown, or growing on land in his occupation at the time of his decease, as well as hay in the yard or barn and the following summer's crop of hay, with the right to sow wheat, beans and barley, according to season, out of his crop on any land not then sown with corn (fallow land), the intention being that she should receive the clear profits of the crop of corn and hay grown the summer after William's decease; all horses, cows, sheep and hogs, and all carts, ploughs and other instruments of husbandry; all firewood; half of the money arising from the sale of the testator's stock of corn and grain, threshed or unthreshed, in his possession at his death in his barns, ricks or other storehouses, and the interest of the other half at four per cent per annum, payable quarterly during her lifetime.

The total of 23 acres presumably represents John's holding which had come to William by inheritance, part of which ought by custom to have gone to John's widow for life for her maintenance. The contents of William's house – especially if she had been living in it – must have seemed more appropriate to Sarah than to William's other relations, and the arrangements regarding the grain crop and farm stock all tend to confirm an element of partnership between the brothers. Nor was this all, for in a separate deed of gift, dated 26 August 1719, William granted Sarah a moiety (a half share) of £353, 'being securities', representing the loans jointly due to the brothers which had been overlooked in the will itself. The reason why William felt it right to give Sarah two houses is explained if it is assumed that the one occupied by John Search, a labourer,[3] had belonged to John Harding.

William's blood relations also benefit by his will, though on a relatively modest scale. His two sisters, Jane Horton and Joyce Webb, get annuities of £5 and £4 respectively. In both cases the money is protected against predatory husbands (an all too likely contingency since the law was on the man's side) by the stipulation that 'no person ... that hath or shall Intermarry with her shall Intermeddle with the said Annuity or have power to demand the same'. This was obviously aimed in particular at Joyce's husband, whose record of financial management did not inspire confidence. Other bequests go to six named 'kinswomen', the testator's nieces, all except one of whom were still unmarried, and two 'kinsmen', identifiable as nephews. Of these, Elizabeth Stallwood and Ann Horton each get £30, Frances and Elizabeth Clarke and Sarah Horton £10 apiece, and Elizabeth Taylor and John and Francis Horton £5 apiece.

Finally come the instructions for endowing the new charity, directed to the trustees of the testator's estate. They are first of all to sell his house in the parish of Princes Risborough in the occupation of Thomas Poynter and to employ the proceeds, together with the residue of the proceeds from the sales of the personal estate, for the purchase of lands towards discharging the two annuities to his sisters and other charges and then to be employed in the trusts specified. The trustees are also to have, for the same purpose, the reversion of the two messuages and of Hardings Elms close and the 23 acres which had belonged to John Harding after Sarah Harding's decease, as well as all the testator's other messuages, lands, etc., in Walton or elsewhere in the parishes of Aylesbury, Bierton, Broughton, Stoke Mandeville, Princes Risborough or elsewhere, and all the residue of the testator's real and personal estate, including debts due on mortgages, bonds, bills or other debts and ready money. How William had come by the house in Risborough is not known, but since no title deeds are listed, it is probably safe to assume that it was another inheritance from the Jennings family, probably through his uncle Francis.

2. The Charity

Then comes the business of setting up the Charity. With the profits of the trust estate the trustees and their successors are enjoined:

(1) to raise the sum of 40s. (£2) yearly to be laid out in buying coats for poor men and women in the precincts or liberties of Walton in the parish of Aylesbury, such coats to be distributed every year on the feast day of St Thomas the Apostle (21 December) to such poor men and women inhabitants as the trustees think the most proper objects of charity, beginning the next St Thomas's Day after the testator's decease. (There were already two Walton clothing charities in existence in 1719 so a larger sum would probably have been inappropriate.)

(2) 'forever hereafter truly and faithfully [to] Distribute and Imploy towards the putting out poor Children Apprentice in such manner as in this my last will is herein after Declared and Directed (that is to say) That the said Trustees or the Major part of them or the heirs or Successors of them shall make choice of such Boys or Girls to be Apprentices as they in their Discretions shall think convenient Provided always the Boys or Girls so made Choice of be the Children of poor Persons settled Inhabitants within the Parish of Aylesbury or Walton.'

Then come more detailed directions for the management of the Charity, all of which are eminently practical. The trustees are to meet twice yearly at the town of Aylesbury on the first Mondays of May and November, or on a day fixed by them at one week's notice, 'to Enquire and Consult about putting out poor Children Apprentice and about procureing fit Masters and Mistresses for that purpose in performance of which I do intreat of the said Trustees to use their utmost diligence and care that the Children … be bound to persons who are Honest of good Moralls Able and well skilled in their severall Trades'. The trustees are to have 25 shillings (£1 5s.) at every half-yearly meeting 'to be spent by them in way of Treat and as an acknowledgement for their Trouble'. They are from time to time to choose two of their number to receive the rents and profits of the lands and apply and account for them and each receiver is to have 10s. yearly for his trouble.

The remaining income is to be employed in placing out poor children, allowing to each child such sum of money, not to exceed £10, as seems 'convenient' to the trustees. Whenever a trustee dies the survivors are to elect a successor to the vacancy by a vote in writing under their hands and seals, attested by two credible witnesses, each person so elected to be a substantial householder living within the parish of Aylesbury or Walton. Trustees are not to be liable for any casual or involuntary loss or miscarriage and shall be responsible only for so much as they respectively receive by or out of the income and on account of the same.

The trustees named – they were also the testator's 'well beloved friends' – are William James, gentleman, Thomas Watson, gentleman, Noah Pitcher, 'chirurgeon' (surgeon), Thomas Williams, apothecary, and Matthias Dagnall, stationer, who are given power to elect new trustees as vacancies arise. Watson is described as of Edgcott and the others as of Aylesbury. The witnesses to the will are Thomas Deering, John Stopp, Thomas Wootton and Joseph Ingram. Stopp seems to have been a neighbouring farmer of that name; Ingram, a Presbyterian, is described in the parish register as a labourer. He was given charge of threshing the grain but died before the work was finished.

The Charity was now in being, but what were the considerations that had induced William Harding to act in this way? One suspects that, as an ageing bachelor, he had already taken a decision about the disposal of his property long before his death and that his financial operations had in some degree been directed to facilitating it. Some of his inspiration may well have come from the bequest of the enormous sum of £5,000 for the re-endowment of the existing free grammar school in Aylesbury under the will of Henry Phillips, who died in 1714. In his will, Phillips, a London merchant, had made provision to enable boys to receive instruction not only in the classics but also in such practical subjects as reading, writing, arithmetic and accounts, 'so as to be fit to go and be apprentices to good trades'.[4]

Here, it may have occurred to William, was a way of building on what had so recently been accomplished. Phillips had entrusted the work, begun in 1718, of rebuilding and enlarging the handsome brick schoolhouse (now part of the County Museum complex), designed to accommodate up to 120 pupils (not excluding Dissenters), to his cousin William Mead, of the Prebendal House in Aylesbury. Since reading and writing were included in the curriculum of the lower, or 'writing', school (there was no necessary progression) and pupils were accepted, free of charge, from an early age, there is every reason to suppose that many of the future recipients of Harding's charity would have spent at least a few years at the school. It may be no coincidence that William James, one of the trustees named in the will, besides being a trustee of the new grammar school foundation, was a close friend of Mead, who left him a large cash legacy of £200.[5]

William Harding must surely also have been influenced by his own experience of public office. As churchwarden and overseer of the poor he had been responsible, jointly with his fellow parish officers, for apprenticing orphan children and children of poor parents receiving parish relief, the object being to get them off the parish's hands while at the same time making some provision for their future welfare. William had been involved in this work as recently as 1712 and his name appears on three surviving parish apprenticeship indentures of that year.[6] He was certainly well aware that, for want of adequate premiums, the future prospects of such children were all too often blighted. Unlike many such benefactors (such as Thomas Hickman, whose almshouses were founded in 1698), William did not limit his charity to the children of persons not receiving parish relief. In this way he ensured that the ratepayers too could not fail to benefit directly from his foundation, hence the generous size of the endowment which he provided.

3. The First Trustees

By calling or status, all William's five trustees belonged to what contemporaries termed the 'middling sort' or above, which, in the context of a market town such as Aylesbury, effectively placed them among the urban elite. Despite the warm terms used of them in the will, one suspects they were probably chosen as much for their public standing and business competence as for friendship's sake.

Though he had strong family connections with the town, William James was apparently not born in Aylesbury. Between 1714 and 1723, however, his name appears in the parish register – along with that of his wife Hannah – among the entries supplied to the vicar by the minister of the Presbyterian congregation in connection with the births of their eight children. He is possibly the same William James who married Hannah Southen at Hedgerley in south Bucks in 1714. His mother, Faith, was one of the three daughters and co-heiresses of Richard Cockman of Aylesbury, who died in 1707, and his wealthy spinster aunt Mary (b.1670) was the last descendant of this ancient Aylesbury dissenting family, some of whom had once been bailiffs of the manor of Aylesbury.[7]

William James's aunt was a woman of considerable fortune. At the time of her death in 1735 she was living in her large and luxuriously furnished house in Aylesbury, apparently alone apart from her maidservant, the aptly named Dependance Lane. William was to be the principal beneficiary and sole executor of her will, made 1734, which also provided for an annual payment of £5 for the support of the minister of the Presbyterian congregation. From his aunt's will we learn that William had a brother, a soap boiler, in London, and he also had connections to the capital through his friend William Mead. He himself seems to have been of independent means. As already noted, he was a trustee of the newly enlarged Aylesbury free grammar school. He had also served as a parish overseer of the poor in 1713. In politics his voting record shows him to have been – as one would expect a Dissenter to be – a strong Whig.[8]

Matthias Dagnall (1658-1736), bookseller and stationer, was the son of Stephen Dagnall, also a bookseller, a prominent local Baptist leader and teacher and the author of many pamphlets expressing levelling opinions. Matthias himself had conformed to the established Church. He and his father had lived at Walton for a time and he was one of the witnesses to the will of William Harding's mother, Elizabeth Harding. He was among the subscribers to the folio edition of Milton's *Paradise Lost* in 1688. Dagnall's account book recording the expenses incurred in building the new grammar school, which he kept for William Mead, is still extant. He had held office as a churchwarden in 1701 and 1702, when he was accused of procuring an illegal rate. Dagnall sold current pamphlets, ballads and prints and his shop would have been a popular meeting place for the better off. One of his son's regular customers was Sir Thomas Lee, 3rd baronet, of Hartwell. Matthias Dagnall too was a Whig.[9]

Thomas Williams and Noah Pitcher (who lived in Walton) were both prominent local medical practitioners. The parish register shows that, like William James, Williams was a member of the Presbyterian congregation which, though shrinking in numbers, was probably still the town's largest and most influential body of Dissenters. He became apothecary to the poor prisoners in the county gaol in 1715, displacing his Tory rival for the appointment. He was dismissed in 1726 for unknown causes but was restored to his post a year later and was still in office in 1730. Williams was also a party to the lawsuit over the grammar school trust. The family monument in the parish church records a long dynasty of apothecaries.[10]

Pitcher's services as a surgeon were also made use of at the county gaol, though apparently on a casual basis. In addition to 'curing' (the word invariably

5 *Accounts referring to William Harding's burial expenses.*

used in the court records) dislocations and contusions, he was required to deal with ulcers, tumours, skin diseases and gangrene. He was a churchwarden in 1715-16; he did not vote in county elections, perhaps lacking the necessary property qualification or wishing to steer clear of party politics.[11]

No information has come to light on Thomas Watson of Edgcott, beyond the fact that he held office as chief constable for Buckingham Hundred in 1692-3 and had 11 quarts of milk stolen from him in 1700, so he may have been a farmer or grazier.[12] As a trustee he is exceptional in not being an Aylesbury resident.

In their capacity as executors the trustees were responsible for proving William Harding's will and for attending to the funeral arrangements, which the testator had left to their discretion. Brief details of the expenses incurred are entered in the earliest trust record book containing accounts of income and expenditure and minutes of orders concerning apprenticeships approved at meetings of the trustees, 1720-38. This is a handsome, leather-bound volume, impeccably written up by Matthias Dagnall, which covers the period 1719-40 and is our principal source for the period. It is in fact a duplicate copy of a lost original, made in 1739 (with additions) for the information of Edward Price (trustee, 1738), whose name is inscribed on the flyleaf; a second, similar volume, the cover of which is embossed with the name 'John Wilkes' (trustee, 1754), is mostly blank.

At the front of the book is a copy of the founder's will, followed by a number of separate accounts related to the executorship; also included are memoranda of elections of trustees to 1754, and summary rentals of the Charity estates for *c.*1739 and 1754. There is no separate minute book as such and it is unlikely that any was kept during this period.

4. *Funeral and Probate – Rebuilding the Farmhouse*

The trustees' first responsibility was to organise the funeral, which was held on 7 December 1719. The accounts show that Thomas Lee, a carpenter, charged £2 5s. for the coffin, while Mr Loddington, the vicar, was paid £1 10s. for his funeral dues and sermon; there were also fees to the clerk and the sexton. Burial took place within the church, as appears from payments to a Mr Oviatt 'for tyth [tithe] and for Mr Hardings grave in the chancel' and to the workman 'for bricks and making up the Deceaseds grave', but, sadly, there is no mention, here or later, of a monument.

Other expenses relate to the mourners attending the funeral and their needs. The modest sum of three shillings was spent on 'a journey to invite friends to the funeral'. Catering was shared out among local tradesmen and shopkeepers, who were mostly paid £5-£6 each, a substantial boost to trade. 'Mr' William Dawney (of the *Crown* inn) charged for 'wine in his last sickness and at the funeral' and 'Mr' Thomas Smith (of the *George*) also supplied wine. Charles Heywood, William Holton, John Edmonds (baker) and Henry Bass provided cake and bread; Charles Goldfinch, described as a tallow chandler (a grocer) in the parish register, was paid a bill for 'mourning &c'.

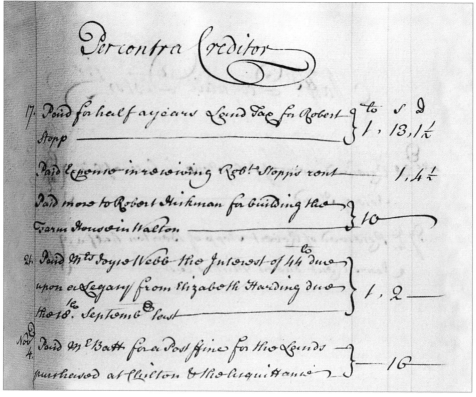

6 *Extract from the accounts showing a payment to Robert Hickman, a carpenter, for expenses in rebuilding the Walton farmhouse, October 1728.*

Bills for unspecified funeral expenses were also paid to 'Mr' Alexander Merrick, a woollen draper of Quaker antecedents,[13] 'Mr' John Wilson and 'Mr' John Goldsworth, the latter, according to the parish register, a linen draper; Merrick's bill was much the largest at £12 1s. 6d. Three pounds in weight of candles were purchased for 1s. 7d. and there is a poignant bill from Silvester Dormer, evidently a hairdresser, 'for one qu[arte]rs trimming of Mr Harding'. Matthias Dagnall was the trustee most involved with the arrangements. His own bill for 'funeral charges &c.' came to a hefty £15 5s. 6d. There was also a bill of £1 11s. 8d. from Thomas Williams 'for physick in his sickness'. The total cost of the funeral came to over £75. It was clearly a very splendid send-off; one wonders whether William Harding would have approved of the expense.

No time was lost in getting on with the business of probate. On 10 December, three days after the funeral, an inventory of William Harding's personal estate was taken by Richard Babham and Thomas Bigg, neighbouring farmers.[14] The total valuation was £1,128 5s., making William a very rich man in local terms – certainly much richer than the average yeoman farmer. Even this total seems to have been an under-estimate, for the accounts indicate that the debts due to the deceased, which in the inventory are put at £648 10s. (including £122 described as 'desperate debts'), or over half the total value of the personal estate, actually amounted to well over £1,000 in securities, notes of hand and book debts. These assets, together with the ready money (£36 10s.), constituted the trust's share of the personal estate, less the sum gifted to Sarah by the deed of August 1719 and her half share of the crop of grain. The farm stock was valued at £351 3s., comprising corn and grain valued at £175 15s., livestock (10 horses, mares and colts, 13 cows and bullocks, 185 sheep and four pigs) valued at £108 8s., and wool, hay and firewood valued at £67. The remainder, £128 12s., was the value of the household goods and chattels, the most valuable single item being the linen, which was reckoned at £56. A few weeks later an application for probate was formally granted in London on 19 February 1720, and the work of executing the will could proceed.

The regular cycle of half-yearly meetings of the trustees in May and November prescribed by the will was adopted from the first, but the accounts of income and expenditure covering the early years have numerous references to expenses incurred at other business meetings, most of them undated, the first being held on 12 January 1720 'at John Reeds', possibly the *King's Head* inn, where a Thomas Read was landlord in 1702.[15] The accounts themselves are often far from self-explanatory in this period. Some of the more obscure entries can be interpreted – if at all – only with the help of outside information, mostly drawn from the 1739 list of deeds and documents, to which reference has previously been made. No annual balances are struck, entries sometimes appear to be inconsistent and possibly incomplete and there are indications that sizeable amounts of cash were sometimes left in the hands of individual trustees.

One priority was to get in cash to cover the inevitable costs of administering the founder's wishes as expressed in the will. The threshing of the corn and the sale of the grain had been put in hand in December and would keep four men constantly employed throughout the winter. The 'Walton farm' was leased to Robert and William March in September 1720, and the Bierton land, to Robert Stopp in November. From the accounts it appears that the annual rents were respectively £50 and £22. More rewarding in the short term was the calling in of loans, and here too good progress was made. In the course of 1720 and 1721 well over £500 was realised in payments of principal and interest due, of which over £400 came from four debtors. In December 1721 the sum of £275 was converted to banknotes, then still a relatively new form of exchange, and early in the following year a further £500 was invested in East India Company bonds for the use of the trustees. Loans continued to be repaid in the following years but some borrowers continued to pay interest and a significant number of loans, mostly small, were still outstanding in 1739.

William's own personal debts were trivial by comparison, being virtually limited to the cost of 'sheep commons' purchased from neighbours to enable him to graze more than his quota of sheep on the common pasture and fallow ground of the manor. Payment of William's legacies to his relations had been dealt with by the end of 1720, but it had also proved necessary for the trustees to take over the executorship of the will of Elizabeth Harding, William's mother, which had still not been wound up nearly two decades after her death (it was proved in October 1720). By January 1721 the trustees were in a position to add to the estate by purchasing 12 acres of land in Walton from John Todd, though no mention of the transaction appears in the accounts. This was the last such addition to the Walton property.

In 1721-2 more than £10 was spent on thatching the Walton farmhouse, explicable as part of the trustees' obligation under the will to execute necessary repairs there. Less obvious is the reason for the trustees' involvement with Harding's Elms, where timber was being felled on a considerable scale by 1725 and the proceeds of its sale, amounting in all to over £80, were being entered as receipts. Not all the timber was disposed of, for in June 1727 payment was made for a stock lock and staple 'to lock up the timber &c. at Marches' and for the cost of 'laying up the stuff at Marches farm'. March was the name of the tenants of the trustees' Walton farm, who on this evidence would appear to have been occupying the farmhouse as well as the land.

The purpose of the timber is made clear by a payment dated July 1728 for 'Expense at the George agreeing with Robert Hickman to rebuild the farm house'. Hickman was an Aylesbury carpenter who also happened to be a trustee of Hickman's almshouses. Earlier the same year a new lease of the Walton farm had been made to John Stopp at an increased annual rent of £60, doubtless reflecting the projected improvements. Work began without delay and on 20 August a payment of 10s. for ale for the workmen 'at the house rearing' (the erection of the main timbers) is recorded. The precise date of completion is not apparent but expenditure continued throughout 1729 and the last payments were made in mid-May 1730.

The total cost came to just over £266, which does not include the value of the timber from Elm Close and of re-used materials. Of this sum a total of

£149 was paid to Hickman. Payments for bricks and lime amounting in total to £60 7s. 9d. were made to Henry Bailey and William Ells, the latter's share being £10. Dagnall's son-in-law John West received £16 4s. for ironmongery and 'Dr Pitcher', one of the trustees, was reimbursed for £35 spent by him 'towards building the Stables & repairs about ye Farm in Walton'. Smaller sums were also paid to Richard Simms, identified elsewhere in the accounts as a mason, including one of 19s. 8d. 'for pitching (paving) the Stable &c', and to Henry Hawkins for '16 Deals', or planks. There are no references to roofing materials as such, but doubtless roof tiles were subsumed under bricks. A few years later, in 1733, a bill for £4 13s. 6d. was paid for thatching done by John Stopp at the farm (also thatched the following year was a new 'mud' boundary wall, a traditional form of construction known locally as 'wichert') and in 1738 a total of some £13 was again expended in thatching John Stopp's farm and his barns at Walton.

The rebuilt house, now used as a school, still stands in Walton Road (No. 23), facing Walton pond. With its facade of vitreous and red bricks and its well-proportioned central doorway with Roman Doric pilasters, it is a good example of an early Georgian dwelling house.

Earlier, the trustees, in accordance with the terms of the will, had sold the house in Princes Risborough for £140 to one Samuel Hiron in 1724. In October 1727 they had also, again in accordance with the will, purchased land in the parish of Chilton, over ten miles to the west of Aylesbury, from Henry Gould, esquire. From later evidence, this property, known as Beany, or Beanhill, Field, comprised some 48 acres of valuable enclosed pasture, which may previously have been arable, for there is a reference in one of the lists of documents to an undated lawsuit involving a Mr Winter, including an Exchequer commission 'to find out ye plowing of Beanyfield'. It was leased in 1729 to Mr Winter for an annual rent of £50, which was clearly a much higher rent per acre than was charged for the Bierton land. From the accounts it appears that it represented an outlay of just over £1,000, a very large investment.

5. *The Pettipher Affair*

In 1720, however, the trustees made a disconcerting discovery which was to complicate the affairs of the new charity for many years to come, and which throws light on some of their actions thus far. This was that Sarah Harding, the founder's sister-in-law and chief beneficiary of his will, had secretly remarried within a month or two of his death. The first hint of this development in the accounts is in connection with the threshing and sale of the grain in store. Under the will, Sarah was immediately entitled to half the net proceeds of grain sold, which, by mid-March 1720, when a balance was struck, came to £132 13s. 10d. A signed memorandum endorsed on the account states that at a meeting of trustees on 14 March the 'moiety' was duly paid to 'Mr Pettipher pursuant to the will'. Mr Pettipher, it becomes increasingly evident from later entries, was not Sarah's servant or agent but her husband.

No record of the marriage is to be found in the Aylesbury parish register but further searching revealed a marriage in an unexpected place which seems to clear up this particular mystery. It records that 'Mr' Henry Pettipher of Banbury and Mrs Sarah Harding of Walton in the parish of Aylesbury, Buckinghamshire, were married by licence at Banbury in Oxfordshire on 31 January 1720, less than eight months after the death of John Harding. How they had come together is a matter for surmise. There was, for example, at least one family of Pettiphers then living in Aylesbury, but it is just as likely that Sarah had links with Banbury, for the surname Gurman (her presumed maiden name) – rare in both counties – is found in Banbury at this time.[16]

Henry Pettipher (also spelt Petifer) was, it seems, a draper, a trade that was both capital-intensive and highly respectable. But if Sarah thought she had made a desirable match she was soon to be disappointed, for when we next catch sight of Pettipher on 20 May 1721 it is as the subject of a commission of bankruptcy included in the 1739 list. It may well be significant that Henry's bankruptcy followed so closely on the bursting of the South Sea Bubble, the first ever major stock exchange crash, which occurred in the months immediately following August 1720. Its effects were widespread among traders of all descriptions throughout the country owing to the proliferation, in this increasingly commercial age, of extensive credit networks, often linked to London wholesalers. Either way, Henry's marriage to a widow of means was – to say the least – convenient in the circumstances, for as another contemporary tradesman, Daniel Defoe, discovered to his cost, the fate of the bankrupt was, at best, extremely unpleasant and, at worst, could lead to a debtors' prison and utter ruin.

It is obvious that her husband's misfortune had implications for Sarah's life interest in the Charity estate, for even if she could raise sufficient cash to pay off his creditors – which is doubtful – there would have been a strong incentive to try to avoid any such drastic step, and it appears that effective action was in fact taken to ease the situation. In August 1722 the Charity's accounts contain a payment for expense incurred 'at signing a counterpart of the Commissioners of Bankrupts deed for Mrs Pettiphers estate'. The precise function of this document is unknown but it evidently exempted Mrs Pettipher herself from the effects of the bankruptcy (presumably because her property was held in trust), because the following year Sarah, wife of Henry Pettipher, subscribed in her own right the Buckinghamshire roll of those taking the oath of allegiance, an obligation which had been placed on all landowners by recent legislation.[17]

Over the next few years there is evidence – much of it derived from the 1739 list of documents – of further negotiations concerning Mrs Pettipher's property, the basis of which would seem to have been that the Pettiphers wished to maximise their financial assets while the trustees were in want of a farmhouse. In March 1724 Mrs Pettipher executed a conveyance, contents unknown, to the trustees and under the same year there is a reference to a 'parcel of notes of hand from Mr Alexander Merrick on Mr Pettiphers account'. In June 1726 expenses were incurred in 'agreeing with Mrs Pettipher for her life in the farmhouse' and in the following March a conveyance was finally executed to the trustees of 'Mrs Pettiphers house in Walton for life'. The *quid pro quo* was another conveyance, also dated March 1727, of 'Mrs Pettiphers lands in Walton and Stoke in trust'; from later sources it is apparent that Mrs Pettipher was in fact given a life interest in the founder's land in Stoke Mandeville (amounting, on later evidence, to over 30 acres) in addition to the house and land at Hardings Elms in Walton referred to in the founder's will.

Mrs Pettipher's trustees were two local shopkeepers, Charles Goldfinch, the tallow chandler, and Alexander Merrick, the woollen draper. Merrick was the tradesman who had provided credit, in the form of notes of hand, in 1724. He was an educated man with some literary pretensions and is the author of an accomplished poem, published in 1737, in praise of the newly improved formal gardens of Sir Thomas Lee, baronet, of Hartwell, for which the grateful Sir Thomas gave him 10 guineas.[18]

As a result of the arrangements entered into, Henry Pettipher seems to have been discharged from his bankruptcy, for in July 1727 he, too, took the oath of allegiance and the following November obtained a certificate that he had taken the sacrament according to the forms of the Church of England, a qualification usually only required from holders of certain public offices.[19] Earlier, in April 1725, the baptism of Sarah, the daughter of 'Mr Henry Pettipher, mercer', had been entered in the Banbury parish register.

Things now seemed to be on an even keel again and the trustees could safely proceed with the rebuilding of the Walton farmhouse. In February 1729 the Aylesbury parish register records the birth of a son, John, to Henry Pettipher, draper, and 'Sara' his wife, the reference to a trade seeming to confirm that Henry was back in business. During 1729 and the following few years the accounts show occasional payments to Mr Pettipher made on the authorisation of one or more named trustees, the largest being £15 in January 1729. Sarah herself is not mentioned in the accounts after May 1730.

But from 1731 there are indications that all was not well again. In March of that year expense was incurred at the *Crown* 'with Mr Pettipher & his lawyer' and thereafter counsel's fees were paid to Mr Pilsworth, a local lawyer. Soon matters were being taken to a higher level. In August 1732 Pilsworth was paid two guineas 'upon his consulting Judge Wills', identifiable as Sir John Willes (1685-1761), afterwards Lord Chief Justice of the Common Pleas, 'upon Pettiphers business'.[20] By 1735 the trustees were in negotiation with Lord North, an influential peer. North's role in the matter is not made clear, but as Francis North he had been M.P. for Banbury from 1727 until his elevation to the peerage in October 1729, and it may be that his patronage of Pettipher stemmed from this connection. The upshot was that Lord North took it upon himself to give a bond to the trustees dated 26 October 1736 'to indemnify them in paying Pettiphers money he being a bankrupt'. The clear inference is that Pettipher had been bankrupted a second time, and was legally barred from receiving money from any source.[21]

Under cover of Lord North's indemnity, measures were put in hand 'to settle Mr Pettiphers account' and in the meantime cash payments to him and to local tradesmen on his behalf become more numerous, amounting to over £140 in 1736-7. They included two payments of £5 in February 1737 'to buy seed for his crop', suggesting that it was 'back to the land' for Henry and Sarah. On 17 June 1737 a payment of just over £25 was made to Pettipher by order of all the trustees 'on a balance of the chief of his accounts'. This settlement was followed in July 1737 by the start of two 'annuities' (soon combined) of £69 and £76 19s. 2d., the former apparently representing the proceeds of the second moiety of corn sold in 1720. These were sums credited to Pettipher, for which interest was paid quarterly at the rate of four per cent per annum, providing together a modest yearly income of £5 16s. After 1737 other advances to Pettipher cease. Two years later the first extant Aylesbury rate book shows 'Pettipher' among the occupiers of land in Walton.

6. New Trustees – the Charity's Finances in the late 1730s

The settlement with Pettipher was complicated by changes in the personnel of the trustees. The first of the original trustees to die had been Thomas Williams, who died in July 1732, aged 67 years. His place had been taken by John Dudley (1694-1745), the recently appointed vicar of Aylesbury. Surprisingly, perhaps, since he was also archdeacon of Bedford and held the prebend of Aylesbury in Lincoln Cathedral, Dudley was a regular attender. His appointment points to a softening of sectarian animosity. Politically Dudley, though a clergyman, was evidently a moderate, for in the county election of 1734 he split his two votes between one of the two Whig candidates and the solitary Tory.[22]

The next three vacancies all occurred in 1736. At a special meeting in June of that year Wilson Williams, apothecary, son of Thomas, was elected in place of Noah Pitcher, deceased, and Matthias Dagnall the younger (1697-1773), stationer, the elder of the two sons of Matthias senior, replaced Thomas Watson, deceased. In November Benjamin Burroughs of Aylesbury, esquire, succeeded Matthias Dagnall the elder, who had died in September, aged 78. In 1733 Burroughs was co-proprietor with John Delafield, a London leather seller, of the Aylesbury waterworks, an (apparently short-lived) enterprise for supplying piped water from the stream near the present Bourbon Street (formerly Waterhouse Street) to subscribers living in the town. He is thought to have been related to Giles Burroughs (or Burrows), of Long Crendon, a London merchant who was High Sheriff of Buckinghamshire in 1745 and who owned land in Walton. Benjamin Burroughs voted the same way as Dudley in 1734.[23]

Thus the only survivor of the original trustees was now William James. More changes followed in quick succession. Benjamin Burroughs died within the year and was replaced in May 1737 by Arthur Hodskins of Aylesbury, proprietor of the *White Hart* inn and wine merchant, who lived at Green End and who was churchwarden in 1720 and again in 1736. He, too, died within a short space of time, aged 53, 'much lamented by all who knew him', according to the parish

Bucks (to wit) At a Meeting of the surviving Trustees of the last will and Testament of Mr William Harding late of Walton in the Parish of Aylesbury in the County of Bucks Yeoman — Deceased held at Aylesbury aforesaid PRESENT Mr Wilson Williams Mr Edward Price Mr Thomas Sheene and Mr Matthias Dagnall for the electing a new Trustee of the said Mr William Harding's Charity in the stead and place of Mr William James the Elder of Aylesbury aforesaid Deceased a Trustee named and appointed in the said late Mr William Harding's last Will and Testament pursuant to the Orders and Directions contained in the said Will Wee the major part of the said Mr William Harding's surviving Trustees do hereby elect nominate authorize constitute and appoint John Wilkes Esquire of Aylesbury in the said County of Bucks a new Trustee of the said Mr William Harding's Charity and last Will and Testament and of all the Powers and Authorities contained in the same in the stead and place of Mr Wm James the Elder deceased In Witness whereof we have hereunto sett our Hands and Seals this Thirteenth Day of August 1754./.

Signed Sealed and Delivered
(being first duly Stampt) in
the presence of
Archdale Williams.
(.23.) Eliz: Williams.

Wilson Williams - - - ⓢ
E: Price . . - - . ⓢ
Tho: Sheene . . -- ⓢ
Matts Dagnall . -- ⓢ

7   *Formal certificate of election of John Wilkes, esquire, as a trustee in the place of William James, deceased, in the form prescribed by the founder's will, August 1754.*

register, leaving a large sum of money for an annual distribution to the poor. He was succeeded in January 1739 by Edward Price of Aylesbury, a lawyer, who was deputy steward of the manor of Aylesbury from 1750 to 1758 or later. He is presumably the Mr Price mentioned as a prospective undersheriff for the county in the Whig interest in 1760. His talents extended to surveying, for he was responsible for making a survey, dated 1758, of the estate of Bedford's Charity, of which he was also a trustee.[24]

The rapid turnover of trustees seems to have left some uncertainty about the Charity's finances in its wake. In April 1737 Matthias Dagnall, the new trustee, found it necessary to call on his brother Deverell Dagnall (1699-1773) to ride to Wendover to ask Mr Hoare to which of the trustees he had paid the principal and interest due on his father's mortgage and the sum due thereon and to make the same enquiry of Mr Norcott at Broughton. Formal notices were also sent to Mrs Pitcher and Mrs Watson to deliver up papers in their possession relating to William Harding's estate. All this is stated to have been done on the orders of Mr James.

Matthias Dagnall had succeeded to his father's role as sole accountant, or receiver. In December 1736 he claimed for 17 years' book keeping, beginning in December 1719, 'by order and direction of Mr Hardings will', at the rate of 20s. (£1) a year, amounting to £58 10s. 10d. Quite how this very substantial bill was arrived at is not explained, but the 20s. a year evidently refers to the 10s. apiece which two trustees acting as receivers were to have yearly under the provisions of the will. About the same time five duplicate copies of the accounts were transcribed in separate volumes, one for each of the trustees, at a cost of £2 2s. per copy, perhaps as a precaution against another such crisis of mortality. It is difficult to see this as anything other than an expensive job-creation exercise for the benefit of Mr Dagnall, but the existence of a large surplus made such expenses affordable and, as matters turned out, posterity has reason to be grateful for his industry. In November 1738 the sum of 10s. was expended 'for a desk and stand to hold the cash papers and other writings belonging to Mr Hardings estate'. Where the desk was intended to be kept is not disclosed; what we do know is that the deeds and papers, or a large proportion of them, were placed in Mr James's keeping the following year.

Evidence of greater awareness of the need for care in recording the finances is provided by formal memoranda of auditing, each of which is attested by three or more of the trustees. The first, dated 9 June 1736, shows a very large cash balance of just under £500 in Dagnall's hands. By 11 November 1738, when the next balance was taken, it amounted to just over £350, allowance being made for a deficiency of £20 which had been discovered 'in the old book kept by the father of this accomptant'. Finally, on 5 January 1741 a balance of £183 12s. is recorded, representing a decline of some £317 in the reserve over a period of four and a half years.

The cost of providing Edward Price with a new volume and engrossing 'all Mr Hardings accounts &c' in it in January 1739 came to £6 1s. The previous month 'Brother Deverell Dagnall' had been paid £8 16s. for 'compleating [updating] the accounts in all the Trustees books', and since Price's volume contains some accounts of later date than this (the series of minutes of trustees' orders ends in November 1738) it is clear that, in his case, some further updating took place. Further expenditure of £2 5s. 6d. was incurred in November 1739 'for making abstracts of writings and fetching them from Mr Watsons of Edgecott', presumably the son of the former trustee.

The accounts end in December 1740 and, although Price survived until 1773 or 1774, there are no later insertions apart from a rental, or 'list of tenants', dated 1754, one of two such lists (the other is undated but on internal evidence was made around 1739), and formal memoranda, duly witnessed, of elections of trustees, which include those of 'Mr' Thomas Sheen of Walton, in succession to the Reverend John Dudley, deceased, in January 1746 and of John Wilkes, esquire, in August 1754, in the place of William James the elder, deceased. There are also the two lists of the writings in the custody of William James the elder in 1739 at the back of the volume, which are written in a different hand from the other material in the book. One list is of documents, relating mainly to the Chilton property, which are stated to have been 'lodg'd', presumably with James, on 22 August; the other is of documents relating to the estate generally, lodged on 7 May 1739.

The second extant book, inscribed with Wilkes's name on the cover, is mostly blank apart from a copy of the founder's will and memoranda of elections, etc., 1737-54, all duplicated in the other volume. Loosely inserted in this volume is a sheet of paper with a list of trustees and dates of appointment, beginning in 1736, which adds the name of Archdale Williams, appointed 1758, to those already known to us. Archdale Williams (d.1766, aged 35), the last of the dynasty of apothecaries, evidently succeeded his father, Wilson Williams, who died in April 1758; he was then still in his twenties. He was also a trustee of Bedford's Charity.[25]

The c.1739 rental shows a total annual rent income of £141 10s. as follows (John Todd's rent, which was left blank, has here been supplied from the 1754 rental):

	£	s.	d.
John Stopp of Walton for the farm there and house he lives in	60	o	o
Anne Barnaby of Walton, widow for a parcel of land she rents there	3	o	o
John Todd of Walton for a parcel of land he rents there	[6	o	o]
Thomas Winter of Chilton, grazier for an enclosed pasture ground he rents there	50	o	o
Robert Stopp of Bierton, farmer for Bierton Closes and a parcel of field land there	22	o	o
Total	141	o	o

Setting aside John Todd's holding, rents were unchanged in 1754, doubtless reflecting the downturn in agricultural prices, which set in around 1720 and lasted until the mid-1740s. John Stopp, who had taken over the tenancy of the Walton farm in January 1728, was still there in 1754 and had also acquired 'meadow ground in the Crofts late in the occupation of Widow Anne Barnaby'. This piece of land had, it seems, been let during William Harding's lifetime to William Barnaby, who in 1719 owed back-rent from 1714 at £3 10s. a year. John Todd's holding in Walton is possibly the 12 acres there purchased from someone of that name in January 1721; 'John Todd farmer' was still tenant in 1754. Here we seem to have an example of an owner-occupier, in this case a smallholder, being transformed into a tenant, a process that was widespread in this period.

The accounts show that Thomas Winter had been succeeded at Chilton by 'Mr Cotes of Ickford' by 1739; in September 1740 Mr Cotes was allowed £1 11s. 'for mending the sheep pens at Beanhill field'. The tenant in 1754 was Daniel Jobson of Ickford, 'grazier'. The trustees had leased the close and lands in Bierton to Robert Stopp, who was paying rent at £6 a year in 1720. He was still tenant in 1738, but had been replaced by Thomas Hill of Aylesbury the following June. The accounts note an allowance of £1 9s. on Hill's rent 'for the poors land at Bierton' in June 1739. The tenant in 1754 was William Parker of Bierton.

I   *Aylesbury from the south, early 19th century. This colour print by Nathaniel Whittock shows the town as seen from the fields of Walton Court Farm. Visible on the skyline are the parish church of St Mary's, the Prebendal House (extreme left) and the County Gaol and Assize Court (centre).*

II   *Aerial view of part of Aylesbury's historic centre in 2000, showing the parish church of St Mary and Church Street. Green fields can still be seen in the Vale of Aylesbury to the north.*

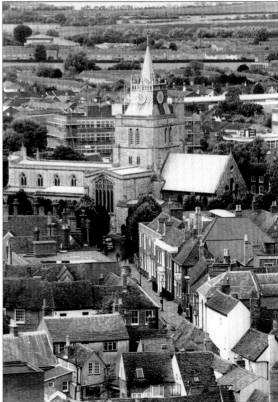

III *'Damn Heart the [Horse] Collar-maker', an Aylesbury craftsman, c.1790. The handwritten caption to this portrait drawing by J. Brett of Aylesbury tells us that its subject was born at the* Three Tuns, *was educated through the industry of his parents and served an apprenticeship at Whitchurch; it also comments on his corpulence, his good humour and his fondness for his pipe and pot. He has been identified from parish records as John Oviatt (1758-1798). Owing to a gap in the records it is not known whether he was a Harding's apprentice.*

The continuing legacy of William Harding's Charity to the inhabitants of Aylesbury. A small selection of photographs representing the many hundreds of community projects which have received financial assistance from the Charity since the 1970s.

IV   *The Roald Dahl Children's Gallery at the County Museum, Church Street. Opened in 1995, it attracts young visitors from far and wide.*

V   *Computer block at the Aylesbury Grammar School, opened in 1983.*

VI   *The Aylesbury Music Centre in Walton Road (incorporating the Roblin Hall), opened in 2001.*

VII *Courtyard of almshouses at William Harding Close, Walton, opened in 1996. The Charity is now responsible for over 30 almshouse units at various sites within the town.*

VIII *Queens Park Arts Centre, founded 1980. Based in the former Queens Park School, the Centre is a hub for many forms of artistic endeavour. It incorporates the Limelight Theatre and is also home to Youth Action. Shown here is a children's clay modelling class in progress.*

IX *Dinner held at the Judges' Lodgings, Aylesbury in April 2001 to mark the retirement of Mr Ernie Roblin after almost 20 years as chairman of William Harding's Charity. Mr Roblin is shown seated with Zena Williams. Pictured standing are (left to rigth): Betty Foster, the late Michael Sheffield, Chester Jones, Susanne Spinks (of Parrott & Coales), John Leggett (Clerk), Les Sheldon, Mike Griffin and Freda Roberts.*

Apprenticeship and the Poor Law
The Parish Economy of Welfare, 1691-1720

Nowadays apprenticeship (French *apprendre*, to learn; Latin *apprendere*, grasp) is associated with any form of practical, in-service, training, especially for the young. But for centuries it had a more specific, institutional meaning, denoting a customary practice of medieval origin by which a young person, usually aged between 14 and 16, was contractually bound to an individual 'master' for an extended period – traditionally seven years – of unpaid labour as a member of the employer's own household in order to learn a skilled trade or calling. The parties to the contract, or 'indenture', were normally the child itself and the prospective master (or mistress), who received a lump sum, or premium, from the child's parent or guardian in return. In this form apprenticeship was deeply embedded in the fabric of society to the extent that, in the words of one of its most recent historians, 'as an institution it reflects the social history of England to a remarkable degree'.[1] Nor was apprenticeship confined to artisans; it was the normal and, legally, the exclusive means of entry into most trades and professions. In the case of the more lucrative occupations the premiums could run to £100 or even more. Richard Jennings would have had to find a sum of this magnitude on his apprenticeship to a London grocer.

In origin primarily an urban phenomenon (there are references to apprentices in the chartered borough of Wycombe as far back as the 15th century),[2] in London and other large towns apprenticeship was regulated by livery companies and craft guilds, in part as a means of controlling the intake of labour. It was also a means of qualifying as a freeman of the borough corporation. For rural areas its legal status came to be defined by the Statute of Artificers of 1563, which codified earlier legislation and made provision for its regulation by the local justices of the peace in each county, who had power to hear complaints and also to punish those found practising a trade without having served an apprenticeship to it. It has been widely assumed by historians that apprenticeship in its traditional form was in steep decline as early as the late 17th century, but recent research[3] indicates that it continued in a relatively flourishing state until the second half of the 18th century, by which time its role in society was being gradually diminished by the growing insecurity of employment among skilled workers deriving from the massive economic and demographic changes associated with the period. Despite this it continued to be a significant institution until well into the 20th century.

The Statute of Artificers was also responsible for giving legal sanction to a new and distinct category of apprenticeship known as parish, or pauper, apprenticeship. This was the compulsory apprenticing by individual parishes of orphans, and other poor children for whom the parish was responsible, under the evolving Poor Law relief system as an alternative to fostering or other forms of maintenance from the parish rates. Here the emphasis was on labour and social discipline rather than on learning a specialised craft, and apprenticeship to agriculture was specifically encouraged. Parish apprentices had masters found for them, who could, if parishioners, be forced to take them on pain of a fine. In 1698, for example, the county magistrates ordered that no fewer than 26 poor children at Brill living with their parents should be apprenticed to husbandry and housewifery.[4] By 1700 parishes were authorised to provide premiums out of the rates, but these, if given, were typically low.

The churchwardens and overseers of the poor normally acted as parties to such contracts. By 1690 the serving of an apprenticeship conferred a legal settlement in the parish where it was served, and it offered a means for a parish to relieve itself of possible future claims for relief. Under existing legislation indigent persons, together with their dependants, could be compulsorily returned to their parishes of last settlement, however distant, even after an absence of many years. There was thus, it seems, a widespread preference for placing out children in another parish.

Parish apprentices were in practice frequently put to unskilled or low-skilled employment: in the rural southern counties of England agriculture was, overall, much the largest category for boys and 'housewifery' for girls.[5] Apprenticeship to these types of employment was not entirely confined to those children who were 'on the parish', though, as we have seen, most 'living-in' farm workers in Buckinghamshire were hired by the year for an agreed sum. What particularly distinguished parish apprentices was that, unlike ordinary apprentices, they could be, and normally were, bound until they were 24 (21 or marriage in the case of girls), and since many were apprenticed as young as 12 (younger than permitted in many skilled trades), or even younger, this often meant a servitude of 10 years or more in practice. Moreover, the terms of their indentures normally did not actually commit the master, or mistress, to impart their own or any other skills, though if the trade specified was a skilled one training was doubtless expected. It is noteworthy that pro forma parish indentures, unlike others, assume duration by the age of the apprentice rather than the number of years to be served.[6] As Dorothy George puts it:

> Though one category merges into the other, a dividing line can be drawn between 'apprenticeship for labour' and apprenticeship for education (not that one excludes the other). In one case the master expected the child's work to be profitable to him and the child expected to be maintained in return for his labour. In the other, a comparatively large fee was paid for the boy's maintenance and instruction and admission into an exclusive trade.[7]

Although circumstances varied – and some parishes seem to have gone well beyond the legal requirements in making provision for their poor children – the prospects of the average parish apprentice were clearly not good. The law did, however, provide some minimal protection for parish apprentices against the worst abuses, the chief being that in order to be legal their indentures had to be individually approved and signed by two justices of the peace. The published proceedings of the Buckinghamshire court of Quarter Sessions contain, in addition to instances of apprentices of both types being prosecuted for mis-behaviour, many examples of employers being called to account for neglecting or mistreating, or even abandoning, their apprentices. Prosecutions of those practising trades without having served an apprenticeship were also common, though their effectiveness may be doubted.[8]

Apprenticeship charities, formed to provide suitable premiums for poor children, are found in many counties from at least the early 17th century onwards. By 1833 well over 50 parishes in Buckinghamshire (out of a total of just over 200), mostly rural, benefited from such charities, the earliest dating from the 1620s and 1630s. Nationally the period 1680-1730 was especially rich in foundations, but new foundations continued into the late 18th century and a very few, such as the Saye and Sele Charity at Quainton, date from after 1800. Most were parochial charities with very small endowments; some others were linked to endowed schools or other forms of charity, and others made provision for more than one named parish.[9]

Such charities can be seen as an alternative to the Poor Law or as supplemen-tary to it. The amounts paid were usually under £5 a year (the sum generally considered adequate to maintain a young person for a year) and were often no more than a parish might otherwise have had to find out of the rates. Their disposal was frequently either in the direct control of the incumbents and/or parish officers of the parish concerned or the money was passed to them by the trustees as required. When Hart's Charity in Buckingham contributed £4 10s. to apprentice John Yerrall, 'a poor boy', to a button-maker in 1714 the churchwardens and overseers of Buckingham – not the charity – were parties to the indenture. On the other hand, many donors excluded children whose parents had received parish relief from benefiting.[10]

Leaving aside the unstated preferences of their current trustees, most ap-prenticing charities were explicitly selective to some degree in their choice of applicants. Unlike Harding's, the majority benefited boys only. Among the exceptions were William Elmer's Charity, Beachampton, founded in 1648, and Thomas Mead's at Princes Risborough (1684), both of which were for 'poor children'. However, Elmer stipulated that the children were not to be apprenticed to an alehouse keeper or to make lace, while Mead, a draper, excluded husbandry. The Saye and Sele Charity was confined to boys 'being legitimate'; in contrast, Hart's at Grendon Underwood was used specifically for apprenticing illegitimate boys and girls, the children of poor labourers of the parish. But whether the premium they provided was large or small, apprenticing charities had the advantage from the point of view of the recipient that their indentures were modelled on the normal, 'non-poor' apprenticeship indenture and not on that prescribed for parish apprentices. In the case of John Yerrall referred to above, for example, the master undertook to teach him the art of button-making. Moreover, the parties to the indenture were the child and the master. As late as 1869 counsel's opinion obtained by William Harding's trustees affirmed that an apprentice, even though an 'infant', was legally competent to enter into such a contract and that it was not strictly necessary for either the trustees or the parents to be parties.[11]

Proportionally to the population, the largest and most generous urban charity was that founded by John Whalley of Cosgrove, Northamptonshire, in 1670 for the benefit of natives of Stony Stratford, a town which in 1709 is said to have had about 1,200 inhabitants, or rather more than half that of Aylesbury. As in the case of Harding's, the amount specified for premiums was 'not above £10', for which, however, only boys were eligible. Whalley's Charity was unique in Buckinghamshire in that any boy successfully completing his time was entitled to a further sum of £10 towards setting him up in his chosen trade (many skilled trades required considerable capital to set up as a master and thus become an independent tradesman). The extent of the landed endowment was over 170 acres but the annual income (around £98 in 1824) was considerably less than that of its Aylesbury counterpart and the number of boys apprenticed annually must have been fairly small. The charity was closely linked to the established Church and to the parish authorities, since the trustees comprised the ministers of three neighbouring parishes as well as two of the churchwardens of Stony Stratford *ex officio*.[12]

We can see how parish apprenticeship was operated in Aylesbury just prior to the establishment of William Harding's trust by analysing the surviving apprenticeship indentures among the parish records. There are 42 in all, covering the years 1691 to 1721 (including three bonds for which the accompanying indentures are missing), of which 15 – over a third – are for girls. Nationally this was a critical period for the treatment of poverty. During the years 1690-1710, a period in which England was involved in almost continuous continental warfare, expenditure on relief escalated to a new level of magnitude, prompting harsh legislation against the poor, which included 'badging' (the enforced wearing of distinctive badges) and the 'punitive' apprenticing of parish children as an alternative to home maintenance and fostering. There is evidence that Aylesbury, where annual expenditure had risen from under £200 in 1670 to a peak of £326 in 1702, was not immune to the backlash, for example in the enforcement of badging in 1697 and the decision of the parish vestry to discontinue subsidising house rents and to compel the poor to live in 'almshouses' which had come under the control of the parish.[13]

Punitive apprenticing in Aylesbury is also suggested by the chronological distribution of the indentures but, if so, it was not of long duration. The annual accounts of the overseers of the poor confirm that, whereas prior to the 1690s the parish officers had routinely apprenticed poor children (one as young as eight in 1686), the number of indentures had rarely exceeded one or two annually. Then, in the 10 months between May 1697 and February 1698, 10 apprentices were bound – almost 25 per cent of the total number of surviving indentures – and the overseers' accounts indicate that the true total was at least twelve.[14] On the other hand, the great majority of indentures prior to 1701, though signed by the justices and stated to be with the consent of the parish officers, are not in standard 'pauper' format: they are in the child's own name and for terms ranging from seven to 10 years. The remaining 32 indentures are spread relatively evenly over the whole period, giving an average of just over 1.5 a year. After 1700, however, a standard 'parish' apprenticeship pro forma of the type to which reference has already been made, was, with only three exceptions, used.

Examples of premiums paid by the parish in 1697, and later, suggest that they were typically from £3 10s. to as high as £5 11s. in the case of boys and from £2 10s. to £3 15s. for girls, which seems to be broadly in line with what is known about practice in other parishes. The ages of the children, where they are stated (which is rarely) or can be ascertained from the parish register, were mostly between 11 and fourteen. Many, if not most, had lost one or both parents. There are several instances of two or more siblings from the same family being apprenticed in succession over a period of years.[15]

Some 20 different trades or occupations are represented in the Aylesbury indentures – a surprisingly high number. In the case of the boys they are tailor (4), papermaker (4), glover, weaver, fisherman, waterman, innholder, victualler, gardener, water carrier, yeoman, husbandman, dairyman, gardener, baker, blacksmith and (tobacco) pipemaker. The dairyman lived at Middle Claydon, an enclosed parish to the north of Aylesbury. The papermaker, who was the same man in all four cases, lived at Saunderton, a village in the vicinity of High Wycombe, where the Buckinghamshire papermaking industry was concentrated, and the indentures in question are dated 1701, 1709, 1715 and 1721, covering a period of 20 years.[16] Papermaking was at this time still largely a craft industry, but by the end of the century large numbers of child pauper apprentices, living in crowded dormitories, had become an integral feature of the new textile factories of the industrial revolution.

For the girls, the trades or skills of their masters and mistresses are labourer (3), husbandman, innholder, widow (a coffee woman), gardener (2), baker, lacemaker, glover, spinster. Some of these clearly do not suggest the imparting of genuine skills, though it is notable that 'housewifery' as such is not included.

Nearly all the employers were local and over half (23) were, or seem to have been, Aylesbury residents. Nine resided in other Buckinghamshire parishes within a radius of ten miles or so from the town (Saunderton, Middle Claydon, Wendover, Chepping Wycombe, Great Horwood, Little Horwood), and one lived in Berkhamsted (Hertfordshire). Only two of the masters were Londoners, a fisherman at Brentford and a waterman at Greenwich. Apprenticeship to either trade counted as apprenticeship to the sea service because in time of war such apprentices were liable to impressment into the navy if over the age of eighteen. Many abuses were alleged in connection with watermen's apprentices in particular.[17]

A few examples from the indentures will suffice. In 1697 William Rolfe, whose father, a labourer, was 'by reason of his great charge and poverty ... unable to bring up his said son', was apprenticed by his father, jointly with the parish officers, to a tailor for seven years; his father undertook to find him shoes and stockings. Joyce North, 'a poor fatherless and motherless child', was bound to John Evett, a labourer, undertaking to serve her master 'in all lawful business' and to behave obediently not only to her master but also his children and family. The master's only commitment was to provide clothing and maintenance. Richard Moore (no. 28) was bound to John Rose of Middle Claydon, dairyman, in 1711 until the age of twenty-four.

Mary Stocker (no. 35), apprenticed to a husbandman at Great Horwood at the age of 14 in 1715 to learn the art of husbandry, was exceptional in that a term of only four years was specified and, in addition, she was to have three days' holidays a year to visit her friends (a most unusual privilege) and a replacement outfit of clothes at the end of her service, the latter a clause often found in 'non-poor' apprenticeship indentures. But Mary, although one of a family of 'parish' children, was not strictly a parish apprentice, since the printed pro forma used was the one appropriate to a normal apprenticeship. Accordingly she herself was the contracting party though the overseers were to provide her clothes. It was probably made possible by a private contribution towards the premium, for an endorsement on one of the three other relevant indentures (nos 25-27) notes that half the £4 premium was paid by the child's friends.

Viewed overall, the indentures indicate that the numbers of parish children apprenticed in Aylesbury were relatively low and that a high proportion were orphans. From 1701 they seem to indicate a greater strictness in conforming to the letter of the law regarding the terms of employment of poor children, but still with some limited scope for flexibility, and in the majority of cases offering at least the possibility that the apprentice would eventually acquire a useful skill. This is less obvious in the case of girls. Here the virtual absence of lacemaking is striking. This skilled domestic craft was the principal resource of the poor in many parts of Buckinghamshire throughout the 18th century. It provided a profitable, if somewhat precarious, employment (it was subject to sharp fluctuations in demand) for women and young children (including boys) on a large scale. In 1698 the number of people in Aylesbury 'which get their living by making of lace' was said to be no fewer than 429, though even this was less than a third of the total claimed for Newport Pagnell, the principal centre for lacemaking in Buckinghamshire.[18]

Apprenticeship to lacemaking was far from unknown in Buckinghamshire. It was favoured by the borough of High Wycombe (usually combined with housewifery) for its poor female apprentices, but for the most part it seems to have been a skill passed on within the family. It was used by the parish authorities as a means of providing work for those receiving relief, including very young children, and to that extent was an alternative to apprenticing. In 1700, for example, the Aylesbury parish accounts record the payment of 2s. for teaching a child 'lace' and there are similar payments as early as the 1670s, as well as payments for hemp and other work materials.[19]

But radical changes were about to take place in the administration of poor relief. By 1720 a number of towns, alarmed by increasing pressure on the rates, which was exacerbated by inward migration from the countryside, had adopted the expedient of permanent workhouses where the indigent could be compelled to reside and those who were able-bodied be put to profitable labour under professional managers. The rationale of these institutions is summed up in the legend over the door of the establishment at Maidstone, opened in 1720: 'Who will not work, let him not eat bread.'

Early in 1721 a proposal by a group of inhabitants to introduce such a workhouse to Aylesbury, on the model of the one recently established at Olney, was brought before the court of Quarter Sessions, owing to local opposition to it which alleged that it was contrary to law. The workhouse, its supporters claimed, would enable the old and impotent to be better provided for, while the young and able would be kept at labour to 'get something towards their maintenance'. This in turn, it was hoped, would make it possible for a stop to be put to the payment of weekly and monthly allowances and of house rents for the poor – an attractive proposition for the ratepayers.[20]

The court gave its approval to the measure, 'subject to the statutes', and the way was further smoothed by a general enabling Act passed the following year. Owing to the gap in the overseers' accounts it is not known precisely when the Aylesbury workhouse was inaugurated but one was certainly in operation by the early 1730s at the latest, for memoranda entered in the parish register under the years 1738 and 1739 refer to John Harding Watford, a hemp dresser, stated to be then governor of the workhouse, and to his predecessor.[21] By the time the overseers' accounts resume in 1756 the 'workhouse test' was no longer being strictly enforced (it was reintroduced in 1759) but spot checks in the accounts between 1756 and 1800 have not produced any references to apprenticeship being undertaken. For much of this period the accounts are in any case uninformative because of the practice of contracting out poor relief on an annual basis.

This was the background to the inauguration of William Harding's new charity. But even if the question of the proposed workhouse is set aside, the creation of a new charitable trust with a gross annual income equal to well over a third of the total amount expended by the ratepayers on poor relief in 1702 could not fail to have an effect upon what has been described as 'the parish economy of welfare', of which the official relief provided from the parish rates was usually only a part, though commonly the largest part.[22]

By the early 18th century Aylesbury had an impressive range of charities whose resources could supplement those of the rates. Ignoring the many smaller charities, some of which were run by the parish officers, there was Bedford's Charity, the oldest, dedicated to the upkeep of the parish highways (its official title was the 'Incorporated Surveyors of the Highways') – and thereby incidentally providing employment – as well as a substantial annual cash distribution. There were also Hickman's almshouses, founded in 1698, with a landed endowment in Walton, the farmhouse of which directly adjoined the Harding homestead on the east, and the free grammar school, recently re-endowed on a scale unsurpassed anywhere else in the country, providing a practical education for over 100 boys. So extensive, indeed, was the range of charities that some contemporaries feared it would add to the town's problems by attracting poor persons into the town. Such at any rate was one of the arguments used by those who were opposed to the enlargement of the free grammar school.[23] It was still being repeated in the late 19th century.

As Aylesbury's first, and only, apprenticing charity, what effect did Harding's have on parish apprenticeship. Did it simply replace it altogether? Unfortunately, the gap in the parish overseers' accounts between 1710 and 1756 previously mentioned leaves some room for doubt, but the abrupt cessation of the series of parish apprenticeship indentures in 1721 (apart from a solitary example dated 1803) suggests that this was indeed the case.[24] Moreover, the introduction of the new, harsh, workhouse system may of itself have militated against the policy of apprenticing parish children, in favour of putting them to work.

V

The Charity in Action

Finding 'Proper' Jobs for the Boys (and Girls), 1720-1740

1. Ways and Means: How the Charity was Run

The first meeting of the trustees for the apprenticing of poor children and for the provision of clothing for the poor of Walton was held in November 1720, and thereafter twice-yearly meetings were held regularly for these purposes in May and November, as prescribed by the founder. The minutes continue until November 1738 (there is a gap between November 1734 and November 1736) and occupy a separate section of the account book. They give the date and place of the meeting, the names of the trustees attending and brief memoranda of 'orders' for the apprenticing of individual children. Additionally, at the November meetings the recipients – one male, one female – of the coats for the Walton poor are named, with individual names recurring at intervals of years.

No other type of business is recorded – though one assumes that other matters were discussed – and the only order of a general nature is one made in May 1737 'that whenever an election of a new Trustee is proposed the four present Trustees be all present (if alive and well)'. The accounts indicate that from 1734 meetings were publicly advertised, evidently to invite applications from parents of prospective apprentices. In May 1735, for example, a notice was placed at the *Queen's Head* (there are no minutes for this meeting) and in October 1737 one was stuck up at the market house.

The venues for the meetings – as well as for other *ad hoc* business meetings – were invariably Aylesbury inns, chosen in rotation, the names of the proprietors normally being given. In 1738-40, for example, they included 'Mr [Thomas] Towers at the Angell', 'Thomas Hill's at the Black Swan', 'Mr Dawney's at the Crown' and 'Mr Eel's at the Red Angel', and also the *George* and the *Queen's Head*, all located in or near the market place. At these establishments, too, the trustees would have spent the twice-yearly 'treat' money provided by the founder on hearty dinners. In contrast, the same drapers provided coats for the Walton poor year after year, Alexander Merrick until 1732, then Matthew Eeles until 1739 and finally 'Mr [Thomas] Smith'.

The individual orders normally give the name of the child and his or her father and the father's place of residence; in cases where the father is deceased this is sometimes stated, or alternatively only the mother's name is given. From

8 *Minutes of orders made at meetings of the trustees held at local inns in May and November 1728.*

1733 onwards, but not before, the father's occupation is usually given as well. Prior to the mid-1730s it is fairly rare for the name and trade of a specific master to be prescribed in the order itself. Instead, the formula most commonly used is that the child is to be apprenticed to 'a proper trade'. By 1738 there are occasional orders that enquiries are to be made concerning the 'character' of prospective masters and mistresses living at a distance, in accordance with the founder's intentions.

In just one or two instances the apprenticing of a particular child is approved with the proviso 'if a parishioner', or enquiry is ordered to confirm parishioner status. This is a reminder that under the founder's will the Charity's benefits were confined to 'settled inhabitants', a technical term which did not necessarily require actual residence in the town; the father of one apprentice is described as 'of Dinton', and another father, according to the accounts, was living in London. Like most market towns of the period, Aylesbury had a high proportion of immigrants, the poorer of whom were, under the Poor Laws, likely to have a 'settlement' in some other parish – often at a distance – which was legally responsible for their welfare and to which they could be compulsorily returned if they became chargeable to the poor rate, though sometimes the home parish elected to send cash relief instead. Permission to reside in such cases was subject to the production of a certificate of settlement issued by the officers of the parish of which the migrant was a legally settled inhabitant, by way of guarantee to the host parish. Residents in this situation were evidently excluded from local charities. 'Certificate men' were also disqualified from voting in parliamentary elections for the borough of Aylesbury.

In the great majority of cases information about masters, premiums paid, etc., is omitted from the orders, but it is recorded – if at all – in the accounts, sometimes after an interval of up to a year, or even longer. Altogether the names of 26 children who were the subject of orders do not recur in the accounts and we cannot therefore be certain that they were in fact all apprenticed, though the assumption must be that they were. All but six of these omissions relate to the period before 1736. The explanation may be that payments made by individual trustees out of Charity funds in their possession were not consistently entered in the accounts in this period. As we shall see, there is outside evidence that at least one boy (Euclid Neale, 1724) whose name is omitted from the accounts was in fact apprenticed to a trade. It is conceivable that the premium for this came from another source, but the cost of apprenticing his brother James in 1727 was definitely paid from the Charity's funds.

Between November 1738, when the orders cease, and November 1740 the accounts are our sole source of information, as they are for a handful of children apprenticed before 1738. In the majority of cases the premium paid was £10, the maximum permitted under William Harding's will. Not infrequently a slightly lower amount, rarely less than £7, is recorded. In one instance in 1725 the sum of £7 is given explicitly 'towards' putting out a boy, suggesting that the parents may have been expected to make a contribution in some cases. Interestingly, no obvious distinction was made between boys and girls in respect of premiums. In late 1737 payment of premiums began to be made in two equal instalments or 'moieties', the second usually after three years, but this practice soon lapsed.

Apprenticing charities were exempt from the Stamp Act of 1709, which imposed a duty of sixpence in the pound on premiums under £50. Surprisingly, it took over six years for the trustees to become aware of this fact, as is clear from a copy of a legal opinion, dated 1727, which is entered separately in the record book. It confirms that premiums were exempt, provided that it was made clear in the indenture that the consideration money was public charity money. The accounts record that Deverell [Dagnall] and 'Cousin Benson' were given two bottles of wine for obtaining the legal opinion to this effect.

2. *The Post-1735 Expansion*

Although the meetings for apprenticing were routine from the start, the number of children apprenticed each year for long remained comparatively small in relation to the charity's gross income of £141 a year, varying between as low as one in 1727 and as high as eight in 1725 and 1730, with an overall total of 72 for the years 1720-35 (allowance being made for some duplicate entries), an average of just under five a year; nevertheless, this is well over three times the average for the earlier 'parish' apprenticeships. In 1736 the number rose to nine. After this things changed even more dramatically and the totals for the following two years – in each of which an additional trustees' meeting was held – were 19 and 21 respectively (an average cost of around £210 per annum), falling again in 1739 and 1740 to 10 and fourteen. Thus as many children were apprenticed in the five and a half years after 1735 as in the previous sixteen. These figures can be compared with annual averages of baptisms recorded in the parish register for the 1720s and 1730s, which were 66.6 and 77.2 respectively. A striking feature of the expansion is the rise in the number of female apprentices from a total of 11, or eight per cent, before 1736 to a total of 30, almost 33 per cent, for the years 1736-40.

What was the cause of this sudden explosion in the number of apprentices? The obvious explanation is that during the earlier period the trustees, faced with heavy financial obligations, actual and potential, in connection with the enlargement and improvement of the endowment estate and, until 1737, the claims of the Pettiphers, had felt it advisable to limit spending on apprenticing. The succession of three new trustees in 1736 may also have had a bearing on the timing of the new, more liberal, policy, which was made possible by a large accumulated cash balance that the trustees chose to spend in this way rather than to invest in the public funds at four per cent. The downturn in 1739 is explicable in terms of declining demand after the initial backlog had been dealt with; shortage of funds seems unlikely to have been the critical factor since, as we have seen, there was still a balance of £183 in hand in January 1741. This being Aylesbury, the possibility that political considerations also played a part cannot entirely be ruled out (there was a general election in 1741). What is clear is that apprenticing on the level of the peak years could not have been sustained indefinitely out of an annual income of £141, which, allowing for landlord's unavoidable outgoings and for incidental expenses, would probably have enabled fewer than 12 children to be apprenticed annually.

3. *'Proper Trades'*

Nowhere in the record is any direct reference made to the parish officers or to parish affairs. The nearest approach to a general statement of policy is the phrase, occurring repeatedly, in individual orders, that the applicant is to be apprenticed 'to a proper trade', varied occasionally to something more specific, such as 'a handicraft trade' or 'any handicraft trade out of the parish' (1726,

1730). Some were even more specific: 'a shoemaker or other proper trade' (1726, 1730); 'a mantua maker at Beaconsfield or elsewhere' (1730); even 'a stone cutter or other proper trade' (1730), implying, it would seem, a degree of choice on the part of the child or its parent. It is noticeable in this connection that sons of artisans were often apprenticed to their fathers' trades or to a related trade; in 1739, for example, the son of Thomas Chilton, a drover and salesman, was apprenticed to a butcher living in Richmond, Surrey, who was possibly a business connection of the father through the flourishing London cattle trade, and William Thorp (1738), the son of a fellmonger, was ordered to be put to a butcher. By their insistence on 'proper' trades the trustees were in effect rejecting the unskilled and also occupations – including, for example, those provided by the town's increasingly prosperous inn trade – associated with parish apprenticeship and these are indeed conspicuous by their absence. The frequent stipulation that apprenticeship should be outside the parish is also significant.

The trustees were in a position to ensure apprenticeship to 'proper' trades, whether in Aylesbury or elsewhere, because, although a designated public charity, they could match the going market rates for 'non-poor' apprenticeship premiums, which in the rural south of England seems in this period to have been in the region of £9 10s. to £15 for boys and £7 10s. to £11 for girls for all trades, figures which encompass a minority of superior trades commanding high premiums.[1] Skilled workers in recognised trades not only enjoyed greater security of employment but could earn up to 50 per cent more per day on average than unskilled.[2]

Judging by the minority of boys, 19 in all, over the whole period 1720-40, definitely known to have been apprenticed to masters residing in Aylesbury, it would seem that only 11 of the numerous male occupations found in the town at this time came within the trustees' definition of 'proper trades'. All of them required considerable skill and training. They were cordwainer, or shoemaker (4), glover, saddler (2), tailor (2), carpenter (2), blacksmith, hemp dresser, twine spinner, baker, butcher and barber-peruke (periwig) maker (3). One of the two carpenters was Robert Hickman (1740), who had been employed in building the Walton farm; he was part of a dynasty of carpenters extending back to the early 17th century.[3]

4. How Poor was Poor?

Given that from the start the average annual number of children apprenticed was so much higher than it had been under the previous parish regime, it is perhaps not surprising to find that the beneficiaries were no longer being limited to the completely destitute. Indeed, as far as our evidence goes the charity may well have served a wider cross-section of society in this period than in any subsequent one prior to the 20th century. As previously noted, prior to 1736 the father's occupation or status is rarely stated but, in all but a few cases, it can be supplied with some confidence from the parish register, which is

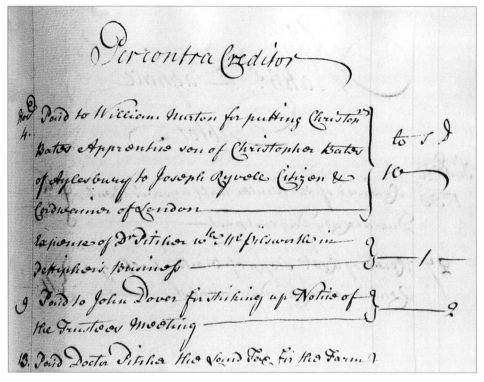

9 *Accounts of payments made in November 1732. The William Nurton named in the first entry was a local carrier who acted as intermediary with prospective employers living in London.*

available in published form for these years. Out of the 72 children apprenticed in 1720-35, 18 can be identified as children of labourers. In addition, the Charity's record book itself identifies five as the children of widows, while in seven cases the father (one of whom is a labourer) is described as 'late of' Aylesbury or Walton, probably indicating that the child was an orphan. Thus the minimum number of children of parents who could reasonably be considered as poor and who benefited from the Charity in these years was 30, an annual average of around two, or under 50 per cent of the whole, though the true total was doubtless higher. During the period 1736-40 the average rose to more than five a year, but this now represented only a third of the total.

The other extreme of the social scale among the fathers of apprentices was represented by James Neale, whose sons Euclid and James were apprenticed in 1724 and 1727 respectively, 'Mr' John Burnham (1725) and Neal Campbell (1739). James Neale has been identified as a schoolmaster who was appointed to the well-paid post of writing master at the grammar school in 1727. Burnham, who died in 1729, was an attorney-at-law, who also practised in the ecclesiastical court for the archdeaconry of Buckingham, a somewhat moribund institution at this period, apart from its probate jurisdiction. He was related to the Bell family, who had been prominent Tories in the 1690s.[4] Campbell is described in 1725 as a mercer (a dealer in fabrics), a trade which required considerable capital.[5] On the face of it, none of the three come within the definition of 'poor', though we know from other sources that Neale had been a prisoner for debt in 1709-10 and it is thus possible that he was still in low water financially prior to becoming writing master.[6] There may well have been special circumstances in the other two cases as well. Young Burnham, who was apprenticed to a joiner in Eton, eventually became a master there and was himself the recipient of a premium from the Charity in 1739 for taking one of his relations, John Burnham, an orphan, son of an apparitor (a summoner in the ecclesiastical court), as an apprentice.

As might be expected, children of what appear to be substantial traders were not particularly numerous. Apart from Mr Campbell, these included a waggoner (Humphrey Nurton), a hemp dresser (James Very), two fellmongers (Thomas Wootton and Thomas Thorpe), a maltster (Richard Stratfold), two farmers (Joseph Giles and Richard Jennings[7]), two millers (Robert Mallard of Walton and John Allen) and a brickmaker (Henry Bailey). One of these, Nurton, was, as we shall see, a special case. But four of the others (Thorpe, Giles, Jennings and Bailey) were deceased and so could be considered to be in a separate category, since the death of a breadwinner, however prosperous, could easily plunge his family into hardship – or even dire poverty – in any period, giving his children a claim to assistance.

Henry Bailey, the brickmaker, four of whose children (two boys and two girls) were apprenticed between 1729 and 1737, had died in October 1728, his wife Susannah having predeceased him by less than three months. Bailey is a significant figure because of his association with Aylesbury's heritage of early Georgian brick buildings, public and private, which are now the most visible reminder of the town's prosperity in that era. His personal circumstances, which are better documented than most, are thus of some interest. Besides supplying bricks for the new farmhouse at Walton – which must have been his last major undertaking – he had been involved in building the grammar school in 1718 and had contracted to supply bricks and lime for the new county gaol and assize courts (the present County Hall building), begun in 1722. This enterprise, a major source of employment for the town, had proved a disaster both for him and for many Aylesbury craftsmen and workmen when work on the building (then in a fairly advanced state of construction) was suspended for lack of cash in 1724, leaving workmen's bills amounting to some £1,908 which were still unpaid 13 years later.[8]

Bailey's will, proved in 1730, shows that he left seven children in all, including four daughters, all unmarried, and also that his affairs, though somewhat straitened, were probably not desperate. His property comprised four houses, or 'messuages', situated near the butchers' shambles in the market place, all of which were, however, subject to mortgage charges. It was left in trust for his eldest son Henry, who also inherited the business, which is not described but was one of several brickfields located in the vicinity of the present Cambridge Street. His other children were to receive £20 apiece out of his estate and an equal share in the moneys owing on account of the county gaol, and were to be maintained and educated under the direction of his trustees, who were in due course to make them apprentices to suitable trades.[9]

Since one of the two trustees of the will was none other than Noah Pitcher, one of William Harding's trustees, the claims of Henry Bailey's children were unlikely to be overlooked. His two younger sons, Joseph, born 1716, and William, born 1720, were apprenticed in 1729 and 1731 respectively, Joseph to a plumber and glazier at Henley-on-Thames and William to Daniel Ryder, a tailor and stay (corset) maker, whose place of abode is not given. Six years later, in 1737, one daughter, Mary, born in 1724, was apprenticed to Elizabeth, wife of Jasper Davis of Aylesbury, a 'mantua maker', or dressmaker, and another daughter, Martha, born in 1721, to Ann Boughton, spinster, also of Aylesbury, described as a seamstress. In each case the premium paid was £10. Since 1737 was the date of the local Act of Parliament for completing the county gaol, which also made provision for paying off the debts still owing for the earlier work done, it may be that no further financial assistance was required by the Bailey family.

The four Bailey children were the single largest group of siblings apprenticed by the Charity in this period, but 11 other apparent instances of more than one child of the same parent being apprenticed have been noted; in all but two cases (Nurton, Reeves) only two siblings were involved.

Between the extremes of property owner and labourer were parents following a fairly wide range of occupations: artisans, craftsmen (carpenters, blacksmiths, shoemakers, saddlers, weavers, a pipemaker), (licensed) victuallers, dealers and the like; two drovers, a 'tripe man', a sexton and a gingerbread man are also recorded. In all there were around twenty occupations, some of which were probably little, if at all, better off than labouring. It is, perhaps, indicative that one of their number was John Footman, the son of a carpenter, who was apprenticed to a Winslow (horse) collar maker in 1724, and whose brother Thomas had been apprenticed by the parish in 1719 to Edward Footman of Little Horwood, a tailor; he is the only direct link with the pre-1720 parish regime.

That not all labourers were solely dependent on day labour is illustrated by William Porter, 'labourer', whose son was apprenticed in 1737. The Charity's account book shows that he was one of two workmen employed by the trustees to thatch the Walton farmstead in 1738 and that he worked for a total of 22 days in April and May 1738 at 20d. (1s. 8d.) a day, a very high rate by contemporary standards, equivalent to more than twice what the workmen who threshed William Harding's grain in 1720 were able to earn. Robert Brunson, or Brownson (1720), was employed in the same capacity in 1721, but in his case the wage rate is not given.

One name that stands out in the category of craftsman is that of Robert Ivatts, a shoemaker, whose son Thomas was apprenticed to Roger Brewer of Aylesbury, a fellow shoemaker, in 1738. Robert is notable as the first of seven successive generations of his family to carry on his trade in Aylesbury. Born

Per contra

Sep: 6 Allowed Mr Coles's Bill for mending the Shoep
1740 penns at Boarnhill Field by order and consent
of the Trustees — 1 .. 11 ..

6 paid for enquiring the Character of Mr Hagsheuo
of Windmill Court near Cork alley Fleet Ditch Barber
in order to putt Jeffery the son of John Peacock
of Aylesbury Cordwainer Apprentice to him — .. 2 ..

22. Pd William Dixon the Smith's Bill for iron work
for the pump done at John Slopp's Farm — .. 16. 8

24. paid the Land Tax for Dunsham platt being half
a year to Lady Day 1740 — .. 3 ..

Expence at receiving John Slopp's rent — .. 1.. 6

10 *Accounts of payments made in September 1740, including payment for obtaining a character reference.*

in the neighbouring village of Fleet Marston around 1700, Robert had been apprenticed to his father and was employed at first in delivering finished goods around the countryside and in Aylesbury. After his father's death in 1720, having been left his tools and a small amount of capital, Robert married and set up in business in Kingsbury, where an Ivatts shoe shop was still to be found until late in the 20th century. Thomas, the son, would eventually inherit the business in 1775. In all, Robert and his wife had 14 children – nine of whom died in infancy – and 11 of them were born by 1740, sufficient justification in itself perhaps for the Charity's assistance.[10]

5. Placement

As already indicated, there was a strong preference throughout, made explicit in individual orders, for apprenticing children to masters residing outside Aylesbury, and this was acted upon. Details of employers are often lacking prior to 1736, but out of the 72 children apprenticed in 1720-35 only one was explicitly put to an Aylesbury employer, while 46 were destined to places other than Aylesbury; the allocation of the remaining 29, six of whom were female, is not known. Thus the maximum that could have been put to Aylesbury employers is 30, or 41 per cent. But the true total was certainly smaller, possibly much smaller, for several destinations, left blank in the text, have been identified from other sources as being other than Aylesbury.

The fuller information available post-1735 shows that in the period 1736-40, out of a total of 73 beneficiaries, only 27 (38 per cent) were apprenticed to masters or mistresses living in Aylesbury, which is higher than the possible maximum in the previous period, and is partly attributable to the increase in the number of female apprentices. As can be seen from Table 1, all but a very few of the 'foreign' employers resided either in Buckinghamshire and the adjacent counties of Oxfordshire, Bedfordshire, Hertfordshire and Northamptonshire, or in London.

Taking both periods together, of the first two categories (Buckinghamshire and adjacent counties) a high proportion of employers were located in market towns such as Winslow (8), Chesham (4), Thame (4), Leighton Buzzard (3), Berkhamsted and Bicester, and the rest mostly in rural parishes within 10 or 15 miles of Aylesbury. London, which at this time drew the greater part of its workforce from every corner of the country, but particularly from the home counties, was the destination of around a third of the total of those apprenticed outside Aylesbury, a proportion that rose slightly after 1735. The addresses of the London employers are sometimes recorded with considerable precision in the accounts.

Table 1. Destinations of Apprentices, Nov. 1720-Nov. 1740

	Aylesbury	Bucks	Adjacent Counties	London	Other	Not Stated	Total
1720-35	1	17 (5)	11 (1)	12	2	29 (6)	72 (12)
1736-40	27 (10)	19 (7)	6 (2)	16 (4)	1	4 (1)	73 (24)
Totals	28 (6)	36 (12)	17 (3)	28 (4)	3	33 (7)	145 (36)

(Numbers in round brackets indicate female apprentices; duplicate entries that appear to relate to the same individual have been conflated.)

Both before and after 1736, the 'proper trades', to which all boys other than those going to London were apprenticed, consisted overwhelmingly of skilled handicrafts, with leather workers (cordwainers, saddlers), wood workers (carpenters, joiners, wheelwrights) and service trades (tailors, butchers, barbers) making up the most numerous groups. Less usual occupations represented were frame wool knitter (in Leicestershire), stone cutter (Oxfordshire), twine spinner, hemp dresser (Aylesbury, 1738), barber surgeon (Leighton Buzzard) and spoon maker (Berkhamsted). The hemp dresser was John Harding Watford, who, according to the parish register, was master of the Aylesbury workhouse for one year to May 1739.

The London trades were more varied in character than the rest, including ropemaker, pack thread spinner, holster maker, glazier, turner and loom maker, bricklayer, tiler, butcher, 'butcher or salesman to butchers in the city' (1731), fan stick maker and tallow chandler. The two most specialised were a mathematical instrument maker (1723) and a jeweller (in Bloomsbury, 1738), to which Samuel Freeman and Neal Campbell were respectively bound. Samuel Freeman's master is given in the accounts as William Carton and the premium paid £10, but this information can be supplemented from the records of the Joiners Company, which show that Samuel was the son of a victualler – information not found in the parish register – and was apprenticed to William Carton, Citizen and Joiner, in July 1723, 15 months after the date of the original order. They also reveal that the premium actually paid was £13, so Samuel's family probably contributed to it. A high proportion of London masters are indicated as members of particular city livery companies, but the specific trade followed is not always stated.[11]

The records of the Dyers Company provide additional information about two other boys. The first of these is the Robert Brownson previously met with (Nov. 1720), who is entered as having been apprenticed to Francis Smith, a member of that company in February 1721; the occupation is not given, but the Charity's accounts state that the master (unidentified) was a silk dyer. The second is Francis Jennings (May 1732), whose deceased father is stated in the order to have been a yeoman. The Dyers Company records confirm that he was apprenticed to Gabriel Kent, a member of the Company, in September 1732, but once again fail to give the actual occupation, which is not recorded in the accounts either. However, the Dyers' records reveal that Francis's older brother John had been apprenticed in the Company in 1727, at which date his father Richard, whose burial has not been traced, was still alive and was presumably responsible for paying his premium.

London may well have been the destination of Euclid Neale (1724), son of James, the schoolmaster mentioned above, born in 1710 while his father was a prisoner for debt, for whom no employer is given and who is not entered in the accounts. He is known from other sources to have become a clockmaker by 1734, by which date he had married.[12]

The female apprentices, in contrast to the males, were restricted throughout to a narrow range of occupations regardless of their place of employment. The vast majority (23) learned the skills of a mantua maker (dressmaker), or the related trades of seamstress (2), tailor (4) and milliner. Only a handful were put to occupations not involving needlework. These were worsted maker (London, 1737), draper (Thame, 1733), glover (1738) and staymaker (1737), the latter two normally being male trades. One enterprising lass, Mary Kingham (1738), herself the daughter of a cordwainer, even received the trustees' consent to be bound to the same trade 'if she likes'. Unlike Mary, most girls were apprenticed either to a single woman or to a married couple jointly. Mantua making was a genteel calling which could be engaged in by the married as well as the unmarried. Only five girls were apprenticed in London, all post-1735.

By reference to the parish register it appears that, overall, the average age of applicants ranged from 13 to 16, though, perhaps surprisingly, there is a significant proportion of applicants as young as 12, and even eleven. Allowance has to be made for possible delays in placing, sometimes indicated in the orders ('immediately', 'within six months', 'within a year', or 'as soon as a master is provided'). Confusingly, in a number of instances entries are duplicated, usually without any cross-reference, when an application is brought forward to a later date. At the other end of the scale, applicants aged 17 or 18 were not uncommon, especially in the 'boom' period after 1735. The apprenticing of young people in their late teens was, it seems, quite usual in London at this period but much less so in market towns.[13] In 1734 Elizabeth Saltmarsh, aged 19, and Sarah Ginger, aged 20, were ordered to be put out to mantua makers, 'if approved by the Trustees'. No further details are found, but in 1738 Mary Green (22) was apprenticed to a tailor at Leighton Buzzard and Susannah Defrane (22) to an Aylesbury mantua maker. Significantly, Susannah's parentage is not given, and she is described simply as 'spinster' in the accounts.

From entries in the accounts we learn that from 1736 onwards it was routine to 'enquire the character' of prospective masters living at a distance, or at any rate in London. The payment made for this information was usually 2s. 6d. In one case in 1738 it was ordered that a boy was to be bound 'after a months liking', but this is the only example of such a trial period to be recorded. Finding suitable masters and mistresses and making the arrangements was, one assumes, primarily the responsibility of the Charity's accountant, first Matthias Dagnall (1658-1736), the bookseller, and then his son of the same name, but there are references to William James being reimbursed for 'putting out' a boy in 1722, and again in 1733, and in 1736 payment was made for apprenticeship business transacted by the order of 'Dr Pitcher' (Noah Pitcher). Personal contacts no doubt counted for a great deal and some London masters may have had Aylesbury connections, an example being Samuel Very, tallow chandler (1736), who was presumably related to the Aylesbury family of that name, several of whom were hemp dressers.

Several references to payments made to William Nurton (he is styled 'Cozen' in 1731, so was probably related to the Dagnalls) indicate that he played an important role around this time. In March 1733, for example, he was paid 'for providing for Christopher Bates boy & finding a master to put him apprentice to in London' and in 1736 he was twice paid for 'returning' (remitting) money and transacting business in connection with London apprentices. Nurton (d.1752) was well placed to assist in this way since he was a waggoner, or carrier, plying between Aylesbury and London. His father, Humphrey Nurton of Aylesbury, was also a carrier, having previously been a licensed victualler (he is so styled in 1728). The apprenticing of three of Humphrey's younger children, one of whom was aged 17, between 1728 and 1733 may well have been the price for similar services performed by him before William took over. The carriage trade was expanding locally in the 1730s, thanks in part to the recent turnpiking of the main London routes. One of William Nurton's regular private customers at this time was Sir Thomas Lee, Bart, of Hartwell, a local notable, whose accounts show numerous large payments to him. Testimony to Nurton's prosperity is the will of his widow, Susannah, who died in 1758 leaving large quantities of luxury household goods, including monogrammed chinaware, to her three nieces.[14]

A few small payments are also recorded for expenses incurred in 'treating' prospective masters or intermediaries at alehouses and just two payments for postage – four 'post letters' from Christopher Bates about putting out his son in late 1732 cost a total of 1s. 2d. But in general, there are many fewer payments for incidental expenses than one would expect to find.

Only in a very few cases is the term of years to be served by apprentices indicated. Presumably it was usually the standard seven years, as stated in the earliest extant example of an original Harding's indenture, dated 1794, but there was obviously room for some flexibility for in 1738 five years is stipulated for one female apprentice and eight for another. It seems to have been exceptional for more than one apprentice to be put to the same employer. The only examples noted were William Wright of Aylesbury, a baker, who received one apprentice in 1737 and another in 1740 (a suspiciously short interval), and Ann Chase, a mantua maker at Chesham, who is listed in 1730, 1737 and again in 1739. It seems unlikely that the mature female apprentices mentioned above would have been willing to work out a full term and mantua makers in particular were, it seems, commonly bound for five years.[15]

6. In Service – and After

Prior to the late 19th century the trustees, with rare exceptions, seem to have limited their activities strictly to those prescribed by the founder's will and clearly expected that their connection with their charges would end once the latter had been handed over to their masters or mistresses. A solitary example in this period of an exception is found in the accounts in October 1725 when 2s. was paid for 'Expence at the George in settling a Difference between Mr Gomme and Widow Pryors Son', the reference being to Abraham Pryor, apprenticed to Christopher Gomme in May 1721. The master's abode and trade are not given, but another boy was apprenticed the same year to a James Gomme of Wycombe, a carpenter.

Doubtless most other apprenticing charities, especially large ones, took a similarly restricted view of their responsibilities, but not all. The trustees of the small Derbyshire apprenticing charity founded by German Pole of Radbourne, 'esquire', in 1685, for example, took steps to obtain an annual report on the 'proficiency usage and behaviour' of their apprentices during their period of service and stipulated in the indentures that their employers should pay them (girls as well as boys) 6d. a quarter by way of wages, as well as a cash sum of £1 or more at the end of their terms.[16]

What kind of future faced the newly apprenticed young person? This is largely a matter for conjecture based on the experiences recounted by the authors of a small number of contemporary autobiographies and on records of litigation and judicial proceedings. We know, for example, that it was normal for children apprenticed to a distant master to make the journey on foot in the wake of the carrier's cart. During their first years of service the newly apprenticed, many of whom were probably already inured to hard work (sometimes as farm servants), often spent much of their time doing domestic chores. Most workshops were small, even in London, and often only a single apprentice was employed, though there might well be one or two other servants in addition.[17]

Although long periods of separation and even complete loss of contact must have been common, apprentices living at a distance from home often contrived to keep in touch with their families either by occasional visits at holiday times with the permission of their employers, or by letter, or both. Some were able to derive comfort and support from friends and relations living in the same vicinity, especially in London. An example is John Taylor, who was apprenticed by Harding's in 1737 to a master living in London, where John's father was already resident. Many had to fend for themselves as best they could. The character of the master was the most important factor for the apprentice's well-being – and that of his wife could also be critical. Complaints of harsh treatment and failure to provide proper instruction were frequent and could lead to the cancellation of indentures by the justices of the peace, but some former apprentices remembered their old masters with affection.

Although they were not legally entitled to any reward other than their keep, by custom apprentices could expect to earn small, but increasing, amounts of money, either as wages or by work done outside working hours, but the costs of setting up in business on one's own, especially in London, were often high, and finding work as a journeyman tradesman could also be difficult and would become more so as the century advanced. We know that at least two of the Harding apprentices achieved the status of master. One was Charles Burnham, already mentioned, who made good in Marlow, perhaps with assistance from his family. The other was Benjamin Bradley, otherwise Bampton, son of a widowed mother, who was apprenticed to John Miles of Aylesbury, a barber and peruke maker, in 1721 and who in November 1730 was paid a £10 premium for taking on Anthony Todd, another orphan, to learn the same trade.

The evidence suggests that a high proportion of all apprentices bound to London masters dropped out altogether. Others on completing their apprenticeships often returned to their home areas, where prospects for setting up as a master might be more propitious.[18] Baptisms in the Aylesbury parish register, 1744-56, show that Samuel Freeman, previously mentioned, who was apprenticed by Harding's to a mathematical instrument maker in London in 1723, later returned to Aylesbury and carried on his trade there. There must have been others.

Some apprentices abandoned their trade after serving their time. William Brandon of Aylesbury, who had served an apprenticeship there around 1720, though without assistance from Harding's Charity, had evidently opted for a military career, ending up in 1766 as a Chelsea Pensioner in London, a haven which was not, however, available to his wife of 45 years. The sequel was that, since Aylesbury (a place with which she apparently had no personal connection) was adjudged to be her husband's last place of settlement, she was ordered to be removed thither while he remained in Chelsea. Situations such as this could lead to expensive litigation between parishes.[19]

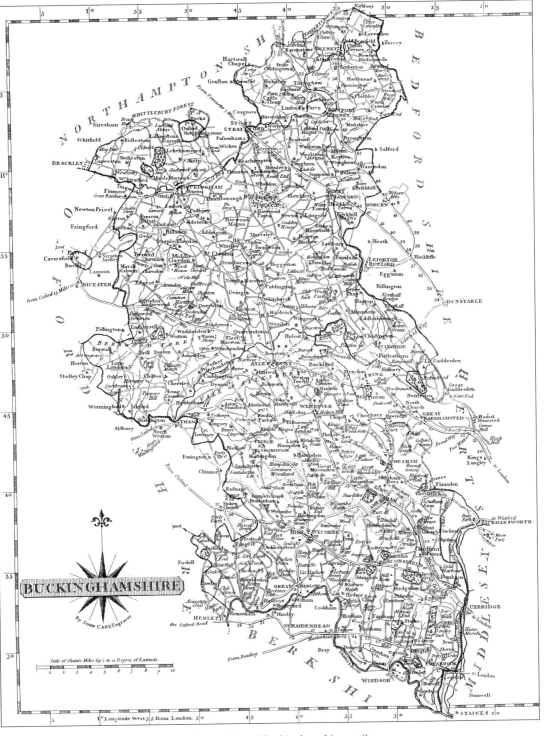

11 *Cary's Map of Buckinghamshire, 1787.*

The experience of one local charity apprentice, preserved in the examination of William Chilton, described as a tailor residing in Quainton, taken before a magistrate in 1725 to determine his place of settlement, is instructive, if hardly typical. Born in Chilton, he had been bound to John Bennet, a tailor living at Great Horwood, by the parishioners of Chilton, who paid his premium of £7 out of 'their charity money', presumably a reference to Hart's Charity, a small apprenticeship charity. Unfortunately, his master had died within six months and the premium had been lost and with it his apprenticeship. The upshot was that his father had arranged for another tailor, Henry Eeles of Quainton, to take his son 'for victuals and bread' for so long as they could agree together. After nearly four years, 'thinking he had served long enough for nothing', William told his master that he would not work any longer without wages and his master then agreed to hire him by the year. He had evidently acquired the skills of a tailor, but without having served a legal apprenticeship and without gaining a settlement. On the other hand, he had become sufficiently useful to be paid wages after only four and a half years of service in his trade, though only by confronting his master. The lesson was that a youth in service had to learn to stand up for himself.[20]

7. The End of an Era?

The two decades following 1720 covered by the apprenticeship records were a period of relative prosperity and stability, with low food prices and a static population level favouring a high demand for labour, particularly in towns. But it was interrupted by Europe-wide dearth and disease in the early 1740s. It is probably only a coincidence that our volume ends within months of the outbreak of Aylesbury's most serious epidemic for more than a century. For in 1742 a visitation of smallpox caused the annual total of burials to soar to 253 – over three times the average for the previous decade and unlikely to be much under a tenth of the total population of the town. Children are likely to have been especially vulnerable. In September 1742 James Neale, writing master at the grammar school, reported to the school trustees that 'so many Boys have dyed and kept away from the school that he knew not how to give the usual list'. One consequence is likely to have been a sharp reduction in the demand for apprenticeships, the effects of which would have been felt for much of the 1740s.[21]

VI

Wilkes and Chancery, 1742-1794
The Unrecorded Years

After 1740 there is a gap in the Charity's own records of over half a century, apart from the memoranda of elections of trustees in 1745, 1754 and 1758 and the 1754 rental already mentioned. Despite this unfortunate lacuna it has proved possible from other sources to reconstruct an outline of at least some of the major developments that occurred during the interval and, in addition, a transcript of accounts covering two years in the 1760s has come to light among records relating to litigation.

The death in 1754 of William James, who since 1736 had been the only survivor of William Harding's original trustees, created a new, and potentially serious, situation. It appears that, legally, the freehold of the Charity estates had become vested in him, by virtue of his survival (perhaps as a result of some unnoticed deficiency in the drafting of the will) rather than in the existing trustees as a body, and since he had failed to make any disposition of it in his lifetime, it was later deemed to have descended to his eldest son and heir, one William James of Winchester, gentleman. Prior to William James's death, John Sheen of Walton, described as a fellmonger, had replaced Archdeacon Dudley as trustee when the latter died in 1745. He was probably a relation of Thomas Sheen the elder, who was one of the trustees of the bequest made by James's aunt, Mary Cockman, to the Presbyterian congregation in 1733.

William James's successor, elected on 13 August 1754, was John Wilkes (1725-97), Aylesbury's most famous resident, then just short of 29 years of age and currently serving his year of office as High Sheriff of Buckinghamshire. Wilkes had acquired the Prebendal estate in Aylesbury through his marriage, in 1747, to the heiress Mary Mead, niece of William Mead, wealthy London merchant and staunch Whig, who had settled in Aylesbury in the opening decade of the century. The son of a London distiller, Wilkes had been brought up as a Dissenter and as a boy had been a pupil at a school in Aylesbury kept by Matthew Leeson, a dissenting minister.

Politically ambitious, Wilkes had intended to stand for one of the two Aylesbury borough seats in the general election held earlier in 1754 but had been outmanoeuvred by his friend and fellow member of the so-called Hell Fire Club, Thomas Potter, and instead had tried unsuccessfully, and expensively, to

12 *John Wilkes, a trustee, as Radical politician. This well-known caricature by Hogarth, dated May 1763, shows Wilkes holding aloft the Cap of Liberty. Beside him are copies of his seditious periodical* The North Briton *which had brought him into direct confrontation with government. By the end of the year – still M.P. for Aylesbury – he had been forced to flee abroad.*

get himself elected for Berwick-upon-Tweed. Wilkes had already been elected a trustee of the Aylesbury grammar school in 1748 – an honour increasingly restricted to members of the local landed gentry – and he became a 'feoffee' of Bedford's Charity, the third of the town's three principal endowed charities, in late 1754 or early 1755.[1]

As an aspiring politician, determined not to miss a second opportunity to stand for one of the borough's two seats, Wilkes's eagerness to serve on local charities was clearly far from disinterested. Public service of this kind – he was appointed a justice of the peace in 1755 and shortly thereafter second-in-command of the newly embodied county militia, of which he became colonel in 1762 – offered obvious opportunities for building up a political interest both by means of 'networking' and by the dispensation of influence and patronage. As far as the charities were concerned, Wilkes's correspondence, frequently ironical in tone, with his tenant and confidential agent, the brewer John Dell, shows that he took considerable pains to try to insert his own supporters into vacancies. In January 1755, writing from London, he alludes to 'the important [underlined] honour conferred on me by the Feoffees' (of Bedford's Charity) in electing him, but is less impressed by their other choice of Sir William Lee, of Hartwell, chiding Dell for neglect: 'I suspect you have been too secure, perhaps lazy; but we will take effectual measures against the next vacancy.'[2]

Dell himself was elected a Bedford feoffee the following July. In December 1755, on learning of another possible vacancy for a feoffee, Wilkes offered to come down post-haste to Aylesbury, if only for three hours, 'for I have all the trusts at heart' – an example of Wilkesean irony. Some three years later he wrote to inform Dell that the Harding Trustees had unanimously elected Archdale Williams, the apothecary, in succession to his father on the plea of a long-standing engagement 'to continue the succession on the same line, whose ancestors the Donor thought at first agreable' (an interesting insight), adding resignedly, 'I am forced to acquiesce'.[3]

Favours for constituents were also an object. In February 1759, by now a Member of Parliament for the town, Wilkes asked Dell to 'mention it to my brother Trustees of Harding's Trust, how kindly I should take it if they wou'd consent to let Mr Edmonds have the vacant Farm'. This application appears from later evidence to have been unsuccessful.[4] Compared to Bedford's Charity, which owned desirable urban property and was also in a position to provide employment to manual workers and to local shopkeepers on a considerable scale, Harding's does not in fact appear to have had a great deal of potential for direct patronage even on the assumption that the other trustees would prove co-operative.

But by 1759 Wilkes was becoming involved in a new form of charity in which he was in a position to exercise sole control himself from the start. As it happened, it too was connected with child welfare, though this time with national as well as a local implications. The previous year he had been elected to the court of governors of the London Foundling Hospital, and it is probably no coincidence that his election coincided with a major expansion of the hospital's responsibilities. In 1757 Parliament had voted funds to enable it 'to appoint proper places in all counties ... for the reception of all exposed and deserted children', a measure which, if fully carried through, would have had far-reaching effects on the whole poor law system.

As it was, its effect on Aylesbury was sufficiently dramatic, for by early 1759 a branch hospital, situated in the Crofts at Walton, a mere stone's throw from the Harding farmstead, was in being. It held some forty children, of whom 14 were aged between 10 and 15 (the foundlings remained in care until old enough to go into service or be apprenticed) and the rest were younger. It was managed, under Wilkes's direction, by a small committee largely composed, it seems, of his own Aylesbury friends and nominees (including the faithful Dell and Dell's future brother-in-law, the Reverend John Stephens, DD, master

13 *Original letter from John Wilkes to John Dell, his friend and confidential agent in Aylesbury, on the subject of the forthcoming general election, January 1761. It makes coded references to the going rate for the purchase of votes. By this date Wilkes, desperate for cash, had already secretly diverted some of the Charity's funds to his own use.*

of the grammar school and one of Wilkes's boon companions), with a 'tame', non-local, J.P. from north Bucks, Walden Hanmer, as chairman, Wilkes himself as treasurer and Robert ('Bob') Neale (son of James), writing master at the grammar school, as secretary.

The story of this short-lived venture, based on original records, has been well told by the late Dr V.E. Lloyd-Hart of Aylesbury in his informative and entertaining little book *John Wilkes and the Foundling Hospital at Aylesbury 1759-1768* (1983),[5] and it is unnecessary to repeat it here in detail. It is clear from the evidence that Wilkes had expected admissions to be made on a local basis, thus maximising his prospects of patronage, but as matters turned out, the planned branch hospitals were established in only six counties and it was accordingly ruled that all the children should be admitted through the parent body in London. As a result Wilkes's wings were clipped (as he put it himself in a letter to Dell), but he carried on nonetheless, telling Dell in October 1759 that he expected the number of children at Aylesbury to double during the coming months, the happy consequence of which, he foresaw, would be 'more money circulating, more dependance created, etc.' and adding, 'I can never myself attend [to] it, but I have set the machine going. You may keep it in the right track,' In this passage Wilkes drops his customary jocular tone and reveals his true motivation with unusual frankness.

By making himself agreeable in various ways Wilkes did indeed succeed in building up a loyal following among the better-off, more independent, voters. But he was to learn the hard way, in 1761, that when it came to a contested election the poorer voters, who formed the bulk of Aylesbury's electorate (there was a household franchise), were not to be influenced by favours alone but 'could only be bought for hard cash', in this instance five guineas (£5 5s.) apiece paid to 300 electors. The experience left him very disillusioned and a great deal poorer.[6]

Meanwhile the decline in the number of children apprenticed by Harding's Charity had evidently continued after 1740, for there had been a large accumulation of surplus cash. At some date prior to 1755 the sum of £164 6s. had been entrusted to Thomas Sheen, one of the trustees, and in January 1756 £250 was invested in Bank of England stock through the good offices of Wilkes, much of whose time was now spent in London, making a total of £404 6s., or just under three times the gross annual rental in 1754.

Unfortunately the trustees had been too trusting in their handling of the surpluses. Late in 1763, when Wilkes, now a national figure following his prosecution for seditious libel and his expulsion from the House of Commons, fled abroad leaving a trail of unpaid debts, it was discovered that he had been systematically misappropriating the hospital funds. At the same time – if not sooner – it came to light that the £250 of Harding's Charity funds which he had so obligingly undertaken to invest for the trustees had never in fact been paid into the bank. To make matters worse, Thomas Sheen's affairs were discovered to have deteriorated to such an extent that he was not in a position to repay the money entrusted to his care.

In 1769 the trustees, now comprising Matthias Dagnall, Edward Price, Thomas Sheen and John Wilkes, together with Thomas Towers, the proprietor of the *Angel* public house, who had been elected in July 1766 following the death of Archdale Williams, became defendants in an action in the court of Chancery. Named as co-defendants in the same lawsuit were William James of Gloucester, gentleman, eldest son and heir of the late trustee (later replaced as co-defendant by his infant son William, represented by his mother Mary James, widow), one Joseph Harding of Aylesbury, said to be the founder's heir at law, and several others whose roles were more formal or peripheral. The plaintiff in the case was the attorney-general 'at the relation of' Henry Russell, Robert Paten and John Bigg, churchwardens of Aylesbury, on behalf of themselves and of the other parishioners of Aylesbury.[7]

The chief matter of complaint alleged was that the trustees for many years past had failed to apply the income of the Charity in a manner that accorded with the testator's intentions and that, although they had accumulated large funds, they were refusing to apply them to apprenticing poor children living in Aylesbury and Walton. The timing of the action is significant and suggests that, despite its adversarial tone, there may have been a degree of collusion about the appeal to Chancery. For on 17 November 1767, almost half a century after the death of William Harding, his sister-in-law Sarah Pettipher had finally died, having outlived both her husbands. This meant that the house in Walton with the garden and close of land adjoining, together with the other land there and in Stoke Mandeville in which she had been given a life interest, reverted to the Trust – thus, it was said, adding £30 to the annual value of the estate, though if the land tax is any guide, the trustees did not get possession of the house until as late as 1786.[8] Her annuity of £5 7s. od., representing the interest on her share of the proceeds of the sale of grain under the terms of the founder's will, also died with her, though its future status seems to have been less than clear. In any case, the questions concerning the vesting of the freehold of the Charity estate and the legal liability for the surplus funds which had been put in jeopardy could hardly be put off indefinitely.

The evidence in the case is interesting not only for the factual information it supplies (some of which has been made use of in preceding paragraphs), but also for the light it throws on conflicting attitudes towards policy on apprenticing in relation to the public interest. The burden of the plaintiffs' case was that, although there were sufficient poor children in Aylesbury parish and suitable masters and mistresses available there to whom they could be apprenticed to enable all the Charity's annual income, estimated (incorrectly) at around £200, to be applied in this way, the trustees had adamantly refused to do so. Additionally, the defendant William James, who had been urged to convey a legal title to the trustees, was alleged to have combined with the trustees and with Joseph Harding and others to refuse to act.

According to the plaintiffs, the pretext given by the trustees for their inaction over apprenticing was that it had been the testator's intention to place children out to masters and mistresses living in other parishes in order that they might gain settlements (the legal right to reside) in those parishes and so be prevented from becoming a charge on the parish of Aylesbury. But experience had shown that this practice would increase the number of poor in the parish instead of lessening it, because persons living in Aylesbury who needed apprentices were obliged to take them from other parishes, 'and that frequently without any premiums at all and seldom or ever so large a premium as the sum of ten pounds'. Moreover, the poor children placed as apprentices in other parishes 'very frequently' returned to, and became chargeable to, the parish of Aylesbury. It was alleged that the trustees also falsely claimed that there were very few poor children in the parish to be placed out and not nearly enough to exhaust the whole of the income and likewise that there were very few 'proper' persons within the parish to take such children apprentices.

More specific charges were that the other trustees ought not to have permitted John Wilkes to take, and apply to his own use, the £250 which he now refused to account for, and for which he wrongly claimed the benefit of the clause in the founder's will exempting the trustees from liability for accidental loss. The same charge applied to Thomas Sheen's application of the £164 6s. to his own use. The defendants claimed that Sheen had, in October 1764, been required to execute a mortgage of his house in Walton to one John Perkins in trust for the Charity, but this mortgage security was very inadequate and Sheen himself was now either indigent or in low circumstances. Finally, the court's intervention was needed since the trustees refused to disclose the full facts of the Charity's finances, and also to 'establish' the charitable trust, by which was evidently meant securing to it the freehold of the landed endowment.

All the trustees except Wilkes put in answers to the complaints. Since Matthias Dagnall was the longest-serving trustee and by his own admission the sole 'receiver' (treasurer) in direct succession to his father, who had also in his time been sole receiver, his answer is the most relevant. Dagnall confirmed that for some years the trustees had had surplus moneys in their hands because proper applications for apprenticeships had not been made to them nor suitable masters and mistresses proposed. He also volunteered that for many years the trustees had distributed many more coats and gowns to the poor of Walton than had been specified by the testator. He had heard that when Edward Price had questioned the trustees' authority to do this, the Reverend John Dudley (d.1745), a former trustee, had given it as his opinion that such distribution was 'equal charity' to putting out apprentices and that the trustees might safely do it, and that the trustees had since relied on this declaration.

The reference to Dudley dates the beginning of the alleged diversion of funds to the early 1740s, since the existing accounts show that prior to 1741 payments for clothing had been within the prescribed £2 limit. It thus seems possible that the decline in the number of applicants for premiums had actually been triggered by a sudden – and temporary – decline in demand for apprenticing caused by the 1742 epidemic to which reference has already been made. Dagnall considered that the trustees ought to be indemnified for their action since it was done with charitable intent and to relieve the distress of the Walton poor. He revealed that the balance in his hands on 4 May 1767 was £107 10s. 6d. (not on the face of it an excessively large amount) and that the gross annual rents and profits had amounted to £141 10s. (the same as in c.1740 and 1754), but that as a result of Sarah Pettipher's recent death the trustees' gross income had increased by £30 on account of the reversion of the property which she had held for life under the will, making a total of £171 10s. Presumably this sum included the Pettipher house and orchard.

Dagnall disagreed strongly with the plaintiffs' views on apprenticing. He accepted that there was so great a number of poor children in Aylesbury and Walton that placing them out would exhaust the whole of the Charity's annual income but did not believe that there was a sufficient number of proper masters or mistresses in the parish, and held that, even if there had been, the trustees had full discretion to place children apprentices elsewhere. This, he believed, was 'a much more proper' course, as had been proved by experience, including evidence of fraud and collusion:

> Defendant saith that in many instances where poor children of the liberty of Walton and parish of Aylesbury aforesaid have been placed out apprentices to masters and mistresses within the liberty and parish aforesaid it has afterwards appeared ... that such masters and mistresses have sometimes taken such apprentices for the sake of the money only and at other times that the money or apprentice fee given by the said trustees to such master or mistress has been ... often divided between such master or mistress and the parent or parents of such child and that such children have afterwards left their places without having learned their respective trades.

Whatever the truth of these allegations, Dagnall's low opinion of Aylesbury employers is consistent with the notorious rapacity of the ordinary Aylesbury electors, as Wilkes had experienced it in 1761.

Dagnall denied that any applications from what he called 'proper' masters and mistresses 'residing out of the said parish of Aylesbury' were ever rejected, while maintaining that any application found upon strict enquiry not to be agreeable to the express direction of the trustees had always been rejected. While the trustees had always used their utmost diligence in placing out poor children, they had, he agreed, sometimes been unsuccessful. Nevertheless he confirmed that it had always been their judgement that it was not only much more for the benefit of such poor children but also for the parish that they be placed out of the parish in order to gain settlements and thereby lessen the number of poor in the parish. Such also had been the practice of former trustees, and such he had heard was the practice in other parishes where money had been left for this purpose. He went so far as to allege that former trustees 'seldom did as [he] believes place out any of the said poor children apprentice to persons residing in the said parish', a statement which cannot be reconciled with the evidence for the 1730s, however true it may have been of the intervening period.

14 *Inscribed flyleaf of Wilkes's copy of the Charity's proceedings (the volume is mostly blank).*

But while the defendant and his contemporary trustees, for the reasons given, had refused to place out poor children in Aylesbury, they had, he claimed, placed out a great number to masters and mistresses living in other parishes, and had never refused applications from fit and proper persons, and had always diligently, and at some expense, enquired into the characters of the applicants. Moreover he believed that very few of the children placed in other parishes had returned and been chargeable. A great part of the Charity's income had been applied in placing apprentices, as appeared in the accounts, but the number varied from year to year.

Regarding the money advanced to Wilkes, Dagnall said that he and the other trustees had for a considerable time believed that Wilkes had placed it in bank stock in the trustees' names, and that Wilkes had even paid him £19 12s. for interest due at Lady Day 1758. He pointed out that at the time Wilkes had considerable estates in Buckinghamshire and elsewhere and was 'in great reputation'. He was now returned from abroad and was living in London within the jurisdiction of Chancery. In the case of Sheen, payment had been made at different times by order of the trustees. His own objection to the loan had been overruled by Wilson Williams, who said that Sheen was worth £700, and he was supported by William James, on the grounds that it was no matter in whose hands the money was lodged provided he was a trustee. Afterwards, when the trustees had reason to believe that Sheen's circumstances were not so good as they had believed, they had applied to him for repayment and when he failed to comply had induced him to secure repayment with interest at four per cent by mortgaging his house. Sheen claimed to have lost the deeds and the property was found to be subject to a marriage settlement. Its value to let was £7 a year.

A supplementary answer by Dagnall incorporates a schedule containing a complete transcript of his accounts of receipts and payments for the 18 months from April 1768 to December 1769. The payments consist principally of premiums for 10 apprentices – two of them female – bound to masters and mistresses who did not reside in Aylesbury (two were apprenticed in 1768 and the rest in 1769), demonstrating that Dagnall's evidence concerning the trustees' policy on apprenticing was literally true, at least for the period covered by the accounts. One of the apprentices was Sarah Pettipher of Walton, apprenticed to Elizabeth, the wife of Thomas Burch of The Lee, a mantua maker. The parish register shows that she was born in April 1754 to John Pettipher and Alice, his wife, and so was probably the grand-daughter of Sarah Pettipher, the founder's sister-in-law.

The destinations of the other apprentices were Great Missenden, Chesham, Weston Turville, London, Oxford, Tring, Wilstone and Northchurch (both in Hertfordshire), and Whichford in Warwickshire. Their employers' occupations were, cordwainer (3), carpenter and joiner (2), mantua maker, mantua maker and tailor (male), baker, plumber and glazier, and wheelwright. Other entries in the accounts show that spending on clothing for the Walton poor was back within the prescribed bounds of £2 a year and that the total spent on dinners at the two general meetings was under £3.

One significant aspect of the evidence in the case is the tacit acceptance by both sides that the apprenticing of poor children was solely a matter for the trustees, with no suggestion that the Aylesbury parish officers either should, or would, exercise their statutory powers in the matter. This apparent abrogation of responsibility gives added force to the plaintiffs' implication that the trustees' high standards in the selection of masters and mistresses were indirectly increasing the number of poor in the parish. For clearly an indigent Aylesbury tradesman, especially one in an unskilled trade, had a stronger incentive than most to seek a 'parish' apprentice from elsewhere, since this was likely to be his only chance of securing a premium, paid by a parish that was happy to rid itself of an encumbrance in this way.

The true situation remains obscure but evidence that *some* pauper apprentices were being 'imported' is not too difficult to find, usually among the records of other Buckinghamshire parishes. One surviving indenture, dated 1797, among the parish's own papers relates to a trade which had become a byword for child exploitation and was the subject of regulatory legislation in this period. It testifies that Robert Bates of Dinton, aged 14, was bound by the parish officers of Dinton to John Fryer of Aylesbury, chimney sweeper, until the age of twenty-one. An earlier example, taken from the records of Quarter Sessions, is Thomas Eyre, apprenticed by the parish officers of Aston Clinton to Robert Ironmaster of Aylesbury only to be removed back to Aston Clinton in 1719 when his master abandoned him and the town after six months. A more chilling example of the potential evils of pauper apprenticeship is the tragic suicide by hanging in August 1738 of Thomas Grenville, probably of Wotton Underwood, who was apprenticed to John Miles of Aylesbury, a gardener, when he was about twelve. After six years with his master he would still have had five years or more to serve.[9]

The schedule of accounts, to which reference has been made, also records the payment in December 1769 on behalf of John Wilkes of £404 11s., being repayment of the £250 principal with interest at five per cent from 5 January 1756. Thus the trustees got their money back in full and Wilkes had extricated himself from further obligation, apart from having costs awarded against him. Having returned from exile in early 1768, he had – despite his outlaw status – been triumphantly elected M.P. for Middlesex, following which he had surrendered himself to justice amid scenes of wild enthusiasm and the soon-to-be-familiar cry of 'Wilkes and Liberty'. Since then he had been holding court to his many political supporters in the King's Bench prison, and it was from prison that he wrote in July 1768 with his usual *sang-froid* to thank his old friend Dell for the gift of bottled beer in which he promised to drink the health of the Dells and of 'the County Town of Bucks and its produce'. Dell was one of 34 of Wilkes's former constituents who, in April 1768, had petitioned against his being deprived of his parliamentary seat for the second time. Among the others who signed were Robert Neale, John Stevens (Stephens) and, rather more surprisingly, E[dward] Price, one of Harding's trustees.[10]

Since Wilkes's debts were said to amount in 1768 to some £14,000, exclusive of fines due, election expenses and maintenance costs, the trustees could count themselves fortunate to have got their money back. In February 1769 the Bill of Rights Society had been founded for the express purpose of securing Wilkes's release from prison by discharging his most pressing obligations. A public subscription was raised and Wilkes himself is known to have used £800, obtained from windfall libel damages, to pay off outstanding Buckinghamshire militia debts described by one historian as 'long a notorious blot on the Wilkes record'. Around the same time, payments were made in settlement of the money misappropriated from the Aylesbury Foundling Hospital as well as the considerable sums still due to the workmen employed on it.[11]

Eventually, in November 1772, the court of Chancery ruled *inter alia* that the Charity should be 'established' (which presumably means legally confirmed) and that 'proper trustees' should be appointed in place of the existing ones. Execution of this decree was entrusted to Master Eames, one of the masters in Chancery, who was also to take an account of the Charity's resources. The master duly reported but the ruling was not made absolute until 1776, by which time all the existing trustees apart from Wilkes were dead: Dagnall and Towers in 1773 and Price and Sheen in 1774.[12] The money lent to Sheen was recovered out of his estate and the annuity paid to the late Mrs Pettipher was confirmed to belong to the Charity. On the other hand, Chancery litigation was notoriously expensive and much of the cost is certain to have fallen on the Charity estate. Already in 1769 Dagnall's schedule of accounts includes a payment of £46 13s. 9d. to Mr Bull, a local lawyer described as 'a solicitor in this case'. Luckily, the substantial sums recovered from Wilkes and Sheen may have been more than sufficient to meet all such demands.

The new trustees appointed by Chancery were (on later evidence) Sir Francis Bernard, William Minshull, Thomas Dagnall, Joseph Burnham and William Brooks. Bernard (*c.*1711-79) was the last governor of the Massachusetts Bay colony, who had been recalled from Boston in 1769. In 1771 he had inherited the Nether Winchendon estate, but finding country life uncongenial, had made his residence in the Prebendal House in Aylesbury, Wilkes's former home, in September 1772. William Minshull (1732-1807) was another scion of the landed gentry, whose family seat was at Aston Clinton, but he, too, was then living in Aylesbury, where he practised as a lawyer. He was Clerk of the Peace for Buckinghamshire, an influential office in the gift of the lord lieutenant of the county, from 1764 to 1787. Thomas Dagnall (1746-92) was the son and heir of Matthias Dagnall and, like his father and grandfather, an Aylesbury bookseller. William Brooks is probably the maltster of that name whose burial is recorded in the parish register in 1784.[13]

Joseph Burnham (1729-99) was another Aylesbury lawyer, who was descended from an old Tory family. The son of a proctor, he himself practised in the ecclesiastical court and was registrar for the archdeaconry of Buckingham by 1780. He was also, by 1765, deputy steward and later, by 1772, steward, of the manor of Aylesbury. He served as churchwarden on more than one occasion. Over the years he acquired a substantial estate in Aylesbury and its vicinity; his elegant residence in Church Street, later known as Ceely House, is now part of the County Museum. A close relation, Charles Burnham, had earlier been a beneficiary of the Charity.[14]

Matthias Dagnall's schedule of accounts of 1768-9 is an invaluable source of information about the Charity's estate at this time. From it we learn that William Bigg of Walton had replaced both John Stopp and John Todd in the Walton farm and the other lands there, and that he also held Dunsham Platt in Aylesbury, that James Lee of Aylesbury had taken over the closes and land in Bierton formerly Parker's, and that John Small of Ickford was tenant of the grassland at Chilton. Bigg had also acquired the tenancy of some open field land in Walton previously occupied by Mrs Pettipher, while Mrs Pettipher's land in Stoke Mandeville had been let to John Smith of Stoke. Her house (the former Hardings Elms) was reported to be out of repair and was, with its orchard, untenanted in 1769.

Dagnall's estimate that Mrs Pettipher's death had added £30 to the Charity's annual income presumably includes both the rental value of her house and the value of her annuity; certainly the rents paid for her other properties seem to amount to less than half that sum. Landlord's outgoings, including land tax at around ten per cent, insurance on the Walton farm, and quitrents, etc., amounted to over £19. A further £5 5s. was taken up by expenses at meetings (£2 5s.), the distribution to the Walton poor (£2) and the cost of writing up the accounts; there was also a payment to the bellman for sticking up a notice of the meeting. This means that the net income available for premiums was well under £120, less than was required for 12 apprentices.

The Bierton property was affected by the parish enclosure of 1780. The trustees, named in the enclosure award as Minshull, Burnham, Brooks and Dagnall (Bernard having died the previous year), were awarded two adjoining rectangular plots, or 'allotments', near the parish boundary with Aylesbury amounting together to some five and a half acres, stated to be in lieu of 13 'computed' acres with right of common. In addition, there were approximately nine acres of old enclosure nearby, presumably representing the Bierton closes

15 *Extract from the entry in* The Universal British Directory *(1790) for Aylesbury. Among the names listed are those of John Oviatt, collarmaker, and (not shown) John Brett, 'limner' (see colour plate no. 3). Overall, the range of trades represented is fairly typical of a market town.*

purchased by William Harding in 1705, and at that time said to comprise 10 acres of pasture.[15] This was the second enclosure award to affect Harding's, the first being the Aylesbury award of 1771, when the trustees received a tiny allotment of one and a half acres in lieu of Dunsham Platt, the piece of meadow there which the founder had been left by his mother.

Of the trustees appointed by Chancery only two – Minshull and Burnham – survived until the Charity's own records recommence in 1794. Virtually nothing is known of what happened in the interval. It is not even certain that successors were elected as vacancies occurred (in 1779, 1784 and 1792); indeed the description of three trustees as 'new' in 1794 strongly suggests the contrary. What we do know is that the large surplus in the trustees' hands, amounting to over £1,000 by the end of the century, can only have been accumulated in this earlier period, indicating either a low level of spending on apprenticing over an extended period or a complete cessation for a number of years. This money is stated in the minutes in 1794 to have been in the hands of Joseph Burnham, described as 'the late treasurer', allegedly on account of a lack of sufficient applications for premiums.

Inevitably a number of questions arise, especially if we assume that there were only three trustees after William Brooks's death in 1784. Why had Joseph been allowed to retain such large sums in his possession? How long had he held them and what use, if any, had he made of them? Burnham was a man with his finger in many pies who rose from fairly modest circumstances to become one of the richest men in Aylesbury. It was undoubtedly to his advantage to have control of large amounts of cash, and not necessarily in his interest to be too zealous about spending them. In the circumstances the possibility not just of lack of zeal, but of deliberate neglect or worse, cannot be ruled out.

Rural Distress and the End of Statutory Enforcement of Apprenticeship, 1794-1845

By 1794, when the first of the Charity's two earliest surviving minute books, properly so called, begins, social and economic conditions were very different from what they had been in the 1720s and 1730s. War had broken out the previous year with revolutionary France, a war which was to last for over 20 years, during which grain prices more than doubled and the value of money declined at a rate unprecedented since the 16th century. Even before this, living conditions in the rural south of England had been deteriorating. The underlying cause was rapid population growth in the second half of the 18th century, but other factors, including the gradual enclosure of the common fields, contributed also. In Aylesbury, where the population had exceeded 3,000 by 1801, unemployed men were already receiving 'outdoor' relief from the parish by the 1780s. By 1795, when the Buckinghamshire magistrates sanctioned the subsidising of wages from the rates in accordance with family size, the pauperisation of a large section of what would now be called the working class was well advanced.[1]

As already noted, two of the five trustees appointed by Chancery were still in office in 1794, namely the lawyers William Minshull and Joseph Burnham. The three 'new Trustees', as they are called in the minutes, who had replaced Sir Francis Bernard, William Brooks and Thomas Dagnall, were the Reverend William Stockins, John Parker and Joseph Brooks. Stockins (d.1827), a local man of humble origins, was master of the grammar school from 1774 to 1806 and again from 1813 to 1817. A Whig in politics, he was to be a regular attender at meetings until 1822. Parker (d.1811, aged 63), who married Thomas Dagnall's widow, was yet another Aylesbury attorney. Brooks is described in a 1792 directory as a 'maltster and farmer'.[2]

The minutes of the first few meetings of the trustees give a distinct impression of new beginnings, tending to confirm that there had indeed been an interruption – long or short – in the functioning of the Charity. In 1794, for example, two meetings were held in January and February, in addition to the prescribed meetings in May and November, in the course of which Stockins and Parker were appointed joint treasurers for the ensuing year – replacing Joseph Burnham, 'the late treasurer' – and it was arranged that future meetings be held at the *White Hart* in Aylesbury on the first Tuesdays in May and November, unless ordered to the contrary. This year was also remarkable for the number of applications for apprenticeships approved, a total of 27 (24 boys and three girls), of whom five were held over until a suitable master

16 *Hand-written indenture apprenticing William, the son of William Green of Aylesbury, deceased, to Christopher Watson of Waddesdon, blacksmith, for seven years, in consideration of a 'premium' of £10 paid by the trustees of Harding's Charity, 1794. This is the earliest example of its kind to have come to light.*

could be found. This was far more than in any immediately subsequent year and well in excess of the gross annual income, suggesting that there had been a backlog of applicants.

Apprenticing was, of course, the principal purpose of the meetings, and the minutes are almost wholly taken up with orders for the placing of individual children. These normally give the father's name, and whether he was deceased, and the name, abode and occupation of the master or mistress. The father's occupation is rarely ever given. The proportion of children identified as fatherless varies considerably from year to year; in 1794 there were 10, or just over a third of the total, an unusually high proportion in this period. In 1797 there were two out of a total of 10 and the average for the five years 1795-9 was under 25 per cent. As we shall see, compared with the first half of century, the range of the apprentices' occupations is considerably more restricted.

One of the orphans apprenticed in 1794 was William Green, aged 13 according to the parish register, who was ordered to be apprenticed to Christopher Watson of Waddesdon, blacksmith. By chance, his original, hand-written, indenture, dated 15 February 1794 – the earliest so far found – survives among the Aylesbury parish records. From it we learn that William's deceased father, also called William, had been a whitesmith (a metalworker or tinsmith). Although

the wording is different, in essentials it is the same as a 'non-poor' indenture, stipulating a seven-year term during which the master undertakes to 'teach instruct and inform' the apprentice in the art or business of a blacksmith and to provide 'meat drink apparel washing lodging and all other things needful or meet for an apprentice' in return for a premium of £10. William signs with a mark, being unable to write his own name, and pledges to faithfully serve his master in all lawful business and to behave himself 'honestly and obediently' towards his master and the rest of his family. Sixty years later a printed pro forma indenture was in use but the terms and conditions – and even most of the wording – were unchanged. William may well have completed his full term since, five years later, his name appears as an apprentice smith under Waddesdon in the Buckinghamshire Posse Comitatus, a roll of men between the ages of 15 and 60, not already serving in a

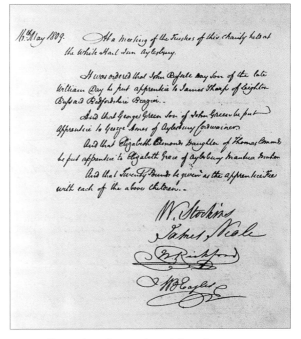

17 *Extract from the second surviving minute book of the Charity, covering the years 1794-1813, showing the minutes of the meeting held on 16 May 1809. They are signed by William Stockins, James Neale, William Rickford and W.B. Eagles.*

military capacity, which was made early in 1798 in expectation of an imminent invasion by the French.[3]

A memorandum in the minutes against another of the entries in 1794 draws attention to an unwritten rule that a child should not normally be apprenticed to his or her parent. Ann, daughter of Thomas and Priscilla Hill, was in fact apprenticed to her mother (no occupation stated), but the note explaining the exceptional circumstances of the case implies a lack of familiarity with normal procedure: 'No instance appears of any child being put apprentice to its parents before nor would it have been done now but on account of Mrs Hills being a relation of the Donor.'

The other related concern of the trustees was the management of the Charity's landed estate. In the absence of regular accounts until 1844, information about income and expenditure is scanty. As we have seen, Matthias Dagnall gave the gross rental income in 1769 as £171, though this may have been an over-estimate since another source gives the figure in 1774 as £145. In 1797, in the course of legal proceedings, the total rental is given as £199.[4] In addition, there was a large accumulated cash surplus by 1794, and one of the trustees' first concerns in the minutes of that year was to put in train arrangements for the investment of £1,000 (five times the gross annual rental) in three per cent consols with the object of increasing the Charity's income. According to the minute book, the money was then in the treasurers' hands 'for want of a sufficient number of applications for placing poor children apprentices'. A further deposit of £200 is recorded in May 1796, bringing the annual dividend to £36. In February 1801 the annual value of the real estate was reported to be as high as £244 and the annual dividend from investments was £36, making a total annual income of £280; there were also cash and other balances totalling £153 at that date.[5]

In 1795 the number of those apprenticed fell abruptly to nine (eight boys and one girl), a third of the previous year's total, and the totals in following years were only slightly higher. In May 1796 the trustees identified the cause, 'it appearing ... that proper masters and mistresses are not to be found at the ... present fee of £10'. Wartime inflation, it seems, had finally rendered insufficient what in William Harding's time had been a generous provision. The remedy adopted on the advice of counsel was to apply to the court of Chancery for leave to increase the premium. Application was made the same year through the agency of Thomas Hatten, an Aylesbury lawyer. The petition recites that 'by reason of the decrease which has taken place in the value of money since the [founder's will] few or no artificers or men in trade of good morals and well skilled ... will now take apprentices with so small a fee as ten pounds ...', and it claims that although 'there are many poor children of settled inhabitants ... whose friends are extremely desirous of their being placed out ... in eligible situations' they are deterred from applying for the charity for this reason. A decree was obtained in February 1801 authorising the payment of premiums of up to £20. The cost in legal fees of obtaining it amounted to over £100. The new premium was the same as that fixed for the new Saye and Sele Charity at Quainton in 1803 (the latter was increased to £30 in 1825). It meant that the number of apprenticeships that could be financed out of current income was now fewer than 14, assuming that the maximum rate was paid.[6]

In the event it was fortunate that the trustees had accumulated such a substantial reserve, for they were about to be faced by large, and apparently unexpected, expenses arising from the enclosure of Stoke Mandeville and Walton in 1797 and 1801 respectively. From the minutes it appears that the total costs, including ancillary expenses, incurred for the two enclosures amounted to more than £650, spread over several years. Additionally, another major expense was incurred in May 1801 when the trustees, taking advantage of a recent Act of Parliament, decided to redeem the land tax assessed on all the Charity properties at a cost of £968.[7] Since the tax was the landlord's liability, the effect was eventually to increase the net income from rents, but in the short term there would have been a net decrease in income of some £36 as a result of the loss of the annual interest on capital invested, which must have been entirely exhausted by 1803.

Meanwhile, the increased premiums introduced at the beginning of 1801 appear to have been having an effect. Apprenticeships, which had declined from an average of 12 in 1796-98, to six in 1799, and to only two the following year, rose to 16 (three of them girls) in 1801, representing an outlay of £320 – considerably more than the gross annual income at that date. Not surprisingly, within three years at this level the trustees found it necessary to reduce the premium to £17 for the reason that the finances 'did not enable them to give more at this time'. Thereafter the amount fluctuated from meeting to meeting. Between 1804 and 1808 it ranged from £13 to £17, returning to £20 between 1808 and 1812, a period during which rents rose steeply. There was no attempt to vary the premiums on the basis of individual circumstances, as some other charities appear to have done. The numbers apprenticed also fluctuated, usually in inverse proportion to the amount of the premium, from as low as nine in 1809 (when the premium was £20) and 12 in 1813 (£18) to as high as 21 in 1807 (£15), averaging 15 or 16 a year. During the same period the number of female apprentices showed a tendency to rise to around a third of the total.

In 1814 the trustees found it necessary to order that 'in future every apprentice put out by this Charity [shall] be expected to board and lodge wholly in the house with the master or mistress'. This rule may have had in mind particularly the minority of children who were apprenticed to masters and mistresses in Aylesbury and who were thus in a position to live at home. But over the previous half century 'living out' (or 'clubbing out', as it was also called) had become an increasingly common phenomenon, even among apprentices living at a distance from home, forcing them to find accommodation in lodging houses and public houses, thus undermining the traditional, familial, concept of the relationship between master and apprentice.[8] Since, as we have seen, the form of the indenture makes no provision for it, living out must have been a private arrangement between the master or mistress and the apprentice and in the majority of cases must have been accompanied by some form of payment in lieu of maintenance.

Equally common by this period, it seems, was the practice of apprentices leaving service after completing as little as four years, or less, of the standard seven years officially contracted for. Between 1750 and 1790 there is statistical evidence of a national downward trend in the number of years served by (non-poor) apprentices from an average of around six and a half in 1750 to just under four in 1786.[9] Buckinghamshire, it seems, was no exception in this regard, for of 15 boys apprenticed by Harding's in 1794, to employers living within the county, only eight can be identified with reasonable certainty in the Posse Comitatus of 1798, and only one of these (William Green) is specifically described there as an apprentice in addition to his trade. This may be partly attributable to inconsistent classification, but most of those boys who were apprenticed in 1795-7, where traceable, are identified as apprentices in the Posse. It transpires, for example, that seven out of 21 boys listed separately as 'apprentices' (no trades given) under Aylesbury in the Posse had been apprenticed by Harding's during 1795-7, while one other Harding apprentice (Joseph Norris, apprenticed to James Neale, draper, one of the trustees) is listed under 'servants'.

The evidence is conflicting, but it is clear that, despite the solemn undertakings of the indentures, the statutory seven-year term had often been disregarded in many trades and crafts, at any rate as far as non-poor apprentices living in towns were concerned. It seems to have been widely accepted in the 17th century, for example, that most trades and crafts could be mastered within three or four years. If an apprentice left of his own accord within that period it was his loss; if dismissed by his master he was entitled to recover some, or all, of the premium paid in the courts. Once fully skilled, he was in a position either to negotiate more favourable terms with his master or to leave him and set up on his own with, apparently, little fear of prosecution.[10] It would seem that by the 1780s rural charity apprentices were in much the same position. Parish apprentices in unskilled or low-skilled occupations, on the other hand, had little or no bargaining power.

The decline in the overall importance of apprenticeship in the labour market generally was recognised by the repeal, in 1814, of the relevant clauses in the 1563 Statute of Artificers. This meant that the obligation to undergo an apprenticeship before practising a trade was no longer enforceable at law. The repeal met with determined opposition from the highly organised skilled craftsmen in the manufacturing districts, but such resistance could hardly be expected in rural Buckinghamshire.[11] Though a significant milestone in the process of 'de-skilling', of itself the Act appears to have had no immediate effect on the popularity of apprenticeship, but it probably encouraged the flexibility in the length of the term served mentioned above.

The minute book of Harding's Charity reveals a continuing strong bias in favour of 'exporting' apprentices from the town, but the policy was no longer

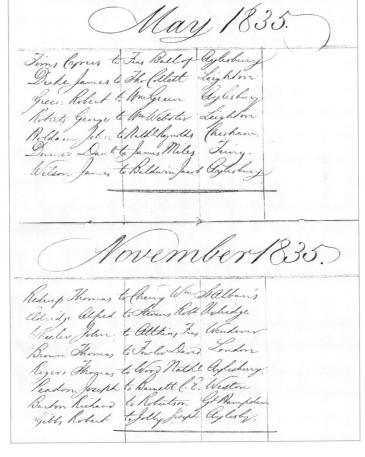

19 *Register listing children apprenticed in May and November 1835. The destinations recorded in column 3 show that a high proportion were still being 'placed' out of the town.*

20 *A few examples of illustrations in* The Book of English Trades, *published by G. and W.B. Whitaker (1824 edition). The trades represented here are (clockwise): cabinet maker, brazier, baker and bricklayer.*

being carried to the extreme favoured in the 1760s. Analysis of the 73 children (including 17 girls) apprenticed during the five years 1801-5 reveals that 31 per cent – 18 boys and five girls – remained in the parish. The destinations of the other 50 may be summarised as follows: Buckinghamshire, 23; adjacent counties, 18; London/Middlesex, 7; other, 2. Of the 41 in the first two categories half went to market towns, comprising Tring (5), Berkhamsted (3), Bicester (3), Buckingham (2), Chesham (2), Princes Risborough, Wendover, Wycombe and – a little further afield – Watlington and St Albans. The 'other' category comprises two boys apprenticed to the felt hat industry in Atherstone, Warwickshire. A striking feature is the reduction of the proportion of apprentices going to London compared to the previous century. It reflected a general decline in such migration. The metropolis was no longer the source of employment opportunities that it had been less than a century earlier.[12]

Aylesbury trades were, for boys, baker, cabinet maker, blacksmith (2), brazier, bricklayer (3), cooper, coppersmith/brazier, cordwainer (4), hairdresser, tailor, wheelwright and whitesmith; for girls, the list only included mantua maker and/or milliner (4) and a 'gloveress'. These trades overlap with the considerably more varied range followed by the 50 children apprenticed to employers located outside Aylesbury. But the distribution of the latter is very uneven, for no fewer than 29 are concentrated in only four trades, namely blacksmith (8), tailor (6) and carpenter (3) for boys, and, for girls, mantua maker/milliner (12). The remaining 21 were apprenticed to 16 different trades, among which were bricklayer, cabinet maker (2), coach spring maker[13] (in London), cordwainer (2), grocer, mercer (London), pawnbroker (London), plumber and glazier, staymaker, and sieve and basket maker. In both lists there is a preponderance of widely distributed craft trades, with woodworking, metal working, leather and clothing especially prominent; 'superior' trades, of which there was a sprinkling in 1720-40, are notably absent with the exception of cabinet maker and, possibly, mercer.

Nineteen of the children – or just under 25 per cent – apprenticed in 1801-5 were fatherless. Of the remaining 54, the occupations of 41 of the fathers can be traced in the Posse Comitatus and in the printed poll book for the borough election of 1804. Some 13 of them are described as labourers; the rest are nearly all artisans of various kinds, the exceptions being two bakers, a waggoner, a licensed victualler (John Shelton of the *King's Head* inn), a chaise driver and a horse dealer. Here, too, there is a contrast with the 1720s and 1730s, when the proportion of parents who were neither labourers nor artisans appears to have been higher.

The death of William Minshull in 1807, after over 30 years in office, severed the last link with the pre-1794 generation of Harding trustees. He was the last lawyer-trustee to be elected for several decades. For the immediate future, control of the Charity would increasingly be in the hands of members of Aylesbury's commercial and political elite, some of them relative newcomers to Aylesbury. The other trustees at this date were the Reverend William Stockins, John Parker, Joseph Pitches and James Neale. Pitches was a farmer and Neale, a draper and

a Londoner by birth, was one of the founders of the recently floated Vale of Aylesbury Bank; he was also closely involved in Aylesbury politics on the popular side in the disputed election of 1802.[14] Minshull's successor was William Rickford (1768-1854), who, with his father (also William), a grocer, had founded Aylesbury's first bank (later known as the Old Bank) in 1795. William Rickford senior (1730-1803), the first of the family to settle in the town,[15] had himself been a trustee for some four years in the 1790s, but had never attended. His second wife, whom he married in 1762, was a daughter of James Brooks, a farmer, presumably the elder of the two previous trustees of that name.

21 *William Rickford (1768-1854), trustee 1808-52. He was M.P. for Aylesbury from 1818 to 1841.*

Neale's bank was forced to cease trading (though with little or no loss to its customers) in 1810 and he eventually left the town around 1818. Rickford, in contrast to his rival, continued in office for over four decades during which time he established himself as Aylesbury's leading citizen as well as its most successful politician, becoming, in 1818, the town's first resident Member of Parliament since Wilkes, under the reforming banner of 'independence of elections'. He remained an M.P. until his retirement in 1841. Like Neale, Rickford was also a trustee of Bedford's Charity, which he and his father are credited with having rescued from a deplorable state of mismanagement.[16] Public service of this kind, together with annual Christmas gifts of beef and coal to the poor, helped to give substance to his claim to be 'the people's friend'.

More prosaically, by the early 1830s – if not before – Rickford was acting as banker to the Charity. Country banking was a new phenomenon and the services of the Old Bank must have been a considerable convenience to the trustees, but there is no doubt that the connection with the two charities was also a matter of importance to the bank. A number of Rickford's supporters and relations subsequently became trustees, beginning with Woodfield Blake Eagles, grazier and political radical, who was a trustee from 1808 until his death in 1852, and Zachariah (or Zacharias) Daniel Hunt, grocer, Rickford's brother-in-law (a native of Suffolk), who succeeded John Parker in 1812.[17]

By 1812, helped by wartime grain prices, and no doubt also as a result of enclosure, the Charity's gross annual rental was reported to be as high as £330, an increase of over £80 on 1801.[18] But a post-war financial slump in 1820-1 hit farmers hard and led to widespread temporary abatements of rent.

In 1822 the trustees agreed to an overall reduction to £300 (a cut of 10 per cent) from Michaelmas. How long the reduction lasted on this occasion is not clear.

One effect of the widespread post-war distress among agricultural labourers was to encourage parish officers and others to take a closer interest in local charities. At the same time charities generally were attracting greater public scrutiny. In 1820 an annotated abstract of Buckinghamshire charities, claiming to have been compared with official returns, was published by a certain T.W. Faulkner of Walton Street, Aylesbury, doubtless one of the town's growing band of Radical reformers, who were to find an effective mouthpiece with the launch of the *Buckinghamshire Chronicle* newspaper the following year.

The declared objective of Faulkner's abstract was to prevent 'the abuses that at the present time, and for many years past, have been existing in the distribution of Various Charities'. It was clearly inspired by other contemporary attacks by political liberals on abuses – real and imaginary – in church and state and, in particular, by recent scandalous revelations concerning major educational charities such as Eton and Winchester and the universities. Unfortunately, the information on trustees, etc., contained in it was well over 20 years out of date and the comments on some particular charities appear wide of the mark. Harding's trustees are given as William Minshull, Thomas Dagnall and Joseph Burnham, all long since deceased, and its estate is stated to be in debt, which was not in fact the case. How much attention the work attracted is unknown, but its price (7s. 6d.) would have placed it well beyond the means of those most affected.[19]

Throughout the 1820s, influenced no doubt by flexibility in the amount of the premium allowed, which averaged around £15-17, but was occasionally as low as £12 and once, in May 1827, went back down to the original £10, the annual number of apprentices were comparatively high at around twenty. In 1827, exceptionally, the figure was 28, of whom 18 were approved in May, when the premium was put at £10, and the rest in November, when the amount allowed was £15, representing an outlay of £330. Some idea of the actual demand is given – for the first and almost the only time – in the minutes for 1830-1. In October 1830 we are told that 21 applications had been received for the November meeting, out of which seven were selected, and the following April that out of 19 applications only five were selected. It is a measure of the inability of the Charity to respond adequately to the increase in population that, at a time of acute distress (the Swing riots broke out in the winter of 1830-1), only 30 per cent (twelve out of 40) of children seeking to be apprenticed could be accommodated.

By 1826, too, the proportion of girls apprenticed was rising again. It was rarely less than a third and sometimes much more. In 1827, for example, 15 of the 28 apprentices were female and, in 1818, 13 out of a total of twenty. This development was probably not unconnected with the gradual decline in the lace trade after 1820, as a result of the introduction of machine-made lace, a decline which reached catastrophic proportions towards the end of the decade. As a result, according to Robert Gibbs, 'Not only were large numbers of able-bodied men out of employment and they and their families being wholly supported by parish relief, but now females could earn nothing; great boys and girls were growing up in idleness.' It was in fact the availability of what Gibbs calls 'cheap juvenile labour' which prompted Robert Nixon, a Manchester engineer, to open a silk factory within the premises of the new parish workhouse near the present Mount Street, around 1830, thus providing some measure of relief. Children were still being removed from school to work in the silk factory as late as the 1870s.[20]

But in November 1832 the trustees decided to adopt a new selection policy designed to reduce the number of female apprentices:

> upon a review of the comparative numbers of male and female apprentices formerly placed out by the Trustees ... and considering the present net income from the Trust estates, [the Trustees] resolved that in future, except in special circumstances, they will not place out more than four female apprentices in the year and will not give a greater premium than £15 with any female apprentice.

At a time of exceptionally high male unemployment the trustees' desire to give priority to boys is, perhaps, understandable, and the fact that girls' apprenticeships were commonly of much shorter duration than those of boys may have been seen as a justification. Nevertheless, the action was contrary to the founder's express intentions and thus probably unlawful, because never submitted to Chancery for approval. A corollary of the new rules was that from then on payment of the full sums of £20 and £15 became standard.

Surprisingly, considering that they were designed to cope with a special set of circumstances, the two resolutions proved long-lived, more especially the resolution relating to differential premiums. A century later the amounts still stood at £20 for boys and £15 for girls. Apart from Rickford and Eagles, the trustees who took these decisions were Robert Dell, a wine merchant, who had replaced James Neale in 1819, Thomas Dell (no relation), brewer, successor to Mr Stockins (d.1827), and John Churchill, grocer and tallow chandler, who had replaced Z.D. Hunt in 1821. All three were associates of Rickford and, like him and Eagles, were actively involved in the struggle to pass the great parliamentary Reform Bill which became law in 1832.[21]

When the Commissioners for Enquiring Concerning Charities visited Aylesbury in 1832 the situation of agriculture was once again acute and the gross rent roll had declined to £289 (£277 net of landlord's outgoings), with the rent on the Chilton property now standing at £90. Worse still, Joseph Read, who in the interval had taken over the tenancy of the Walton farm in addition to his previous holding, was reported to be over three years in arrears with his rent – although he had paid £250 on account – and the Charity was in deficit to Rickford for £69. In their very comprehensive report the Commissioners give the average number of children apprenticed annually as about fourteen, adding that, 'The trustees are careful to select respectable persons as masters and mistresses'. But although mention is made of the Chancery decree of 1801,

22 *View of the offices of Parrott & Coales, solicitors, Clerks to William Harding's Charity, in Bourbon Street, by Nina Ribeiro. Founded in 1775, the firm acquired its present name in 1917 (see also p.102).*

nothing is said about the new rules on the allocation of premiums, which must have been introduced after the Commissioners' departure, since the report states that the net income is spent by the trustees 'in apprenticing boys and girls, selected by themselves, at premiums of £20 each'.[22]

In a separate entry under Walton we are told that the sum of £5 was spent annually by Mr Woodford B. Eagles, one of the trustees (who lived in Walton), in the purchase of five sets of clothes, each containing either a coat worth £1 or a gown and other clothes of the same value, which were distributed by him around Christmas to five poor persons of the hamlet.[23]

A crisis point was reached in May 1835 when, following Read's failure to pay off his rent arrears, the trustees recorded that there were no funds in hand to pay any premiums. Nevertheless six boys were selected for apprenticing with £20 apiece out of the first moneys to be received and eight more the following November at the same rate, to be paid 'so soon as the funds allow'. But even premiums of £20 were no guarantee against sharp practice by masters. In May 1836 it was resolved that, to prevent the recurrence of frauds which have been practised on the trustees, and to ensure the proper treatment and instruction of apprentices, in future one half only of the premium would be paid on execution of the indentures and the rest (the 'second moiety') after three years. Payment of apprenticeship premiums by instalment, occasionally employed by the trustees in the 1730s, had in fact been prescribed by law in 1768.

The precise nature of the frauds is not spelt out, but may well have included a further shortening of the term served. Payment in two instalments (which had occasionally been enforced in the 1730s) remained the rule thereafter and is recorded in a separate summary register of apprentices and of employers and their places of abode commencing in 1826, but with the column provided for the second moiety left blank until 1837. In the first two years no fewer than seven of the second moieties were forfeited, but after this forfeitures were comparatively infrequent, suggesting that the policy had proved effective.

There are also – as well as some unexplained blank spaces – very occasional brief entries to explain non-payment in particular cases, such as 'App[renti]ce married' (1847); 'Runaway' (1849); 'Clewley [the master] failed' (1851).[24]

An earlier rule, made in 1797, had required character references to be produced for all masters not personally known to the trustees, and there is evidence that it was still being enforced in the 1880s; this rule, too, was not altogether new since payments had occasionally been made in the 1730s for expenses incurred in obtaining 'characters'.[25]

For the remainder of the 1830s the annual number of children apprenticed remained steady at 14, rising to an average of around seventeen in the 1840s. During the same period the number of female apprentices exceeded four on only three occasions and it was often as low as two or three. These averages represent annual outlays of around £260 and £320 respectively, compared to a gross annual income from rents of under £300 in 1833. Clearly spending was still close to the limit of what could be afforded out of income, implying a probable excess of demand. But from around 1840 the situation began to alter. Not only was social distress becoming less acute (or at least better controlled) following the implementation of the New Poor Law in 1835, but the outlook for agriculture was improving and, with it, the prospect of improved income from rents. In November 1840 the trustees felt able to raise the rent on the Chilton property to £114 a year, and William Fleet, who had been paying £30 a year for the land in Stoke Mandeville, was now to pay £35. The following year the minutes record a balance in hand of £373; by 1852 it had risen to £569. A corner had been turned.

There is scarcely any mention of routine administrative arrangements in the minutes until the 1840s. In November 1842 the purchase of a deed box is recorded and later, in May 1850, a ledger for tenants' accounts. This has not survived, but accounts of receipts and payments are available from 1844; they are not always easy to interpret. We know from later references (in 1851 and 1852) that meetings for auditing the accounts were sometimes held at the Old Bank but this may be connected with the election of Rickford's nephew and partner, another Zachariah Daniel Hunt, to be a trustee in 1848 in succession to John Churchill, who had left the town. References to the clerks occur in the earliest bank pass book, which records payment of Edward Prickett's bill in 1841 (£28 18s.) and of that of 'Rose and Prickett' (£27) in 1846.[26] These partnerships were predecessors of Messrs Parrott & Coales, the present clerks to the Charity.

The minute book makes no mention of Prickett until 1852, when, 'it being intimated that Mr Prickett, one of the clerks to the Charity, was about to leave the country', it was ordered that he be requested to deliver up 'all deeds, books and papers that he has belonging to the Charity to Messrs Rose and Parrotts [sic]'. The outcome of this order proved disappointing, for at the next meeting, in November 1852, Rose and Parrotts (the new clerks) reported that 'Mr Prickett had delivered over to them the probate will of William Harding, an old minute book and numerous miscellaneous papers … but no title deeds'.

The Story of Elm Farm and the Post-Enclosure Charity Estate, 1798-1914

The so-called parliamentary enclosure movement, which began in the 1740s and lasted for over a century, reaching a climax between 1793 and 1815, has left an indelible imprint on the landscape of today, not least on that of north Buckinghamshire. As a result of independent initiatives, thousands of local Acts of Parliament authorised the redistribution of the open arable fields and commons within individual parishes through the agency of specially appointed enclosure commissioners. The initiative for this legislation came, almost invariably, from the larger landowners, who stood to gain most from the improved agricultural productivity resulting from the rationalisation of farms and holdings. Smallholders and landless labourers, who often had a greater stake in the status quo, usually had relatively little say in the matter.

Among those who benefited indirectly from enclosure were the local surveyors and lawyers who provided the technical expertise required to put the process into effect. William Minshull, one of the Harding's trustees, had acted as clerk to the commissioners for the Hartwell and Stone enclosure of 1774-7. Another of the trustees, Joseph Burnham, was successively solicitor and clerk to the enclosure commissioners for Aylesbury (1771), Whitchurch (1771-2) and Bierton (1779-80) and – exceptionally for a lawyer – was himself a commissioner for three other enclosures during the 1790s. Such officials, as well as others possessing the necessary capital and contacts, were also often in a position to profit by investing in land in anticipation of enclosure. Both Burnham and William Rickford were in this category and Rickford was also banker for at least six enclosures.[1]

The Charity's estate was affected by four separate enclosures, those for Aylesbury, Bierton, Stoke Mandeville and Walton (1801). Only the outlying property in Chilton, which had been enclosed in a much earlier, non-parliamentary phase of enclosure, was unaffected. At Aylesbury the amount of land involved was fairly insignificant and at Bierton, too, it was relatively small, comprising mainly old enclosure, resulting in an award of a total of 14 acres in two blocks adjoining the main Aylesbury road, one of which is described as old enclosure and the other as an allotment (land allotted in lieu of open field land and/or of common rights).

In the case of Stoke Mandeville, where the commissioners were at work by November 1797, the holding was more substantial. From the trustees' minute book we learn that it was agreed to ask for an allotment adjoining 'Walton field', evidently with the intention of making the estate more compact, and also – as was common – to accept a reduction in the size of the allotment in return for exoneration from payment of tithes on the property, an obligation which normally fell to the tenant. The result, incorporated in the enclosure commissioners' formal award, was a single rectangular allotment of just under thirty acres fronting to the west side of the Wendover Road and at right angles to it, a little to the south of the Aylesbury-with-Walton parish boundary and extending west as far as the Stoke Road.[2] Costs, in addition to £42 10s. 9d. due for general expenses, included £111 for fencing, a total of £153 10s. 9d. – a sum that would have weighed heavily on a small owner-occupier.

Hard on the heels of the Stoke enclosure award came that for Walton, which, although dated 1801, was already well advanced in November 1799.[3] Walton, as a separate hamlet with its own set of common fields, had not been included in the Aylesbury enclosure of 1771. Now, 30 years later, the centuries-old system of communal agriculture familiar to William Harding was finally abolished, and the landscape of the hamlet completely reordered. In the table of reference on the enclosure map (the earliest large-scale depiction of Walton) the trustees are credited, under the heading of 'Old Inclosure', with two existing homesteads and, additionally, with three separate holdings under 'New Allotments'. One of the homesteads (plot no. 40), containing over three quarters of an acre, is directly opposite the present Walton pond, on which can be identified the present no. 23 Walton Road, located at the front right of the plot, together with three other buildings, presumably outbuildings, one of which also adjoins the street, leaving a large gap between it and no. 23. The other homestead (the former 'messuage at Hardings Elms') is a slightly larger plot (no. 18), of just under an acre, on the south side of Walton pond, containing the 'New Inn' (now the *Broad Leys* public house), fronting to the Wendover Road. Adjoining it to the rear is an allotment (no. 19) 'in Elm Close' made to one John Rolls.

Of the three 'New Allotments', one is very large, comprising 111 acres in the former Dean field (plot no. 124) at the southern extremity of the parish, extending from the Wendover Road on the east to the Aylesbury – Stoke Road on the west, with its southern boundary precisely aligned with the jagged boundary of the ancient parish. It was separated from the Charity's holding in Stoke Mandeville by only a short distance, though they continued to be farmed separately, then and later. The other two are small appendages to the two homesteads. Plot no. 104 is an allotment of one and a half acres in the Crofts and is a square plot directly to the rear of no. 23 Walton Road. Plot no. 80, of a little over two acres, is described as an allotment (the only one) in New Close and adjoins the *New Inn* on the south, with a long frontage to the Wendover Road. The Crofts had been an area of extensive common pasture extending from Walton Road as far north as the Bear Brook, and adjoining the

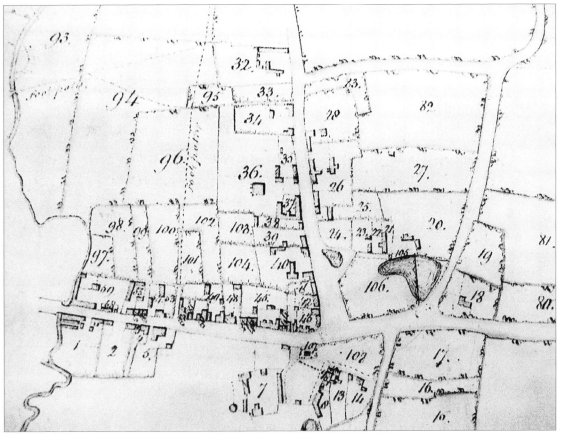

23   *The village of Walton as shown on the map to accompany the Walton enclosure award of 1800 (north is to the left of the map). William Harding's old farmstead (at No. 23 Walton Road) is shown as plot 40. As a result of the Enclosure Act, the lands belonging to it, previously scattered, were replaced by a consolidated holding known later as Elm Farm.*

present Exchange Street. In contrast, New Close had clearly been carved out of the former Bedgrove open field long before 1801, so that 'new allotment' is a misnomer, the inn and the plot evidently forming one ancient smallholding.

In total, the Charity's Walton estate now amounted to 115½ acres, making it the fourth largest in the hamlet. The two largest properties were those awarded to the Reverend John Pretyman, whose lands comprised 192½ acres in lieu of rectorial tithes pertaining to the prebend of Aylesbury – an example of an entirely new farm created by enclosure – and William Rickford, Esq., who received 200 acres as 'lifehold' tenant of the manorial estate (Walton Court) pertaining to the prebend of Heydour-cum-Walton, and an additional 17 acres of freehold.

The expenses of the Walton enclosure were much higher than those for Stoke Mandeville. The sum of £314 10s. 4d. was paid to a Mr James by order of the enclosure commissioners, presumably for general expenses, and further payments for fencing (including subdivision fences) and related expenses amounting to £191 15s. 3d. spread over the following three years can be identified in the Charity minute book.

Even before the enclosure had been formally completed, the farmhouse with the pre-existing old enclosures, the allotments in Dean field and the Crofts, together with the small piece of land (one and a half acres) in Aylesbury township, were leased to William Bigg, the existing tenant, for four years at an annual rent of £135. At the same time 'the house called the New Inn', with the orchard and New Close, were let on a yearly tenancy to William Rolfe for £12. The *New Inn* public house was the former Pettipher residence. It was first licensed in 1778 to Elizabeth Gouge, who had been succeeded by a James Rolfe by 1786.[4]

The return to peacetime conditions in 1815 was bad news for farmers, especially arable farmers, to whom wartime high prices had brought unprecedented prosperity, but it was the financial slump which set in after 1820 which caused the greatest distress. In November 1821 Mrs Fanny Biggs of the Walton farm, widow of William, who owed one and a half years' rent, was granted a reduction to £120 (more than 10 per cent of the amount agreed in 1799), conditional on paying off the arrears by the following May and assuming responsibility for keeping the premises in repair. The following September a special meeting of the trustees was called to consider further applications from tenants for reductions and it was agreed that, as from Michaelmas 1821, the rents should be: Fanny Bigg (for the Walton farm), £120; Joseph Read (for two closes of land totalling 14½ acres in Bierton), £33; Thomas Monk (for the *New Inn* and land), £16; William Fleet (for 30 acres of arable in Stoke Mandeville), £31; Mrs Catherine Shirley (for 47 acres of enclosed pasture in Chilton), £100. The total gross rental income was thus £300, compared to £200 in 1801 and £330 in 1812.

The granting of such rent relief by landlords was widespread at this time. It was usually intended to be a temporary measure only, but, as in this instance, sometimes proved long-lived. By the late 1820s conditions for farmers were, if anything, worse than before, largely, it seems, because of the heavy burden of the parish poor rate levied on houses and land, which in Aylesbury, after dropping from a peak of over £6,500 in 1817 to £3,480 in 1823, had again risen to over £4,600 by 1826. By 1832 the rent roll had declined to £289, with the rent on the Chilton property now standing at £90. In addition, as previously noted, Joseph Read, who in the interval had taken over the tenancy of the Walton farm in addition to his previous holding, was reported to be over three years in arrears with his rent, and, although he is said to have paid £250 on account, he was still in arrears in May 1835. Read was not wholly dependent on farming, since he owned a brickfield in Aylesbury.[5]

By 1840 matters were improving. In November of that year the rent on the Chilton property, by then in the occupation of William Claridge Harding, was increased to £114 a year and William Fleet, who had been paying £30 a year for the land in Stoke Mandeville, was now to pay £35. A surviving draft shows that a lease of the *New Inn* and just over three acres of land had been granted to Mark Price in 1838; the rent is not stated in the minutes, but is given as £25 in 1852.

Despite threats of legal proceedings, Joseph Read was still over a year in arrears with his rent in 1843. The trustees' forbearance with this difficult tenant was to be matched many times in the future. On this occasion their patience seems to have at last run out, for in August 1846 the minutes record that William Perrin was granted a lease of the Walton farm, with an allowance of £60 to cover improvements, including the cost of fruit trees planted and of drainage tiles. Landlord's expenses for improvements of this kind were a considerable charge on the estate at this period and represent an appreciable diminution of the gross rental. Read continued in possession of the two closes in Bierton. In 1851, aged 72, the census return shows him living in Cambridge Street and farming a total of 90 acres.

Perrin had, in fact, already been in occupation by 1844, for the accounts show that he paid a year's rent of £120 (£115 9s. net) in May 1845. What both the minutes and the accounts fail to indicate is the building of a new farmhouse, on what was later to be known as Elm Farm, around this time. It was part of the logic of the parliamentary enclosures that the redistribution of land holdings should be followed by a 'great rebuilding', as farmhouses in effect migrated away from the nucleated villages that characterised the old way of farming, to reappear on the newly created, compact farms that had been carved out of the former open fields. This phenomenon is observable in the Aylesbury area, as elsewhere, but it proved a surprisingly long drawn out process. At Walton, for example, the 1851 census shows some seven or eight farmers and smallholders still resident in the village at that date, though not all were living in specialised farmsteads.

In the absence of large-scale maps of the area between the 1820s and the 1870s, our first clear evidence of the move to a new site is a fire insurance policy dated 1844 in the name of William Perrin, a chance survival among the Charity's records. It relates to a farmhouse at 'Walton Field' with a barn, stable, hovel and other farm buildings, including a cottage in the same occupation 'all communicating near' and all brick and tiled. This can only refer to the new farmhouse shown on later OS maps as situated on the new farm, set back from the Wendover Road and accessible from it by means of a lane.[6]

Further confirmation of the location of the farmhouse is found in Kelly's 1847 directory for Buckinghamshire which lists William Perrin, farmer, at Wendover Road, Walton. Perrin's lease may have allowed a reduced rent over a period of years on condition of his building being a farmhouse, which would explain the absence of any reference to building works in the accounts. The minutes show that Perrin under-let the farm to Charles Bennett, of Stoke Farm, Stoke Mandeville, the same year. Ironically, since Stoke Farm was situated only a short distance to the south of the Walton property on the Wendover Road, Bennett had no need to reside in the new farmhouse and the 1851 census gives the sole occupiers of 'Walton Farm', which is the next entry after the *Three Pigeons* public house on Wendover Road, as George Parsons, an agricultural

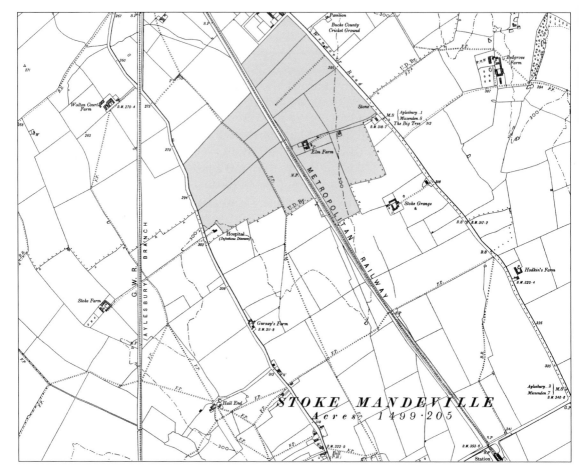

24 *Elm Farm, Walton, on the 6-inch OS map of 1900, showing the line of the Metropolitan Railway from Marylebone, opened in 1892. Note that the farm's zig-zag southern boundary coincides with that of the ancient parish of Aylesbury.*

labourer, aged 22, and his wife Fanny. Further changes of tenancy followed in quick succession. In May 1851 Perrin's lease was assigned to James William Platt, who in turn assigned it to Thomas William Morris the following year (he paid two years' arrears of rent in 1852).

Overall, the period between 1845 and 1879 was a golden age for English agriculture and Buckinghamshire shared in the prosperity. By 1855 the rent of the Walton farm, which had been £120 in 1845, stood at £140. Ten years later it was £182, reaching a peak of £190 in 1878 – a rise of over 50 per cent over the whole period. The rents of the other estate properties also rose substantially – if less spectacularly. In May 1852, following the death of William Fleet, the land in Stoke Mandeville was surveyed and re-let to John Weedon of Stoke at an enhanced annual rent of £40, with an allowance of £20, spread over three years, for drainage tiles. All this would change after 1879 with the onset of the prolonged depression in arable farming caused by the appearance on the market of huge quantities of cheap American grain.

Prior to 1879 the only serious threat to the new prosperity was a visitation of cattle plague – the deadly Rinderpest – in 1868, much the most serious such outbreak of cattle disease prior to the 1960s. The accounts show that two of the tenants were subjected to a local rate raised to pay compensation for the compulsory slaughtering (for which allowance was duly made in the rents), but there is no indication that any were directly affected.[7]

T.W. Morris, who was to be the tenant of the Walton farm for over 30 years, lived at Bedgrove House in the adjoining parish of Weston Turville, so, like his predecessor Charles Bennett, had no need of the new farmhouse on Wendover Road. This explains why at the 1861 census, and again in 1871, 'Walton Farm' appears to have been occupied by two labourers and their families. In an extant copy of a renewal of his lease in 1876, Morris is described as 'of Bedgrove ... farmer'. The new farm itself is not named, being described simply as a 'plot or allotment' in part of the former open field called Dean Field.[8] Neither does it have a name on the first edition OS 25-inch sheet surveyed in 1877-8, which shows a small complex of buildings with one range facing towards the Wendover Road, two similar-sized right-angled ranges at each end, and a large orchard behind.

In the 1876 lease the farmhouse is stated to be 'newly erected', but this is clearly an exaggeration, such as is not infrequently found in such documents. Surprisingly perhaps, in view of the general drift away from tillage in north Buckinghamshire post-enclosure, it was still very much an arable farm at this date. Strict husbandry covenants are imposed, including the use of the four-course system of cultivation. Significantly, too, provision is made for the possibility of some of the land being required for a railway.

Seven years later, in May 1884, a new 14-year lease was granted to Henry Landon of Aylesbury, farmer. The rent was fixed at £66 10s. for the first two years and £166 10s. thereafter – a reduction of some 12 per cent, in recognition of the downturn in the price of grain; the husbandry covenants were similar to the earlier lease. As before, the farm has no name in the lease but the first reference to 'Elm Farm' appears in the accounts the same year.[9]

The original Harding farmhouse, the present no 23 Walton Road, had evidently been included in the leases to Morris and his predecessors and sublet. From the 1851 census enumerator's book it would seem that it was again being used as a farmhouse at that date, for, although in the absence of house numbers identification is uncertain, the then current rate book appears to show that the occupant (as a subtenant of William Terry) was a William W. Thorne, a farmer of 195 acres. Thorne was the tenant of the newly created 'tithe' farm awarded to the Reverend John Pretyman at the enclosure and so could have been in want of a temporary farmhouse. In 1862 the trustees granted a formal lease of a 'messuage being an ancient farmhouse', with the outhouses, buildings and gardens belonging to it, to Edward Terry, brewer, of the nearby Walton brewery for seven years at an annual rent of £30. The draft lease states that it had been previously in the occupation of Joseph Read and 'lately' of T. W. Morris, but does not list the actual occupants. The area of the property is given as 3 roods 19 perches (about seven eighths of an acre), which agrees fairly closely with that given in the 1801 enclosure award (3r. 20p.).[10]

Terry was required to undertake to repair the hall and sitting room of the house with new oak flooring within 12 months, and to be responsible for keeping the property in repair at his own cost. A Frederick Rogers is listed as the occupant in an Aylesbury street directory for 1879. Prior to this, in or around 1862, the garden at the extreme rear of the premises (plot no. 104 in 1801, being the allotment in the Crofts) had been let for £4 a year to W.T.D. Eagles, whose house, now no. 9 Walton Terrace, it adjoined; it was later sold to him in 1879 for £306. Eagles was a son of the former Harding's trustee.

Tenancy changes to the other estate properties were also relatively infrequent. The land at Stoke Mandeville was occupied by successive members of the Bennett family until around 1873, when it passed to R.W. Welch, who was still there a decade later. Following the death of W.C. Harding in 1871, the Chilton land was let first to Robert Paxton and then, by 1879, to Richard Roadnight. The 14-odd acres in Bierton passed to William Read after Joseph Read's death in 1857, and then, by 1868, to Thomas J. Hinds, who already held the small piece of land in Aylesbury. The accounts show that the *New Inn* was tenanted by Edward Terry, brewer, in 1860.

The onset of the agricultural depression in 1879 led to immediate 'temporary' abatements of rent payments on all three larger holdings, abatements which, as the 1884 lease demonstrates, tended to become more permanent over time. In 1888 the total gross rent roll of the Charity properties was £452, but the amount actually received after abatements and allowances for repairs done, etc., was £408 11s.; a further £17 (gross) was received in allotment rents at Bierton.[11]

At Elm Farm (as we may now call it) Henry Landon continued as tenant for many years, despite the discouraging state of farming, as did Francis Pursell, who succeeded at Stoke Mandeville around the same time, and Richard Roadnight at Chilton. Landon, who came from a family long associated with the carriage trade on the Grand Union Canal, also farmed other land locally; a John Landon, doubtless a relation, was farming at Walton Farm, no 59 Walton Road, in the 1870s.

In 1892 the Metropolitan Railway extension finally arrived in the area, via a route that took it within a stone's throw of the farm complex, on the west. In 1893 rebuilding was approved by the Charity Commissioners at a cost of £530. It seems clear from the 1899 Ordnance sheet (OS 2nd edn) that the existing farmhouse was not in fact demolished, but several new structures on the east and west sides were presumably added at this time. The sale to the railway company brought in £1,330, payment of which was made in the form of government securities, which, for legal reasons, remained lodged in the High Court for many years (they were still there in the 1920s), but the annual dividends were a useful addition to the Charity's income.

The old farmhouse, No. 23 Walton Road, which had been leased to the brewery company, was let in 1890 to C.A. Lippincott, who was manager of the Anglo-Swiss Condensed Milk Company (afterwards Nestlé), since 1870 one of Aylesbury's largest employers (mainly of female labour), whose factory survived at the corner of High Street and Park Street until 2005, when it was demolished. The rent was a substantial £40 a year. Between 1887 and 1913 directories show the actual occupant as D.T. Dent, described in the 1891 census as a coffee roaster. Lippincott himself, a New Yorker by birth, was living round the corner at no. 13 Walton Terrace ('Wyoming Houses') in 1891. No. 23 was eventually sold to the Anglo-Swiss Company in or around the year 1922 for £1,550.[12] The land in Bierton, leased to Thomas Haywood by 1888, now consisted of only 10 acres. The remaining four and a half acres there had been laid out as allotments in 1886 under the Allotments Acts; this involved sinking a well at a cost of £26. The rent income was high, relative to the area, but administrative costs were also high. Harding's was not the only Aylesbury charity to provide allotments, for which there was obviously a big demand at a time when the town's population was again expanding rapidly.

The *New Inn*, and the smallholding which went with it, was the first substantial portion of the Charity's landed endowment to be disposed of voluntarily. Its sale was, seemingly, a result of the crisis in the Charity's finances caused by declining income coupled with rising demand. The accounts indicate that it was sold around 1891, but do not show the price received or the name of the purchaser, who, on the evidence of the later (1895) sale particulars, seems to have been James Gurney of Aylesbury, a gentleman of independent means, who purchased it in November 1891; the price may have been £1,834, since a share certificate for this amount bears the same month and year. Prior to this, the tenants had been the proprietors of the Walton brewery since 1861: firstly Charles Terry, then Edward Terry and, finally, Wroughton and Threlfall, at a rent of £35 yearly.

The sequel to this transaction was that in July 1895 the whole property was offered for sale by auction as 'Freehold building land admirably adapted for the erection of villa residences ... and a ... Freehold Inn ... "The New Inn" ... occupying an important frontage to the Main Road ...' The inn itself, comprising just under one acre, is stated to be on a lease to Salter and Co., brewers, of Rickmansworth at £50 a year and it sold for £750. Among the amenities listed are a bar with bay window, bar parlour, sitting room, commercial room, three bedrooms, a stable, loose boxes, cart shed, hen house, two pig sties and timber valued at £15. The rest of the property is set out in 13 building plots (including one previously sold, not numbered), 11 of which have frontages of 40 feet to the road, and one of 52 feet. New building on the lots is restricted by covenant to private dwellings only. The aggregate sale price, including the plot sold privately, was £965, making a grand total of £1,715, which is less than the sum lodged with the High Court. Within a few years, building work was well under way and the 1899 edition of the OS 25-inch map shows that many of the original plots had been subdivided by that date. Thus the *New Inn* property played a not insignificant role in the ribbon development of middle-class housing along the Wendover Road, which was a feature of Aylesbury's expansion in the 1890s.

Meanwhile, the long-continued agricultural depression was bringing about changes at Elm Farm. In 1905 Henry Landon came to the conclusion that milk production was now a more attractive proposition than arable farming and decided to register as a cow keeper. This had serious financial implications for the Charity because new sanitary regulations, enforced by the Aylesbury Urban District Council inspectors, required buildings of a higher standard for dairying. The architect's estimate for repairs and additions was £350, but the total cost seems to have been nearly twice that amount. The Charity Commissioners gave their consent, subject to Landon's agreeing to pay an increased rent and the replacement by the trustees over a 20-year period of investments sold to pay the cost.[14]

The cost of the new outbuildings was partly offset by the sale to the UDC in 1907 of several acres of farmland fronting on the Stoke Road for use as an isolation hospital. A few years later, in 1911, Landon reported that his well had failed owing, he believed, to the deep well sunk by the 'new factory' (the Bifurcated and Tubular Rivets works in Stoke Road, built in 1910 and soon to be one of Aylesbury's largest employers). The upshot was that the trustees were compelled to contract with the Chiltern Hills Spring Water Company for a mains supply. Urban expansion was beginning to impinge on Elm Farm.

IX

New Departures
The Charity in the Victorian Era, 1845-98

Between 1852 and 1930 there is an extended gap in the minutes, with the exception of a rather illegible draft volume covering the years 1897-1912. This means that for the whole of this period, apart from what can be gleaned from general sources, we have to rely principally on the treasurers' account books, now supplemented by a quantity of surviving loose papers. These consist of a few draft leases and the like, as well as much larger quantities, arranged in annual bundles, of bills and vouchers (1859-89) and duplicate apprenticeship indentures (1850-95), the latter testifying to a generally good standard of literacy by the invariably neat signatures of the children concerned.

For most of the Victorian period the trusteeship was dominated by bankers, lawyers and other professional men. William Rickford died in 1854, having ceased to attend trustees' meetings after 1850. His nephew, Zachariah Daniel Hunt (1848), was for a time chairman of the Old Bank, which in 1853, following amalgamations with other local banks, became the Bucks and Oxon Union Bank (it was taken over by Lloyds in 1903). Hunt was joint treasurer of the Charity from 1852 to 1870. The other banker was Rickford's grandson, Herbert Astley Paston Cooper, the younger son of a Hertfordshire baronet, who had joined the Old Bank in 1855 aged 19, becoming a director within a short period of years.[1] He too served as joint treasurer from 1870 to 1885 or later. Paston Cooper was extremely active in the public life of Aylesbury and in the late 1870s was a member of the nine-strong Local Board of Health, which since 1849 had been the town's principal organ of local government, being the direct predecessor of the Urban District Council of 1894 and the Borough Council of 1917. He was a strong supporter of the established Church and was a trustee of three other local charities.

Lawyers appointed in the 1860s and 1870s were Richard Rose (by 1860), E.R. Baynes (1867) and Henry Watson (1875), all three local solicitors. Rose was a great-nephew of Joseph Burnham. Like Paston Cooper, he was a member of the Local Board of Health. Watson is listed as clerk to the same board in the 1853 county directory. Baynes was later clerk to the lieutenancy for Buckinghamshire and, from 1880 to 1888, Clerk of the Peace for the county. He too acted as joint treasurer for a time.

25 *Counterpart indenture on printed pro forma apprenticing Thomas Chapman to William Franklin of Wendover, tailor, for seven years, in return for a premium of £20 paid by the Charity, 1850. It differs little in essentials from the earlier manuscript version of 1794 (illustration no. 16).*

Apart from bankers and lawyers, the only other long-serving trustee at this time was James Crouch (1869), of Court Farm in Walton, who, like Paston Cooper and Baynes, was also a trustee of the Aylesbury Free and Endowed Schools, as the grammar school foundation was now officially designated. He was chairman of the Aylesbury Market Company in the 1890s. New trustees towards the close of the century included four prominent professional men, C.H. Watson (by 1889), another solicitor (the last for very many years), Charles Hooper (1883) and Woodfield Eagles (1892), surgeons, and George A. Lepper (1895), veterinary surgeon, as well as Edward Terry (1881), farmer and grazier. Hooper, another Rickford relation, was Medical Officer of Health for the town for many years; Eagles, the grandson of an earlier trustee, was a surgeon at the Royal Buckinghamshire Hospital; Lepper had been involved in setting up the Aylesbury Corn Exchange and Market Improvement Company in the 1860s.[2] Overall, however, the town's business sector, including larger retailers and builders, which after 1870 was expanding rapidly, was under-represented in this period. The names of the nonconformist families which had become prominent in the public life of the town since the 1820s do not appear.

Between 1801 and 1851 the population of Aylesbury had doubled to just over 6,000, but, as we have seen, the number of children apprenticed annually did not keep pace.[3] The total for the five years 1846-50 was 76, an annual average of 15 – almost the same as for the years 1801-5 (when the total was 73) – comprising 60 boys and 16 girls and representing an average annual expenditure of around £280. Of this number 31 children were apprenticed to Aylesbury residents, seven more than in 1801-5, but still well under half the total.[4]

Despite the arrival of new forms of transport, Aylesbury's market town economy had not radically altered in the first half of the century, so it is perhaps not really surprising to find that, allowing for some differences of terminology, the occupations of the 31 children apprenticed to Aylesbury employers also show a high degree of continuity. They were bricklayer (3), butcher (2), confectioner (2), cabinet maker, coachmaker, currier (leather dresser), dressmaker (9), grocer, plumber-and-glazier, printer (3), shoemaker (2), straw bonnet maker, tailor (2), wheelwright, whitesmith/coachmaker. Only the three printers stand out as different in kind. They were employed by the three or four county newspapers now being published in the county town, which were made more viable by the arrival of the railway in 1839. The large number of dressmakers and the solitary bonnet maker reflect the high proportion of female apprentices (nine out of 16) who stayed in Aylesbury. Dressmaking was the sole specifically female occupation sufficiently numerous to merit separate classification in the Aylesbury section of Musson and Craven's county directory of 1853.

The occupations of the 45 children apprenticed outside Aylesbury were: baker, blacksmith (3), bricklayer, carpenter (and builder) (4), coachmaker (2), confectioner cooper, dyer and scourer, miller, milliner/dressmaker (4), pawnbroker, plumber and glazier, saddler and harnessmaker, shoemaker/cordwainer (16), tailor (2), turner, wheelwright (2), not known (2). A few of these occupations, notably the dyer and the pawnbroker, were exclusive to London. The most notable development is the expansion in the number of leather workers; otherwise the range of occupations is not markedly different from the beginning of the century. Destinations were now Buckinghamshire, 16; adjacent counties, 20; London, nine. There was thus a 50 per cent increase in those going to London, a reversal of the earlier trend, though the total remained proportionally low. Once again most of the others (20 out of 34) went to local towns, but this time Leighton Buzzard stands out above the rest with nine apprentices; the others were Banbury, Berkhamsted (3), Henley, Luton, Princes Risborough, Thame, Tring (2) and Wendover (4).

The availability of a published transcript of the 1851 census enumerators' books for Aylesbury[5] makes it possible to obtain a fuller understanding of the circumstances applying to children who were apprenticed to Aylesbury employers. A check on the names of all those apprenticed over the eight years 1844-51 leads to a number of conclusions, which can be summarised as follows:

(1) The range of ages in 1851 is consistent with apprenticing at the age of 15 or 16, according to the official 'binding' dates. But some children clearly began their apprenticeship up to six months – or even longer – before the official date. One, James Ingram, enrolled as an apprentice to a saddler in November 1851, was already an 'apprentice saddler' by 30 March 1851 (census night), being then aged fourteen. Three other children apprenticed in 1851 have the appropriate occupation in the census, though only one of them, a wheelwright, is described as an apprentice.

(2) With few exceptions, apprentices did not normally serve much (if at all) beyond the date on which the second moiety of their premium was paid to their employer, which was almost invariably three years after the date of apprenticeship. Of 22 apprentices (four of them female) bound during the four years from May 1844 to November 1847 only three, one (a printer) bound in 1845 and two in 1847, are described as apprentices in the census. None of the three was then 'living in' with his master. Of the remaining 19, nine were no longer resident in Aylesbury in 1851: three had married, one (apprenticed in May 1845) being termed a 'journeyman', implying a completed apprenticeship; and the other six – all living with parents or other relations – are described in the census simply by their occupations (but see point 4 below).

(3) A very few apprentices to skilled trades served for four years or more. Samuel Walter, the printer referred to in (2), is a case in point. Apprenticed to James Pickburn, printer and publisher of the Tory *Bucks Herald* in May 1845, he is described as an 'outdoor apprentice' in the census, even though a second moiety had been paid in May 1848. Another printer, Samuel William Sanford, one of the three who had married by 1851, had been apprenticed to John Rolls Gibbs, printer and editor of the rival *Aylesbury News*, in May 1844, but his second moiety – very exceptionally – was not paid until May 1850, so he must have served at least six years. Joseph Johnson and John Fellows, both apprenticed in May 1847, the first to a coachmaker and the second to a bricklayer, were still apprentices in March 1851, and Johnson's second moiety was not in fact payable until May 1851.

(4) Finally, 'living in' with employers was still far from dead in 1851, even in the case of apprentices living in their own home town. Of the 22 Harding's apprentices (nine of them female) bound to Aylesbury employers in the three years from May 1848 to November 1850, payment of whose second moieties was still pending on census night, 20 can be traced in the census returns. Eleven of these were living with their employers (two of whom were also relations) and are described as 'apprentice' in the column for relationship to head of house. The remaining nine were living with parents or relations. Significantly, only four of the latter group are explicitly called apprentices in the 'occupation' column. Clearly, apprenticeship was inherently more likely to be consistently recorded as a relationship than as part of an occupation, making the census an unreliable guide to 'outdoor' apprentices.

26 *Receipted bill for men's and women's clothing purchased at Longley & Sons, drapers and house furnishers, for the annual distribution to the poor of Walton, 1888. The shop shown on the billhead is the New Road (now High Street) branch of this fashionable establishment and its appearance reflects the growing availability of manufactured goods locally.*

Altogether, 20 Harding's apprentices – 14 boys and six girls – are listed as apprentices in the census. The individual returns afford fascinating glimpses of the domestic arrangements of those who were living with their employers. Maria DeFraine, aged 16, had been apprenticed to Arabella Webb (36), a dressmaker, in November 1849. In March 1851 she was living in Walton Street with her mistress and her mistress's husband, John (46), a tailor, their unmarried daughter Mary Ann (24), also a dressmaker, and another apprentice, Mary Butler (17), born in Edgcott. Maria's father, Joseph (39), was a hairdresser living in Cambridge Street (then a working-class area) together with Maria's mother and two younger brothers, aged 15 and thirteen.

In contrast, Ann Fryer's mistress, Elizabeth Turnham, a milliner, was a spinster aged 32, living in Market Square with her unmarried sister, aged 30, also a milliner, and their 11-year-old nephew, a 'scholar'. Also staying in the house was William Olliff (28), an Aylesbury-born policeman, unmarried, who is described as a visitor, but may have been a lodger. Aged 18 in 1851, Ann had been apprenticed in November 1848; her parents had apparently moved away from Aylesbury by 1851. Like Arabella Webb, Miss Turnham (but not her sister) is one of the 18 Aylesbury milliners and dressmakers listed in the county directory of 1853, a list that is far from complete.

Perhaps the most unconventional apprenticeship was that of George Newton, aged 18 in 1851, who had been bound to Ann Hedges, a 'shoemaker', in May 1849. She appears in the census as a widow, aged 55 (probably of James Hedges, shoemaker, Market Street, listed in an 1842 directory), living in Market Street, and is listed as a shoemaker employing 13 men, a uniquely large business of its kind for the town in 1851. The other members of the household are a boy of 12, described as a 'scholar', and a female house servant of 20, from

Whitchurch. George's own father Samuel, aged 40, was a cordwainer (shoemaker) living 'behind the Red Cow', a public house in Buckingham Street, with his wife, three daughters and two other sons, all aged between one and 19, and a lodger, aged 23, also described as a cordwainer.

A wider perspective on apprenticeship locally can be gained from a computer analysis of the 1851 census statistics for Buckinghamshire as a whole (population 163,732), and for Aylesbury in particular.[6] It shows a total for the county of 698 apprentices, of whom the vast majority (632) were males, but owing to the bias in the data (see above, p.116) the true total is likely to have been considerably higher. Distribution is broadly in accord with that of the population. Aylesbury's total of 61 (50 male, 11 female) is the second highest after the much more industrialised High Wycombe (96) and represents just under 10 per cent of the 12-19 age group in the town. Thirty-one (22 male, 9 female), or just over half the total of the Aylesbury apprentices listed, were born in the town, and of these 20 (65 per cent) were Harding's. The majority of the 11 other Aylesbury-born apprentices were apprenticed to craft trades, but one boy was bound to a linen draper and at least three others seem to have come from well-to-do backgrounds, while one of the three girls was apprenticed to her father, a carrier, and another was the daughter of a salt merchant.

27 *Character reference for George Gladman and Richard Michael Cousens, drapers, of White Cross Street in the City of London, as prospective masters to an apprentice, late 19th century.*

28 *Engraving of Messrs Hazell, Watson and Viney's new Aylesbury printing works, opened in 1877, from H.J. Keefe,* A Century in Print *(1939). This craft industry provided many new openings for apprentices and it gradually came to dominate the Charity's expenditure on premiums.*

The birthplaces of the remaining 30 apprentices may be summarised as follows: Bucks (13, 1 female); adjoining counties (7, 1 female.); London (1); other (8); Scotland (1). Some of those in the 'other' group came from as far afield as Ramsgate, Stroud and Cambridge. A high proportion of these 'incomers' were concentrated in service trades, notably those of grocer (8) and draper (6), both of which could probably command high premiums. At the other extreme of respectability were three 'sweep apprentices', two of them living in the same lodging house, one from Quainton and the other, aged 11, born in Worcester. Over half (18) of the apprentices listed in this category were living with their employers.

The Charity's increasing income from rents after 1840 (£322 gross in 1845, rising to £350 by 1855) combined with static, or reduced, spending on apprenticing led to a gradual accumulation of surplus funds. It would have been open to the trustees to use the surplus to increase the amount of the premiums, perhaps with provision for differential payments according to trade, etc., as had been practised to some degree in the 1720s (the Saye and Sele charity at Quainton had increased its premium to £30 by 1833). In addition, or alternatively, the arbitrary quota for female apprentices – never envisaged by the founder – could have been increased or abolished. Instead, beginning in 1855, they chose to invest it in Exchequer bills and similar interest-bearing securities, thus increasing income still further (the annual income from interest was around £35 or more by 1860). By 1868 the Charity's total income was reported to amount to £490, comprising £447 in rents and £43 in dividends and interest on investments, which by now had grown to £1,450.[7]

It may have been the existence of this growing reserve which, in November 1856, prompted the trustees to submit a draft 'Scheme', or new governing instrument, to the new Charity Commissioners, giving themselves enlarged powers, the nature of which are not stated; the Commissioners' reply, received in February 1858, was obviously not encouraging, for it was decided to take no further action for the present.[8] Most likely the Commissioners had advised against too hastily undertaking new binding commitments which might limit the Charity's freedom of action should the demand for apprenticeships suddenly increase.

Nevertheless, beginning in 1859, and with the consent of the Commissioners, who in 1853 had taken over many of the powers formerly exercised by Chancery in regulating charities, the trustees gradually began to enlarge the range of expenditure in the fields of education and social welfare other than apprenticeship. First, the annual distribution of £5 to the poor of Walton, which appears to have been increased to £10 around 1849, was increased to £25. Next, in 1860, an annual prize book fund of £15 and upwards was inaugurated for the newly reformed Grammar School, and in November of that year Mr Dell, Mr Rose and Mr Hunt are recorded as having 'attended the [public] examination of the scholars and subsequently distributed prizes to them'. In addition, regular gifts of books for the school library were made. In 1867, too, an annual subscription of £10 to the Buckinghamshire Infirmary (later the Royal Buckinghamshire Hospital) was begun.

Then, in August 1869, an approach was received from the Grammar School trustees, to discuss 'the educational needs of the neighbourhood', the immediate objective being the provision of a new, less cramped, site for the school. In response, the trustees agreed to consider a contribution of up to £2,000 of the estimated £5,000 required.[9] The project came to nothing, having apparently been overtaken by the crisis affecting the Aylesbury elementary schools, caused by the passing of the 1870 Education Act, which made the provision of adequate elementary school accommodation mandatory in every parish. If this requirement could not be met by voluntary effort, the alternative was the establishment of statutory, non-denominational school boards with rating powers. Opposition to the threat of school boards came mainly from Anglicans and in some parishes frantic efforts were made to increase voluntary school provision – sometimes in the face of determined opposition from nonconformists – in order to avert their imposition.

According to Robert Gibbs, it was the vicar of Aylesbury, Archdeacon Edward Bickersteth, a churchman of national reputation, who came up with the idea of supplementing the voluntary subscriptions by a grant from Harding's Charity, an idea which found favour with the nonconformists also.[10] The trustees were favourable and the Charity Commissioners, who could be dilatory, evidently made no objection to such a drastic *ad hoc* variation of the Charity's objects. The grant was apportioned to the existing schools in accordance with the amount of accommodation each provided. The Anglican St Mary's National School and the non-denominational British School in Pebble Lane, which was rebuilt and enlarged at this time, each received £700, and further grants of £50 and £120 went to the Church of England schools in Walton and Cambridge Street, a total of £1,570, realised by the sale of consols, and thus disposing of the greater part of the Charity's investments at that date.

From 1874, too, an annual subscription of £50 was paid to the 'Aylesbury Joint Schools'; this was in addition to the Grammar School prize fund previously mentioned and it brought to over £100 the total annual amount of income devoted to objects other than apprenticeship. A precedent had been set. Harding's had become – if to a limited degree only – a patron of popular, classroom education, but as things worked out, it was to be a long time before it went further down this road.

Between 1851 and 1881, while the population of Aylesbury continued to grow (though at an uneven pace), the number of children apprenticed was declining. Throughout this period the average annual total of Harding's apprentices was 15 or less, representing an outlay of around £280; it only exceeded 20 (around £380 a year) on two occasions and in 1855-6 it dipped to as low as nine. From 1869 onwards the decline is more pronounced, with totals varying consistently between 10 and 14 for the whole of the 1870s.

The obvious reason for the decline (assuming that the trustees were not restricting the entry) was the gradual decline of many traditional craft occupations, such as boot and shoemaking (of which 30 practitioners are listed under Aylesbury in Musson and Craven's county directory of 1853) as a result of competition from manufactured

29 The Aylesbury Charities, *by E.T. Mackrill (Aylesbury, 1889), a one-man inquiry into the state of the town's charities based on the statutory annual returns of the Charity Commissioners. Mackrill was a trustee of Harding's from 1903 to 1907.*

goods, including ready-made footwear and clothing, which an expanding rail network was making ever more widely and cheaply available.

Also declining by the late 1850s was the proportion of children apprenticed to masters and mistresses not resident in Aylesbury, with very few going to London in particular. By the late 1870s the number of children apprenticed outside Aylesbury was very small indeed and the practice appears to have almost ceased altogether by the early 1890s. Apprenticing at Aylesbury was thus coming to be a much more parochial affair than formerly. This development, though it may owe something to the abolition, in the 1860s, of the old Poor Law settlement system and still more to increasing local employment opportunities after 1870, was probably in large measure a casualty of the gradual decline in the centuries-old tradition of living-in apprenticeship. It is paralleled by the virtual disappearance of living-in farm service in the same period.

Change was very gradual. Throughout the 1860s and 1870s traditional craftsmen, such as carpenters, blacksmiths, coopers and tailors, continued to make up the core of employers, though shoemakers and tailors are increasingly rare after 1870 and had virtually disappeared by the 1880s. There is an increase in the number of retailers: principally grocers, drapers, and confectioners. There is also a sprinkling of skilled specialist trades. To printers were added watchmakers (1876, 1879), an upholsterer (1875) and, significantly, a gas fitter (1874). The printers were particularly active as employers. G.T. DeFraine of the *Bucks Gazette*, for example, had a throughput of no fewer than seven apprentices between 1869 and 1879.

But the event of greatest significance for the future of the Charity was the advent to the town of printing on a scale hitherto undreamed of, signalled by the appearance of the names Hazell and Watson (later Hazell, Watson and Viney) among the employers in 1868. Hazells, who had just moved into vacant small factory premises in California, a recently developed area adjoining the present railway station, were large-scale industrial printers specialising in book production. The firm had brought a core of five employees with them from their London headquarters in 1867, but almost from the start they were taking on up to three local apprentices yearly as they gradually expanded their Aylesbury operations. Appropriately, the very first of the Aylesbury apprentices was Richard Moscrop, member of a family of silk-weavers that had migrated to Aylesbury from Yorkshire in the 1830s, to pioneer the Aylesbury silk factory. In 1879, by which date the number employed had increased to 90 (it would reach over 650 by 1914), the firm moved to a new, enlarged, factory site on the Tring Road close to the new condensed milk factory, opened in 1870, and the numbers of boys apprenticed through the Charity started to rise.[11]

Book printing, with its numerous associated trades, including electrotyping, bookbinding and gilding (though many of the apprentices are described simply as 'machinist' or 'machine minder'), had a long tradition of apprenticeship and, more importantly for Harding's, it was one of the major craft industries in which the practice continued to flourish. By the late 1890s Hazells accounted for a third of all boys apprenticed annually. The partnership between the Charity and firm was to last for over a century.

In contrast to the growing variety of openings for boys, apprenticeship for girls was still overwhelmingly confined to dressmaking. As earlier, many of the mistresses were married and they often took on apprentices at very short intervals of years. Sarah, the Aylesbury-born wife of Frederick Fidelio Lehmann, jeweller and watchmaker, a native of Germany, who kept a shop in the market place, is named as an employer in 1871 and again in 1872, 1875 and 1876.

Light is shed on the selection process at this time by an undated list (in two versions) of half-yearly applicants, which on internal evidence can be ascribed to the year 1881, containing the names of 15 children, five of them girls, giving ages, names of parents (three had lost a father) and of prospective employers.[12] Four were aged 14, nine were 15 and two as old as sixteen. Eight are annotated 'G[ood]', three 'Subject to enquiry', three 'Postponed' and one

'Declined for reasons'. One is further annotated 'In bad health – to be stood over'. The accounts show that 10 of the 15 were apprenticed (all but one to Aylesbury employers) in 1881-2 and that nine remained in post long enough for the second moiety of the premium to be paid. Here is evidence that the numbers applying to the Charity at this time were not greatly in excess of the numbers actually apprenticed.

Valuable information – as well as an indication of local opinion about the town's charities in this period – is provided in a 48-page pamphlet, *The Aylesbury Charities*, published at Aylesbury in 1889. Edward T. Mackrill, the author of the pamphlet, was born in London in or about 1840, settling in Aylesbury around 1870. Trained as a gas fitter, he established himself as a gas engineer with premises in Kingsbury. He was thus, in his profession at least, a thoroughly modern man. He was a member of the Local Board of Health in the 1890s and became a trustee of Harding's in 1903.

This impressively thorough study reproduces, together with critical analysis and comment, abstracts of the current annual statutory returns made by all the town's charities to the Charity Commissioners (with some reference back to earlier returns from 1856).[13] Mackrill's avowed intention, as stated in his introduction, was to overcome 'the difficulty hitherto met with by the working classes in obtaining reliable information on the subject'. From this circumstance, he maintains, had arisen 'the widespread belief in this district that Charities have frequently been diverted from their legitimate objects'. In his introduction Mackrill also makes the point that, 'At present the charity administration is thought to be very much under the influence of a "ring", as the same names appear, over and over again connected with the whole of the Charities', and he advocates that all trustees should be both resident and elected. He expresses strong disapproval of cash doles as a form of charitable giving as being demoralising to the recipients and likely to attract 'thriftless or incompetent persons from adjacent districts, to the serious injury of the older residents'. His misgivings on the latter score were shared by Archdeacon Bickersteth.[14]

In the section on Harding's Charity, Mackrill is scathing about the donations made to the Aylesbury schools in 1871-2, criticising the trustees for spending large sums 'for the benefit of institutions never contemplated by the donor, or by earlier trustees of this Charity'. He also questions the investment of such a large proportion of the income (a total of over £4,000 since 1856), and while he concedes that 'it is perhaps only fair that the income of the property should be increased at intervals so as to adequately meet the needs of an ever-increasing population', he speculates with heavy sarcasm that the trustees may have in mind 'the generous assistance of "a thousand or two"' to relieve the funds of the schools in the future. But in calling for it all to be spent on apprentices he ignores such considerations as fluctuating demand and the proper size of premiums, and nor does he declare an interest as an employer who had benefited more than once from the Charity. In the summary accounts the number of grants to apprentices in 1888 is given as 40, but this figure is misleading since it includes both moieties of the premiums.

Mackrill's figures show that the Charity's total expenditure for 1888 was just under £700, of which £482 was spent on apprenticeship premiums, £25 on clothing for the Walton poor and a further £80 on other forms of giving (joint schools £50; Grammar School prizes £17; infirmary £10). Administration and legal charges accounted for £44 15s. (eight per cent of the total), and repairs and landlord's works not deducted from rents for £28. Income consisted principally of rents amounting to £408 net (£452 gross) and a total of £126 from dividends on investments totalling £3,256, leaving a deficit of £147 which required the sale of consols to that amount in order to bring the account into balance. Also mentioned is £16 income from four and a half acres of land laid out as allotments in 1886.

Mackrill's pamphlet came at another turning point in the Charity's affairs, for by the early 1880s the annual number of children apprenticed had begun to rise again. This trend was particularly marked during the years 1887-94, when the totals for first moieties paid were usually in the high twenties, reaching the unprecedented level of 30 (£580) in 1888 and 1892; second moieties were somewhat lower, indicating a measure of wastage. A major contribution to the increase was made by Hazell, Watson and Viney, who were now giving employment to six or more apprentices annually. To what extent – if at all – the rise was linked to the depressed state of agriculture after 1879 is unclear.

What is clear from Mackrill's figures is that, although the Charity could draw on a sizeable reserve of investment capital, spending at the current rate could not be sustained indefinitely without additional income. The accounts seem to show that, instead of restricting spending, the trustees continued to dip into reserves, for between 1888 and 1898 sales of consols to the value of around £100 or more are recorded in many years and the annual accounts were usually either just in balance or slightly in deficit.

Fortunately for all concerned, additional income was forthcoming as a result of the sale to the Metropolitan Railway Company in 1892. The proceeds were invested in £1,330 consols, which, for legal reasons (apparently against the prospect of purchasing other lands in lieu of those sold), were required to be lodged with the High Court. Further substantial investment capital was obtained from the sale in 1891 of the *New Inn* and the land belonging to it. These gains were offset by the cost of building work at Elm Farm, amounting to over £550. Nevertheless, the improved financial situation enabled the trustees (ignoring Mackrill's views) to respond positively in 1893 to a new appeal to local charities to assist in making provision, linked to the Grammar School, for the higher education of girls. Fortunately, perhaps, they were never called upon to make good their promise of 'a substantial sum'. Around the turn of the century investments stood at £3,781, producing a return of some £94 yearly.[15]

The Town Hall Connection

The Charity after Local Government Reform, 1898-1956

The local government reforms of 1894, which established a uniform system of elected rural and urban district councils, had a profound indirect effect on the constitution and personnel of some parochial charities, including Harding's. In 1897, acting in accordance with powers conferred by the Local Government Act, the Charity Commissioners issued a draft Scheme for the Charity which authorised the Aylesbury UDC to appoint up to three representative trustees, in addition to the existing five 'co-optative' trustees, who would hold office for the duration of their term as councillors but could be re-appointed. Not unreasonably, the trustees suggested that, if there had to be representative trustees, two would suffice, but this was of no avail. The UDC insisted on its full quota and the first representative trustees, appointed in November 1897, were Henry Gunn, William Smith and R.W. Locke.

The long-term effect of the new arrangement was to confine the trusteeship largely to serving and former members of the town council, for it became normal practice that when a vacancy arose among the co-optative trustees one of the representative trustees was elected to fill it, leaving the council to appoint a replacement representative. As a result, it would seem that by 1909 only two of the five permanent trustees (Lepper and Eagles) had not previously held office as a representative. On at least one occasion, in 1909, co-option took place before the trustee concerned had formally resigned as a representative. The Charity doubtless benefited considerably in various ways from the connection, though possibly at the price of a certain loss of independence. E.T. Mackrill (who was himself co-opted in 1903) would presumably have approved of the UDC's involvement with local charities in this way.

At the same time – and the two things are clearly related – the social background of the trustees began to change. To a much greater extent than formerly they were drawn from the ranks of Aylesbury's growing number of small and medium-sized tradesmen and merchants. No fewer than five of those who took office between 1897 and 1905 (four of them UDC representatives) were in this category, comprising a butcher (William Smith), a confectioner (J.C. Garner), two builders (R.W. Locke and Thomas Green), and an electrical engineer and dealer (Mackrill). For obvious reasons, the building trade was

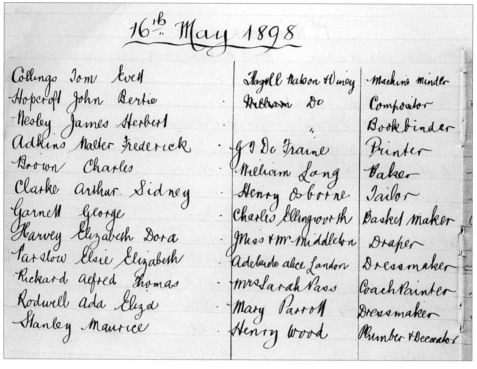

16th May 1898

Collingo Tom Evell	Hazell Nalson Henry	Machine minder
Hopcroft John Bertie	William Do	Compositor
Neoley James Herbert	"	Bookbinder
Adkins Nalter Frederick	Go De Fraine	Printer
Brown Charles	William Long	Baker
Clarke Arthur Sidney	Henry Osborne	Tailor
Garnell George	Charles Ellingworth	Basket maker
Harvey Elizabeth Dora	Miss & Mr Middleton	Draper
Tarstow Elsie Elizabeth	Adelaide alice Landon	Dressmaker
Rickard alfred Thomas	Mrs Sarah Pass	Coach Painter
Rodwell ada Eliza	Mary Parrott	Dressmaker
Stanley Maurice	Henry Wood	Plumber & Decorator

30 *Half-yearly list of apprentices and employers, May 1898. By this date, in contrast to earlier practice, virtually no children were being apprenticed out of the town. Note that four of the 12 children listed (33⅓ per cent) were apprenticed to the printing trade.*

particularly buoyant in the town at this epoch, though builders, so-called, were a relatively new phenomenon. Green may have belonged to a family of that name who had been carpenters in Aylesbury for generations. Locke, who was to become Aylesbury's first mayor when the town acquired a borough charter in 1917, was also in business as a brick manufacturer and coal merchant with headquarters at Hartwell. The enterprising E.T. Mackrill (d.1907) had moved with the times since 1889.

Two trustees of this era whose names are still widely remembered are Alfred Rose and Giacomo Gargini. Rose (1928), a farmer, was a trustee for over 25 years. The rubicund Mr Gargini, who was serving as mayor when appointed in 1935, was the enterprising proprietor of the *Bull's Head Hotel* in Market Square. Other long-serving trustees included T.W. Lepper (1901-38), veterinary surgeon, who succeeded his father, G.A. Lepper, as a co-optative trustee; T.E. Jenns (1918-*c*.1935), of Jenns and Sons, house-furnishers; V.H. Jarvis (1914-46), of the well-known High Street drapers business; and Thomas Buckingham (1923-51), a justice of the peace, who lived in Bicester Road.

Though they cover only a short span of years, the draft minutes 1897-1912 previously mentioned are much fuller than the laconic record of meetings that survives for the first half of the 19th century. There was also more to record, for the number of meetings held annually increased to eight at this time. In addition to information about rents, investments, etc., complaints from and about apprentices are occasionally recorded. In April 1901 Maurice Stanley, apprenticed in May 1898 to Henry Wood, plumber and decorator, complained that he was not being taught his trade. He and his master were summoned before the trustees and it was decided to defer payment of the second moiety of the premium. In 1903 an apprentice was discharged for dishonesty and his indentures were accordingly cancelled. Insubordination and poor time-keeping were the reasons given by the Bucks Advertiser Company for dismissing one of their apprentices in 1909. In April 1907 Frederick Longley (of Longley's, the High Street drapers) complained that Elsie Hearn, apprenticed the previous October as a dressmaker, was 'unmanageable and defiant'; he was advised that he must summon her before the magistrates and compel her to fulfil the terms of her contract. Similar advice was given to at least one other disgruntled employer.

Occasionally the trustees had to take account of an apprentice whose term had been disrupted through no fault of his or her own. In such cases steps were taken, where possible, to arrange, or approve, a transfer to another master. Sometimes the apprentice made his own arrangements. In May 1906 William Reading, aged 16, was apprenticed for five years to Charles Ellingworth, a basket maker then living in Highbridge Walk. In December 1909 his master reported that he had left his employ in consequence of bad trade, but later offered to take him back. It transpired that in the interval William had managed to obtain employment as a journeyman with another basket maker in Leighton Buzzard and no further action was required. Basket making was an ancient Aylesbury craft which had benefited from the requirements of railway transport.

In March 1898 a letter was received from Messrs Malcolmson and Son, whose address is not given but was evidently not Aylesbury, stating that, while they could not accept Henry Glover as an 'indoor' apprentice as proposed, they were prepared to receive him as an 'outdoor' apprentice and to pay him a scale of wages for five years. In the end it emerged that Glover would be 21 in three years and that the trustees could not, or would not, apprentice him beyond that age. Malcolmsons accordingly agreed to pay him wages for the three years of his apprenticeship (as a machinist, according to the register of apprentices) at the rate of 10s. per week for the first year, rising to 12s. in the third.

It seems to have been this incident which finally prompted the trustees into revising the existing terms of apprenticeship. The pro forma indenture then in use was clearly unsatisfactory because it was designed for the traditional 'indoor' form of apprenticeship, and also for a term of seven years, both of which had become obsolescent, leaving unresolved the legal position regarding whatever unofficial alternative arrangements were adopted. Outside advice was sought and it was decided to adopt the form of apprenticeship already in use by the Oxford charities, a form that enabled the agreed weekly wages for each year of an agreed term of apprenticeship to be inserted in advance.

Before the decision was taken, a meeting had been called of the children to be apprenticed, together with their prospective masters, 'to see what arrangements can be made with them as to the wages the apprentices are to receive in lieu of the present covenant to provide them with all things necessary for them during … their apprenticeship'. These 'binding days' continued to be held twice yearly thereafter for many years and are the first recorded example of the children themselves being consulted collectively on anything.

From now on, too, the agreed future wages for each child, together with the other relevant details, are written into the minutes; unfortunately the absence of minutes between 1912 and 1932 means that this unique record of wage scales is incomplete. The wage rates that are recorded at this time suggest that Henry Glover had received relatively generous treatment, though wages varied considerably even within the same occupation. Examples taken from the 1898-9 entries include Frank Cheshire, apprenticed to a blacksmith, to receive 5s. a week at 16 rising to 12s. at 21; Frederick Paton, apprentice compositor at Hazell & Co., 4s. at 17, rising to 10s. 6d. at 21; Rosa Moore, apprentice dressmaker, aged 16, 3s. rising to 5s. over a three-year term; Florence Hannard, apprentice draper, aged 15, 1s. rising to 3s. over the same term.

Many apprentices were 16 or even 17 at this time and the duration of their service was consequently limited, especially as a period of at least five years was apparently still normal for a really skilled trade. When Hazell & Co. wrote in October 1898 suggesting that the apprentices should be bound at an earlier age they were informed that the trustees were unable to do this 'in consequence of the numerous applications'. In April 1901 Hazell's representative reiterated that the firm did not want boys to be apprenticed to them after the age of sixteen. The situation may have been complicated by the custom by which aspiring apprentices in the printing trade served a preliminary probationary period as a 'printer's devil'.[1]

31 *Advertisement in a* Kelly's Directory *for 1899. Cycle engineers begin to figure in the lists of apprentices around this time.*

The average annual intake of apprentices declined after 1900: from 24 in the late 1890s, to 18 or 19 for the whole of the period 1900-14, and sinking to 11 during the years 1915-19. After the war, numbers failed to regain their pre-war level, averaging just over 16 throughout the 1920s, despite an increase in the premiums (the first in over a century) made in 1924 in response, it was later said, to demand from employers. From now on boys would receive £30 and girls in proportion. The increase was made without consulting the Charity Commissioners (who did not discover it until many years later), as were increases in the amounts spent on the Walton poor in these years. Throughout the 1930s the average number of apprentices was between 16 and 17 annually, but this conceals considerable fluctuations, including a sharp dip in the Depression years 1932-3, when the figures were 10 and 11 respectively.

New trades slowly continued to appear and old ones (such as blacksmithing) to diminish or disappear. The first cycle engineer appears in 1904 and the first motor engineer noted (E.C. Little) is recorded among the employers in 1908. Printing and, to a much lesser extent, a few other skilled

32 *As these advertisements of 1913-14 indicate, some traditional trades continued to flourish and a few, like basket making, even underwent a modest revival.*

trades were becoming gradually more dominant. Of the 71 boys apprenticed in the five years 1906-10 just over half (36) were bound to printers, mostly to Hazell's, but also to G.T. Hunt, G.T. DeFraine, the Bucks Advertiser Co. and others. The remainder were distributed as follows: building trades (7), coach building (6), motor engineer (4), food retailing (4), engineer/electrician (3), miscellaneous (11). Within the latter category the professions were basket maker (2), clothing (2), hairdresser (2), bootmaker, blacksmith, chemist, and cycle engineer (2).

A generation later, analysis of the 79 boys apprenticed in 1935-9 shows an even greater concentration on a limited number of skilled trades, as follows: printing (35), building trades (11), engineers/electricians (11), motor engineers (10), other (12). The last category includes gents outfitter, ironmonger, butcher, and

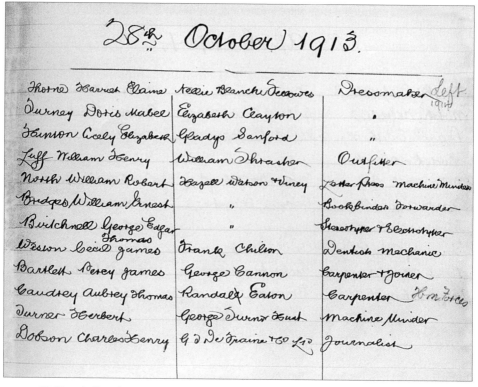

33 *Half-yearly list of apprentices, October 1913. Dressmakers are still quite well represented at this time but their numbers steadily declined thereafter. Journalist and dental mechanic were new arrivals and were never especially numerous.*

boot and shoe repairer. It is a measure of the importance which printing had assumed in the town's economy at this period that in 1939, out of a population of 13,000, over 1,600 people were directly employed in the trade, 1,175 of whom worked at Hazell's.[2] Although Aylesbury would retain its ancient cattle market until 1987, it was clearly no longer a simple market town.

Another striking feature of the period was the decline in the number of girls apprenticed, from an annual average of five and a half in the late 1890s to just under three between 1900 and 1914 and fewer than one (13 out of 220, just under six per cent) in the period 1915-29. Throughout, employment was exclusively in dressmaking, apart from a few milliners and drapers.

Nationally, apprenticeship had long been contracting. In 1920 only 13 per cent of boys aged under 21 were apprenticed, and in 1926, even in the industries where apprenticeship was supposed to be the rule, which were principally the metal industries, woodworking, building, printing and the retail trades, only 20 per cent of employers had apprentices in training. Aylesbury was thus not unrepresentative of general trends in apprenticing.[3]

During the whole of the period to 1932 investment income rose steadily to offset receipts from rents, which rarely exceeded £375, so that total income rose from an average of around £470 from 1910-14 to over £700 from 1928-32. The stock market collapse of 1933 brought a sharp reduction in dividends and thereafter income hovered around the £600 mark for some years. However, since expenditure on premiums was relatively low, averaging under £330 a year until 1924, and £400-£460 thereafter, annual accounts were consistently in surplus, some of which appears to have been invested.[4]

From 1930 the minutes of trustees' meetings are again available. They show that, contrary to their earlier attitude, the trustees often went to a good deal of trouble to try to resolve grievances between employer and employee. It was not unusual for an apprentice, often accompanied by a parent, to be summoned to attend a meeting of the trustees, together with his employer or his employer's representative, to be solemnly admonished by the chairman and made to promise to mend his ways. In 1935 a young motor mechanic was proving a liability because, although admitted to be willing and honest, it was alleged that 'he is very forgetful and this leads to customers' instructions not being carried out, resulting sometimes in the loss of such customers'.

Sometimes it was the apprentice who complained that he was not receiving appropriate instruction and it was the employer who had to promise to do better. In a few cases the indentures were cancelled. On one occasion it was suggested to a boy's parents that their son might improve his time-keeping if they took more interest in his welfare.

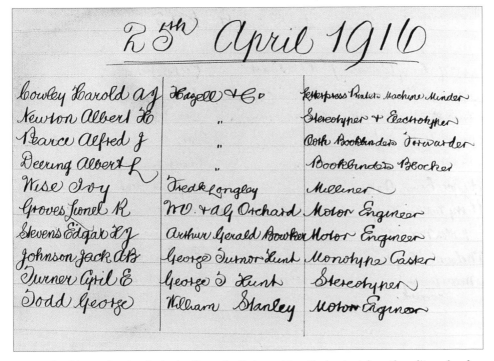

34 *In this wartime intake in April 1916 all those apprenticed, apart from the solitary female apprentice, are either printers or motor engineers.*

The advent of the Second World War brought new problems, with some apprentices going into the forces and normal trading disrupted. One apprentice complained of being left alone in sole charge of a garage at Bierton while his employer was more lucratively employed in tractor-ploughing for the War Agriculture Committee. The father of another requested his release for the duration of the war 'to enable him to obtain work in one of the Bicester Road factories', referring to the temporary factories engaged on war work located there which paid good wages. One far-sighted businessman, Mr Payne of A. & F. Payne, whose apprentice had volunteered for the RAF, was reluctant to commit himself to taking him back 'owing to the uncertainty of what was to happen to small businesses after the war'.

Demand for apprenticeships fell still further after 1945, and in 1949 the decrease in the number of applications was given as the main reason that the Charity's income was not being fully spent.

Apprenticing was, of course, not the trustees' only form of expenditure. Even before the First World War the £10 limit on the cost of providing clothing for the poor of Walton was regularly being exceeded. This additional expenditure provided an outlet for surplus income, but it could also be justified by the increasing population of the area, which now included the Tring Road factories and much of the adjoining, post-1870, lower middle-class and working-class housing development, as well as earlier development in the Walton Street and Wendover Road areas. The amounts spent on distributions fluctuated but during the war years averaged over £40 annually, and between 1918 and 1924 was in excess of £70, reaching £104 in 1924 and £117 in 1927. Dresses for the women and coats for the men were, as earlier, provided by local shopkeepers.

During the Depression years, 1930-5, the numbers relieved averaged 32 annually, falling thereafter to well under twenty in most years. Addresses of recipients extend from Southcourt (a post-war development) on the west to the Tring Road on the east, with Chiltern Street, Albert Street, Highbridge Walk, Old Stoke Road and Walton Street among the streets most frequently mentioned. Names of individuals recur only every third year. In 1949 the interval was extended from three years to five and the following year to six. Ages, given in the 1950s, were all over sixty.

During the First World War farming had suddenly become a vital part of the nation's resources and farmers benefited accordingly. After 1918 rents held up better than might have been expected. In 1920 the total rent income was £387, compared to £398 in 1915, declining to £373 in 1924. At Elm Farm rent remained stable at £155 a year from 1910 onwards and, following Henry Landon's death around 1923, it actually increased to £190 under the new tenant, Frank Evered, equalling the peak years of arable farming prior to 1879. Then, in July 1932, after a half year which Evered claimed was 'the worst for farming he had ever experienced', an abatement of 25 per cent was allowed for the following year. In the meantime over £270 was being spent on improvements to the farmhouse, including a bathroom, hot water supply and cesspool, a sum equivalent to one and a half year's rent.

Elsewhere rents either declined or remained static. At Chilton, Richard Roadnight, who had inherited the tenancy from his father in 1910, was paying only £80 a year by the end of the decade, compared to £115 in 1924, and P.A. Leader at Stoke Mandeville was constantly in arrears with his rent of £40, despite repeated threats of legal action. At Bierton the rent was reduced from £35 to £30 in 1937, by which date total annual rent income was averaging less than £340.

In these circumstances it is scarcely surprising that by 1934 the trustees were actively exploring the feasibility of disposing of Elm Farm. It was a question which was to engage much of their time from now on. In October 1932 there had already been an enquiry from a builder interested in acquiring land fronting the Wendover Road. In the following year it was decided to commission a survey of the property with a view to future development for building purposes, in harmony with the new town planning schemes for Aylesbury borough and rural district councils. Discussions on the subject were held with the Charity Commissioners, in which the trustees expressed them-

35 *Advertisement for Bowker's garage in Cambridge Street, taken from the Aylesbury directory for 1925-6.*

selves strongly in favour of selling the farm as a whole rather than piecemeal, as proposed by a consultant. Meanwhile, in 1937, the tenant was authorised to have a caravan camping site on part of the land – an example of what would now be called 'diversification'. The trustees were also in favour of selling at Bierton, where an offer of £2 per square foot for road frontage had been received in March 1934.

In 1939 the whole matter of land sales was overtaken by the advancing shadow of war. In July of that year a local land agent acting for the Ministry of Health informed the trustees that a site of 20 acres was urgently required for an emergency hospital and that the portion of Elm Farm fronting the Stoke Mandeville Road and adjoining the existing isolation hospital was the most suitable location. In the event the Ministry agreed to purchase 30 acres running back to the railway for £3,000. The conveyance was executed in October 1939; the tenant received compensation of £50 and a reduction of £50 in the annual rent.

Two years later, in December 1941, the Ministry purchased another 22 acres for £3,060, leaving the farm approximately half its former size. The tenant, now S.G. Evered, was again compensated, and had his rent reduced to £104. As a result of these transactions the total rent roll stood at just under £300 and income from investments now permanently exceeded income from rents.

After this the issue of the future disposal of the estate properties receded again for some years, apart from an offer from the new Milk Marketing Board in 1944 to purchase the land at Stoke Mandeville for £2,000. The offer was adjudged insufficient and nothing more seems to have come of the matter. In 1943 the farmhouse at Elm Farm was found to be in a state of collapse, and urgent, expensive repairs had to be undertaken.

Even more serious was the discovery in 1950 of structural defects so serious as to require a complete rebuilding of much of the farmhouse at a cost estimated at £1,000 or more. To complicate matters, it transpired that the tenant had sublet the house to his elderly parents and was himself living in one of the farm buildings, which he had converted into a bungalow without permission. As rebuilding was considered uneconomic, it was agreed to seek the consent of the Charity Commissioners for a sale to the tenant.

In 1951 the farm, described as pasture land on a subsoil of heavy, ill-drained clay, was valued at £5,500 for immediate sale without rebuilding the farmhouse, but as the trustees realised that this price would not be acceptable to the Charity Commissioners it was agreed instead to let the property to Mr Evered for an increased rent, fixed at £175 in 1953, leaving the question of further work to the farmhouse in abeyance. It had been noted by the valuer that the trustees had already spent £800 on the property since 1942, which was not far short of the aggregate rent received in the same period. It is interesting to compare the 1951 valuation with the approximately £8,000 realised by Bedford's Charity in 1955 on the sale of 25 acres of allotment land in Buckingham Road, the last remnant of that charity's once quite extensive land holding.

By 1954 several developers were showing an interest in Elm Farm and two offers of £9,000, one of them from the tenant, were communicated to the Charity Commissioners. The latter observed, reasonably enough, that if the sale took place the investments held for the Charity in fixed securities would be even more heavily weighted than before. It was further observed that:

> it was certainly the experience of the past that Charities which had retained their investments in land had usually preserved the real value of their endowments much better than Charities which had converted their lands into fixed interest earning stocks.

On the other hand, the Commissioners acknowledged that a time might come when the value of a certain holding was so abnormally high that it would be beneficial to sell and perhaps reinvest the proceeds in, presumably cheaper, land nearby, and they emphasised the potential higher value of building land in a borough whose population was destined to increase. A report from W. Brown & Co., the estate agents consulted, confirmed that offers of £9,000 were

𝕿𝖍𝖎𝖘 𝕴𝖓𝖉𝖊𝖓𝖙𝖚𝖗𝖊 witnesseth that

Philip John Roche   son of

James Frederick Roche and Gertrude May his wife   of

Aylesbury, in the County of Buckingham, *Assistant TimeKeeper* with the consent of his

Father   testified by his executing these Presents, doth put himself

Apprentice to Edward Peach Gilkes Jane Gilkes William Henry Edward Gilkes
Ronald Arthur Elliott Gilkes and Leslie Harold Elliott Gilkes (trading
as Gilkes and Sons) of Aylesbury aforesaid Builders

to learn the Art or Business of a   **Carpenter and Joiner**   and

with them after the manner of an Apprentice to serve from the   22nd   day of

October   one thousand nine hundred and   **thirty four**   until the

~~20th~~
~~twenty second~~ day of ~~October~~ June   one thousand nine hundred and
forty one
~~thirty nine~~   during which term the said Apprentice his Masters faithfully shall

serve, their secrets keep, their lawful commands everywhere gladly do; he shall do no damage to his

said Masters, nor see to be done of others, but to the best of his power shall let or forthwith give

warning to his said Masters of the same; he shall not waste the goods of his said Masters, nor

lend them unlawfully to any; he shall not do any act whereby his said Masters may have any loss

with their own goods or others; he shall not during the said term, without licence of his said

Masters, either buy or sell, or absent himself from his said Masters' service unlawfully but in all

things as a faithful Apprentice shall behave himself towards his said Masters, and all theirs during

the said term. And the said *W.* Gilkes and Sons

in consideration of the sum of Fifteen Pounds to them paid by the

Trustees of HARDING's Charity, Aylesbury, at the time of executing this Indenture, and of the further

sum of Fifteen Pounds to be paid by the Trustees to the said *W.* Gilkes and Sons

(subject to the proviso

hereinafter contained), at the expiration of three years from the date hereof, making the sum of

Thirty Pounds, out of the Funds of the said Charity, do hereby for themselves, their Successors, and

Assigns, covenant and promise to and with the said   ~~Gilkes and Sons~~

Philip John Roche   that they the said *W.* Gilkes

and Sons   shall the said

Philip John Roche   in the Art or Business

of a Carpenter and Joiner   which they the said

W. Gilkes and Sons   now use,

after the best manner that they can, teach, instruct, and inform, or cause to be taught, instructed

and informed, paying the Weekly Wages hereinafter mentioned, namely:—   June

not less than   10/- per week until the 20th ~~22nd~~ day of ~~October~~ 1935
                                                                         June
        "   "   12/-   "   "   20th ~~22nd~~   "   ~~October~~ 1936
                                                                         June
        "   "   14/-   "   "   20th ~~22nd~~   "   ~~October~~ 1937
                                                                         June
        "   "   16/-   "   "   20th ~~22nd~~   "   ~~October~~ 1938
                                                                         June
        "   "   18/-   "   "   20th ~~22nd~~   "   ~~October~~ 1939
        "   "   20/-   "   "   20th   "   June   1940
        "   "   25/-   "   "   20th   "   June   1941

36 *Apprenticeship indenture of Philip John Roche as a carpenter and joiner to Gilkes & Sons,
builders, Aylesbury, 1934. The premium paid by the Charity was now £30, living in was a thing of
the past, and the employer had to undertake to provide weekly wages according to an agreed scale.*

on the low side and drew attention to the definite decision, taken since 1951, to expand the population of the borough to 38,000. In these circumstances, they counselled, it would be better to wait until the new Town Plan had been approved, when it might be found that some – if not all – of the land was zoned for development: 'In that event it could become very valuable.'

In 1937 the Charity Commissioners had belatedly woken up to the fact that the trustees were exceeding the official amounts allowed for premiums for apprenticeships and for distributions to the poor of Walton. They were informed that the premiums had been raised some 14 years earlier in response to representations from employers to the effect that increases in the wages being paid to apprentices had made the premiums inadequate, that Walton parish (the ecclesiastical parish created in 1848) had increased greatly in size, and that the cost of clothing had also risen. In response, the Commissioners proposed a new Scheme, or governing instrument, to regularise the application of the income. The figure suggested by the Commissioners for the clothing distribution was rejected by the trustees as less than the annual amount spent for the past 11 years and they suggested a discretionary power to spend up to £100 in any one year for the purpose.

Further discussions followed. The limit of annual expenditure on Walton was apparently compromised at £50. The existing premiums were confirmed, as was the reduced annual subscription of £25 to the local church schools, which had been adopted following the 1902 Act under which the county council became responsible for education, and the £10 subscription to the Royal Bucks Hospital (discontinued on the introduction of the National Health Service in 1947). Up to £10 was allowed for the Grammar School prize fund, and up to £20 to nursing and kindred institutions. Provision was also made for payments not exceeding £25 annually, out of a residuary fund of amounts, for the advancement in life of, or the provision of working tools and equipment for, young persons under 21 years of age. This last clause (6b) was a new departure and contained the germ of future developments. The Scheme was approved in February 1939.

After the war the trustees decided, in 1947, to request the Charity Commissioners to amend the 1939 Scheme to enable the capital fund to be used for building housing accommodation for the elderly (much needed at the time), but this application met with a blunt refusal. Two years later, in March 1949, the trustees, noting with regret that income was not being fully spent, mainly owing to the decrease in the number of applications for apprenticeships, decided to apply for authorisation to spend £200 annually on clothing, instead of £50, and £50 on school subscriptions.

This application received no reply until April 1951, the delay being attributed to pressure of work consequent on the introduction of the National Health Service. The trustees were informed that existing trusts could only be varied if the income could not be applied in accordance with those trusts, and it was suggested that applications for grants under clause 6 of the current Scheme be invited by means of advertisements in the local press. The following March letters to the press designed to publicise the Charity were proposed, and it was conceded that if there was still no response at the end of two years the trustees should renew their application.

Discussions were accordingly renewed in late 1954. This time the Commissioners produced a Scheme, proposed for a charity in Derbyshire, which they thought might be adapted for Harding's. Its purpose was to provide grants for the further education of boys and girls under 21, including those going to universities: 'it would thus bring within the scope of the Charity an additional strata [*sic*] of the population'. Eventually the Commissioners produced the draft of a joint Scheme, drawn up in consultation with the Ministry of Education, for discussion. The original version split the income into three parts, one part applicable for the benefit of the poor and two parts for apprenticing and 'advancement in life' and various other purposes, but this was simplified, and apprenticing as such is not specified in the final version. There were now to be seven co-optative trustees, while the number of appointed trustees was reduced to two, one to be appointed by the borough council and the other by the county council as Local Education Authority, serving for five years. The first co-optative trustees under the Scheme were to serve for life, their successors for five years only. The small annual allowance still paid to trustees under the founder's will was deleted by agreement.

In April 1955 the trustees considered the latest draft. They noted that the major part of the endowment was apportioned to the educational foundation under the control of the Ministry of Education, that the trustees of both foundations (the educational and the eleemosynary) would consist of the same persons, and that the old distinction between Aylesbury and Walton would no longer apply. Among the mainly minor amendments proposed was one to enable the transfer of surplus funds from one foundation to another if required. These were duly settled and the Scheme came into force on 26 January 1956. It still forms the basis of the Charity's constitution.

PART III
WIDER HORIZONS

The End of Apprenticeship, 1956-1978

The seven life trustees named in the 1956 Scheme were Alfred Rose, W.H. Palmer, Charles Harris, F.B. Howard, C.W. Ivatts, W.G. Brown and Joseph S. Holland of Wendover, the latter replacing J.J. Evett, who had recently died. Their respective occupations were (or had been, for all were retired) farmer, printer's reader, railway official, draper, shoe shop proprietor, architect and company director. With the exception of Alfred Rose none of them had held office before 1944. The first two representative trustees were Colonel F.W. Watson (d.1966), representing the county council, and W.T. Fewkes for the borough council.

All the original life trustees had resigned or died by 1966. Alfred Rose, who resigned in 1962, had served for almost 35 years. Among their successors were Mrs Zena Williams, who succeeded C.W. Ivatts in 1961 as the very first female trustee, and Mrs Olive Paterson, who replaced T.S. Holland the following year and acted as chairman from 1966 onwards. Mrs Williams was the daughter of an Aylesbury master butcher; Mrs Paterson was the wife of a former managing director of the Rivets company. Others who came to office in these years included Harold Crookes (1966), a former town clerk, Dr G.W.H. Townsend (1969), formerly county Medical Officer of Health, a strong-minded Irishman with a Dublin accent, and the first and last medical man to serve as a trustee for many years, (Alfred) Ernest Roblin (1969), of the Aylesbury engineering business that bears his name, R.S. Pearce (1971), a farmer from Stoke Mandeville, the last trustee to be appointed by the old borough council, whose rather abrasive style must have enlivened many a meeting, and F.A. Burch (1974), a former borough treasurer. Membership of the two local authorities was not confined to the representative trustees: Mrs Williams was a member of the borough council and held office as mayor in 1958, and again in 1971, and M.W. Buckingham was serving as mayor when co-opted in 1962.

With hindsight, the principal theme of this period is the transformation of the Charity's financial resources through the sale of its landed endowment, but the process was long drawn out and the magnitude of the opportunity became apparent only gradually. In 1956 a windfall payment of £1,886 was received as the compensation payable for the refusal of planning permission for the Bierton property. In 1958 the 45 acres at Chilton, described as 'good sound feeding pasture', was sold to Aubrey Fletcher Estates Ltd for £3,700. Then, in 1962, came a major breakthrough when Aylesbury Borough Council itself decided to purchase the 10.2 acres of land at Bierton for development. The valuation price was £47,000, a sum greatly in excess of anything so far realised.

Meanwhile the saga of Elm Farm dragged on. In October 1957 an outline application for development was refused planning permission on the grounds that it was 'premature'. Brown & Co. recommended no further action for six months in view of the current credit restrictions and the probability that the borough council was more likely to extend development to the north and east of the town than to the south. Two years later, in 1959, offers of up to £75,000 were being received from private developers, and Aylesbury Borough Council was intimating that it wished to acquire the property by private treaty. However, sale by public auction, jointly with Hickman's Charity, whose allotment land adjoined Elm Farm, was agreed in principle to be the best option. A professional valuation, obtained in 1960, was now £250,000. In 1961 an appeal against refusal of planning permission was requested, and a further application in late 1962 was again refused. In 1964 yet another appeal met with the same fate, and it was decided to accept a renewed offer from the borough council to negotiate.

In February 1965 an offer of £265,000 (£5,000 an acre) for the whole of Elm Farm was accepted, subject to the approval of the Ministry of Education, but Hickman's trustees reported that the Charity Commissioners would not permit them to sell at this price since advertisements had produced an offer of £9,000 per acre. In February 1967, following joint negotiations with Hickman's, another joint application for planning permission, this time phased over a period of years, was submitted, and was finally approved in early 1967. Further meetings were held with Hickman's to work out the details. The trustees were particularly concerned, for example, to see that the proposed new school should be sited on Harding property, and also to retain ownership of the existing access, or 'cattle creep', from the site under the railway line to the Stoke Mandeville Hospital. In July 1971 the first 7.75 acres of Elm Farm was sold separately to the county council for £174,000 as a site for the school, and it was agreed to request the Ministry of Education to name it after William Harding.

More joint meetings with Hickman's trustees followed. Then in 1972 a tender of £955,000 from Sunley homes for Hickman's field and part of Elm Farm was accepted and the money paid into a temporary joint account pending apportionment. In November 1974 an offer of £1,071,000 from Bryant Homes Ltd and Gough Cooper Ltd for the remaining 32 acres of Elm Farm (the name survives as that of a new residential housing estate) was accepted subject to Ministry approval. The conveyance was signed the following year. Payment of the purchase money was delayed by a dispute over an alleged right of way but was finally completed in December 1975. The following year the joint fund was apportioned by agreement on the basis of acreage, Harding's share being in the region of £2,000,000.

However frustrating, the long delays in disposing of the bulk of the Charity's property (there remained some 25 acres in Stoke Mandeville parish and four and a half acres of land let as allotments in Bierton) at least enabled the trustees to adjust gradually to the daunting realities of a vastly expanded scale of giving, as well as to experiment with the new powers and opportunities provided by the 1956 Scheme. Up until the sale of the Bierton land in 1962 the annual income had risen considerably, but not dramatically, and even after that date, when the capital had increased by over £50,000, the rise in annual income was far from astronomical until 1971, when the sale of the school site increased it to a new order of magnitude.

Even after 1956 applications for apprenticeship premiums continued to be received. Annual numbers varied from as few as three in 1956 to over fourteen. After 1957 details of the individual wage agreements are no longer entered in the minutes. When it was revealed in April 1962 that applicants for apprenticeship to Hazell's had in reality already taken out their indentures before applying, the firm explained that the premiums paid by the Charity were used to augment wages during the early years of service; it was decided to continue to make use of the Charity's own form of indenture as before.

During the 1970s apprenticeship in its traditional form was fast disappearing everywhere for a variety of reasons. Later, in the 1990s, the government, alarmed at the serious decline in the national skills base, and finding that the various youth training schemes that were a feature of the 1980s had a bad reputation, would launch a so-called 'modern apprenticeship', lasting from two to three and a half years. The results were mixed, partly, it was said, because the culture of apprenticeship had finally been lost. But that is another story.

Formal industrial training projects were already receiving help from the Charity in the 1970s. In 1974 a grant of over £30,000 was made to the Aylesbury Industrial Group Training Centre Ltd, for additional equipment for their workshop. The Centre had been established at Gatehouse Close with the help of the Engineering Industrial Training Board and was financed in part from training fees paid by employers. Its membership comprised some 60 Buckinghamshire engineering firms, large and small, about a third of which were located in Aylesbury. The trainees, too, were drawn from a wide area. In view of the Charity's history it can be seen as a peculiarly appropriate beneficiary, and it was to receive further substantial grants over the years for machinery and equipment. Between 1981 and 1998, for example, the total given in grants would exceed £120,000. The training fees of a number of trainees from Aylesbury were also paid.

Much of the trustees' time at meetings held during the first five years of the new Scheme was taken up with requests for student grants, including grants for school fees, books, equipment, musical instruments and travelling expenses. The applications were not especially numerous but they required individual consideration. Assessment of need must sometimes have been difficult, especially as family background and circumstances varied widely and some of the applications were for children of middle-class parents attending private boarding schools. In October 1958 it was agreed to adopt a regular system of cross-checking applications with the Chief Education Officer as a first step towards greater consistency. Most grants were in the region of £30 to £50, but some talented youngsters – students of drama and music among them – received grants amounting to several hundreds of pounds. In 1973 one former student who had been helped to obtain a training in secretarial skills wrote expressing the wish to pay back the money. The trustees expressed their delight at the sentiment but suggested that a small donation would suffice!

37   *The last of Elm Farm, 1973. Aerial view of the residue of the Elm Farm property (c. 32 acres), offered for sale in November 1973. Stoke Mandeville Hospital is on the far left of the picture.*

Applications for grants for working tools for apprentices and trainees, as well as for books and instruments both scientific and musical, had begun to be received in early 1962, and by 1966 as many as 25 were coming in annually. After some initial enquiries a maximum grant of £15 per person for working tools was thought appropriate, raised to £25 in 1969; by the 1990s it had reached £250. These grants became a regular item of expenditure and gradually replaced the payment of apprenticeship premiums as such.

In October 1960 a request was received for a grant for school prizes for the new Girls High School which had been hived off from Aylesbury Grammar School a few years previously. It was decided to give £10, the amount given to the parent institution, and this too was repeated in following years. Grants for prizes eventually became routinely available to schools in general on request.

By 1962 the Charity's growing resources were attracting requests for larger sums, mostly from schools and institutions to cover 'one-off' expenditure for special purposes. In that year up to £100 was promised to

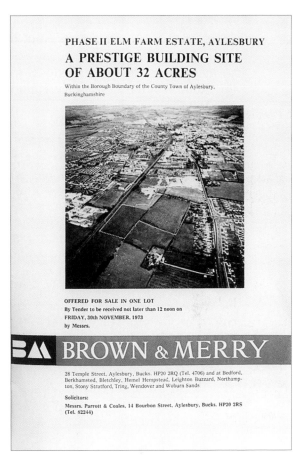

38 *Photograph of the sale notice for the Elm Farm property (c.32 acres), offered for sale in November 1973.*

Quarrendon School towards the expense of a new swimming pool, and in the following April a grant of £250, the first of many, was made to the Grange School for a sixth-form conference it was organising. Nevertheless, reference was being made the same year to 'the necessity for ways and means to be devised for distributing the increased income among suitable beneficiaries if they can be found', and Col. Watson, the county council's representative, undertook to discuss the matter with the chief education officer with a view to forming 'a plan which would enable the trustees to dispose of the income in accordance with the Scheme'.

No formal plan is known to have been adopted at this time but the number and variety of applications gradually increased and by 1966 it was being found necessary to increase the number of annual meetings from two to four in order to cope with them. The trustees themselves took the initiative in December 1964 in approaching Charles Pope about the requirements of the Aylesbury orchestral and choral societies, with which his name is so closely associated and which contributed greatly to the cultural life of the town. The upshot was an immediate grant of £100, followed in later years by more and larger benefactions, which still continue to be made. Among the other recipients of grants around this time were the Aylesbury Festival of the Arts (an annual event for many years), Beech Green nursery school, and local branches of the Girl Guides and the Red Cross. In 1969 an approach to the Aylesbury College of Further Education (now Aylesbury College) led to the presentation of the Harding Prizes for catering, hairdressing, business studies and engineering.

By 1973, with vastly increased funding assured, larger grants in the thousands of pounds were becoming more frequent. The new Aylesbury Youth Action organisation, launched in 1970 with a grant of £600, was given £2,400 to enable it to appoint a co-ordinator and a community service volunteer. Youth Action was aimed at involving pupils from the town's secondary schools in community work and was closely associated with Aylesbury Grammar School and its headmaster, Keith Smith, who was chairman of the organisation until his retirement in 1992.[1] In the same year £8,000 was promised towards the cost of an adventure playground for handicapped children at the Manor House hospital, later to be known as the Jonathan Page adventure playground. Both these ventures were unusual in that they received continuing support with staffing and equipment over extended periods, the playground until 1986, while Youth Action was still a recipient at the end of the century.

The year 1973 also saw a grant of £46,000 to the Grammar School towards the costs involved in providing a lecture hall for science and drama and for holding sixth-form conferences. This seems to have been the first major grant of its kind. It was capped the following year by a grant to the high school of £61,800 to assist in providing additional music and drama facilities.

An example of a much more modest grant, but one not lacking in significance, was the £100 given to the Aylesbury Community Relations Council in 1973 for educational visits for pupils attending the English language centre. Two years later a further grant was given for a summer play.

The year 1973 also saw a sizeable grant to the county council to help pay for an additional room at the new schools planned for the Elm Farm site, later to be designated a special annexe for handicapped children. The previous year the trustees had renewed their application to have the schools named after the founder. In 1974, when the new William Harding First and Second Schools had been inaugurated, the trustees were in touch with the headmistresses to see if anything more could be done for the children. They must have been a little surprised to be informed that the one amenity which the children most missed on transferring from Queens Park, their former school, was a wall in the playground against which to play their games. This modest request was eventually supplied.

When news emerged in 1974 that the Prebendal House, one of Aylesbury's most historic buildings, was about to come on the market it led to considerable excitement in the town. It was soon brought to the attention of the trustees that the parents' association of the Prebendal School, which had occupied the building for many years, were anxious to set up an educational trust to buy or lease the property, which comprised some four acres of land. The trustees considered that it would benefit the town if the school were to continue and decided to investigate the feasibility of purchasing it with a view to leasing it for this purpose. The Charity Commissioners did not raise any objection, evidently considering the property an acceptable investment. On the basis of an expert valuation it was agreed to make a bid of £130,000, an amount which it was thought could probably be met from accumulated income, but the bid proved insufficient and no further action was taken.

The house was to come on the market again some five years later, in mid-1979, having been restored in the interval as a private residence by Lady Rosebery. The recently formed Aylesbury Society felt that it should be secured for the community and approached the trustees to see if the Charity could assist, but perhaps because of the asking price – £500,000 – the trustees were disinclined to pursue the matter.

Meanwhile the trustees, in their capacity of eleemosynary charity, continued to provide annual distributions of clothing and bedding for the poor, and also made use of their wider powers under the 1956 Scheme to purchase furniture, fuel and other comforts for the sick and the needy, though, despite what the new Scheme said, distributions until 1978 seem to have been confined to Walton.

In the 1950s meetings for distributions were still being held each October at the *New Inn* (now the *Broad Leys*) public house in Walton, where the trustees personally interviewed applicants. As Sue Spinks, who started with Parrott & Coales in 1960, recalls, coats, dresses and shoes were requested, and sometimes blankets and sheets. At one point the trustees solemnly discussed whether to award two blankets rather than one, since the cost of a coat or a suit – made to measure, usually at Spraggs, the drapers – considerably exceeded that of one blanket. One of the trustees would then undertake to purchase the required items and these would be delivered to the *New Inn* in time for collection on or near St Thomas's day, 21 December, the traditional distribution day.

From 20 or 30 a year in 1950, the number of applicants for clothing continued to grow, and by 1956 the trustees were compelled to borrow the use of a committee room from the borough council to enable all the elderly applicants to sit down while waiting to be interviewed. Distribution of the clothing and bedding was transferred to the office of the Clerks, Parrott & Coales, in Bourbon Street, where Mrs Spinks vividly remembers the piles of clothes, blankets, sheets and shoes which arrived prior to 'distribution day'. The last such distribution in kind took place in 1964. After this, following a brief experiment with a voucher system, a cash gift – originally of £7, raised to £10 in 1975 – was substituted; it was paid at first by postal order and later by cheque. By this time the number of applicants had increased to more than a hundred.

39 *The* Broad Leys *public house, Walton, formerly the* New Inn. *It was sold by the trustees in or around 1891 (see p.112) but was still being used as the venue for the Charity's annual distribution of clothing to the poor as late as the 1950s.*

The first application for help towards the cost of transport was received in 1977. The trustees were 'concerned that elderly persons were prevented from attending social and civic functions in the evening for lack of affordable transport'. They decided to fund the hire costs of coaches or minibuses for this purpose, but not of taxis, and for evenings only. At the time 11 clubs or societies were eligible but before the end of the century the number was nearer thirty. Long before then, too, the rules had been relaxed to include daytime outings and excursions, and nowadays taxis, too, are funded if appropriate. This little-known – and relatively inexpensive – aspect of the Charity's activities has helped to brighten a great many lives over the years.

Early in 1975 the trustees discussed the possibility of funding a large capital project such as sheltered housing or almshouses with the new funds. It was felt that new powers might be needed and this led to the appointment of a sub-committee of three (Paterson, Burch and Townsend) to consider ways of spending income and also a more equitable division of funds between the educational and the eleemosynary foundations. The following year arrange-ments were made for further consultation with the Charity Commissioners about amending the existing Scheme in order to enlarge the objects of the Charity.

In 1976 the trustees were informed by the county council of a project to make the former Queens Park School premises available for youth and community purposes in association with Aylesbury Youth Action, with a request for a grant of £25,000 to equip and furnish the new centre. This was the beginning of the Charity's long and continuing involvement with Queens Park and with what eventually became the Queens Park Centre for the Arts.

Another major beneficiary at this time was Aylesbury's ancient parish church of St Mary's, where urgent restoration work, carried out in 1978, provided an opportunity for extensive remodelling of the interior to incorporate facilities for a community centre. The Charity's contribution to the appeal was £100,000, the largest single grant yet made by it.[2]

In October 1978 the trustees' representations in favour of broader powers finally bore fruit in a new Scheme under which the two branches of the Charity were reunited under the oversight of the Charity Commissioners. Briefly sum-marised, the principal objects of the Charity were now to be:

(a) To benefit residents in the Charity's almshouses,

(b) To provide relief in need,

(c) To provide special benefits of any kind not normally provided by the L.E.A. for any maintained school or any college of education, or any institution of further education in, or substantially serving, the town,

(d) providing scholarships and maintenance allowances tenable at schools, universities, colleges and other institutions of further education (including professional and technical), for persons under the age of 25 years resident in Aylesbury.

Additional objects separately specified include making travel grants to indi-viduals in furtherance of their education; assisting those entering upon any profession, trade or occupation by providing them with outfits, clothing, tools, instruments or books, or by paying their fees, travelling or maintenance expenses or by such other means for their advancement in life to enable them to earn their own living as the trustees think fit; providing facilities of any kind not normally provided by the LEA for recreation and social and physical training for beneficiaries receiving education at all levels; and making grants to any charitable voluntary organisation in the town for advancing the education of, or improving the conditions of life for, beneficiaries by developing their physical, mental and moral capacities through their leisure-time activities.

Subsumed under the heading of Relief in Need was the continuing annual cash distribution to elderly residents. As in the 1956 Scheme, relief given under this heading in particular cases was, in principle, to be non-recurring. All the Charity's giving was subject to a caveat in clause 42 of the Scheme that income should not be applied directly in relief of public funds, but only to supplement such relief – a distinction not always easy to make in practice. The trustees had already developed their own rules against making grants for building work or for vehicles, and there was also a strong presumption against grants to pay salaries, except as a 'pump-priming' exercise, and always on a year-to-year basis.

The first of the objects, still purely an aspiration, since the almshouses were as yet unbuilt, was the only radically new departure, but the third, explicitly sanctioning grants direct to schools and colleges, was also a significant advance. In keeping with the spirit of William Harding's original bequest, the principal beneficiaries – directly or indirectly – were still the young and the old, but there was now greater clarity and flexibility than hitherto about the ways in which assistance could be delivered.

In the Major League
The Charity in the Computer Age, 1978-2000

1.Getting Organised: Almshouses and Education, 1978-1990

The first meeting of the trustees held under the new Scheme of October 1978 took place in December of that year. The trustees, all but one of whom had been continued in office, were Fredrick Burch, Harold Crookes, Reginald Francis, Mrs Olive Paterson, Richard Pearce, as nominee of the Aylesbury Charter Trustees (successors to the recently defunct Aylesbury Borough Council), David Rimmer, representing the county council, Ernest (A.E.) Roblin, who was to be chairman from 1983 until his retirement in the year 2000, Dr George Townsend and Mrs Zena Williams.

The following six or seven years would see a succession of changes through death, resignation or completion of terms of office, and by March 1985, of the original nine, only Roblin, Williams and Pearce remained in post. Mr Burch died in 1979 and Mrs Paterson the following year. Their successors were Mr W.T. Philbey of Jowett's, ironmongers, the last of Aylesbury's old-fashioned town centre shops, and Mr R.A. Wyatt, a retired bank manager. Later newcomers included Mrs Gillian Miscampbell (1982), the county council's nominee, who became chairman of the County Education Committee in 1985 and was later chairman of the county council, and Mr G.B. Ravens (1985), a former county treasurer.

For the whole of the period covered by this chapter the trustees' principal underlying problem was more than ever that of spending the Charity's vastly increased, and steadily increasing, annual income as it accrued. With the help of expert advice, and in a share market that was generally favourable to long-term investment, the Charity's portfolio of investments had risen in value to £4.5 million by 1985, producing an annual return of £759,000.[1] By the late 1980s, despite its limited geographical scope, Harding's was being listed among the country's major charitable trusts, even if it remained a comparative minnow in this particular pool. From 1987 onwards the Charity's London brokers considered that their client's holdings justified a regular personal visit to Aylesbury in order to present a verbal annual report to the trustees, incorporating a wide-ranging survey of world financial trends and investment opportunities.

In these circumstances it is hardly surprising that spending – as well as sometimes fluctuating sharply from year to year (in 1982 grants totalled £51,000 and in 1985 £239,000) – lagged well behind income in most years, thus producing sizeable surpluses over extended periods. Such surpluses in turn generated additional income, thus in a sense compounding the problem. For surplus income could not legally be simply added to the Charity's permanent endowment, and nor could it be allowed to accumulate indefinitely without questions being asked by the Charity Commissioners.

Although small and medium-sized grants continued to be the rule, in order to spend up to, or near, their current income it was becoming increasingly necessary for the trustees to find a constant succession of major projects to fund which were both in conformity with the Scheme and at the same time did not contravene their own self-imposed rules – adopted at a time when income was much smaller – against grants for building expenses, for salaries (except in special circumstances and for limited periods) or for vehicles. This was not always an easy task.

Policy matters were much on the trustees' minds during 1980. In August there was a general discussion on financial policy and the view was expressed that some degree of planning of specific expenditure was desirable. It was felt that the trustees had contented themselves with a passive role, with the result that funds tended to be unevenly distributed. In particular, some schools made repeated applications while others never applied. To improve matters it was agreed that an annual budget based on an estimate of income over a five-year period should be attempted. It was also agreed to obtain reports on individual children applying for grants for private education. There seems to be no evidence that the five-year plan was in fact implemented, but Mr Wyatt produced a detailed budget in following years.

Earlier the same year, the more radical idea of commissioning a professional social survey to determine areas of need had been mooted by Dr Townsend, who had some professional experience in this field and was a strong advocate of positive action on the part of the trustees. An approach was made to the Department of Sociology at Bedford College, London, but the cost – estimated at £45,000 as well as expenses for secretarial assistance for some two years – was felt to be too high, and the trustees decided to rely on their own knowledge, and on the assistance of both the recently formed Aylesbury Association for Community Care and of other local organisations.

In retrospect it may have been a lost opportunity. Too much positive action of the kind envisaged by Dr Townsend might have had its dangers; nevertheless the trustees themselves lacked the leisure for sustained reflection on social priorities and an objective professional analysis could at least have helped to provide additional detailed criteria against which to measure proposals submitted. The information would surely have been useful to other local agencies also. By the time the decision was taken, in December 1980, Dr Townsend had already resigned. A stickler for correct procedure, he had taken exception on principle to the co-option of Mr Pearce while still a nominative trustee before he had resigned his nominative status, a manoeuvre which had been regarded as unexceptional earlier in the century. Over time, a number of standing orders and guidelines were evolved to ensure greater regularity, mainly in respect of more routine forms of giving, including the imposition of financial 'ceilings' on allowances for tools, etc., and the 'means testing' of parents seeking educational grants for their children.

One opening for positive action, for which specific provision had been made in the new Scheme, was that of providing almshouses for the elderly. But it was not until February 1980 that the trustees at last learned that several plots of land were available in St John's Street, Aylesbury, close to the town centre, which might suffice for some 12 or 13 almshouse units. Negotiations were begun, but some of the owners proved recalcitrant, with the result that the land was not finally acquired until early in 1982. In the interval the trustees belatedly realised, through the vigilance of Mr Pearce, that a piece of land near the so-called cattle creep off Wendover Road on the new Elm Farm residential estate was still in the Charity's ownership and could provide a site for 10 to 12 additional units.[2] The estimated reserves earmarked were £250,000 for the St John's Street project and £200,000 for the development of the land at Elm Farm. In the event both sites were developed simultaneously by the same contractor.

Encouraged by the provisions of the new Scheme, the number of applications for grants, large and small, being received from schools and other educational establishments was increasing from 1979 onwards. Owing to the rapid expansion of post-primary education in this period, there was a fairly constant demand from Aylesbury's six secondary schools, led by the Grammar School with the Girls' High School not far behind, as well as from the College of Further Education (now the Aylesbury College of Education), for additional specialised facilities of many kinds, ranging from swimming pools and tennis courts to units devoted to the teaching of music, art and science. Pressure of demand was such that some individual schools had to be discouraged from too frequent applications. Steps were also taken to ensure that applications (as well as grants) were channelled through the county council as local education authority, instead of being received direct as hitherto. This procedure helped to consolidate the close relationship with the LEA which came to be such a dominant feature of the Charity's activities in following years.

One of the most far-reaching influences on education – as on society generally – during the 1980s would prove to be the gradual dissemination of the new information technology. Some senior schools had already been experimenting with computers as early as the 1960s, but it was a long time before their full potential for education was fully appreciated. It is thus hardly surprising that an application from Aylesbury Grammar School in July 1980 for funding for some additional computers met with a refusal, the trustees considering that 'the College of Further Education was a more suitable place for tuition in computer work and that equipment ought to be concentrated there for those who intended to pursue a career in that discipline rather than installing it piece-meal in individual schools'.

Eighteen months later, in February 1982, with the backing of the LEA, the Grammar School tried again with a more ambitious request: a grant towards the provision of a 'computer centre', consisting of seven specialist rooms for computer skills, to be based at the school. 'Computers,' the trustees were informed, 'were becoming all pervasive in all aspects of teaching,' and skill in the science 'was vitally necessary for the country and its industry,' This time a grant of £60,000 (the final total seems to have been nearer £100,000) was approved, conditional on the centre's being open to all selective and secondary schools in Aylesbury. When the splendid new building was opened the following year it was described by *The Times* as providing 'the best computer facilities of any school in the United Kingdom'.[3]

The same year a substantial grant of £13,000 for computer equipment was made to the Girls' High School, again with the support of the chief education officer, and in April 1983 the College of Further Education was given £50,000 to fund the setting up of one of two 'word processor rooms', though in this case payment seems to have been deferred for several years. The trustees were told by the college that there was an increasing call for training on these machines.

Computers were in many ways an ideal subject for grants since they were still new and unproven enough to be considered as an 'add-on' in educational terms which the LEA had no clear obligation to provide. Thus they did not contravene clause 42 of the Charity's Scheme. In contrast, an application from the Grange School in May 1983 for £14,300 for a language laboratory was refused, the trustees being 'of opinion that the equipment should be provided by the County'. The other relevant characteristics of computers were expense and rapid obsolescence. They would soon come to occupy a large part of the Charity's grant budget.

Apart from grants to schools, throughout the whole of the period many medium-sized grants, often amounting to £5,000 or more, and in one or two cases to as high as £25,000, went to churches and to scout groups and other youth organisations, usually towards the cost of equipping new halls and headquarters. Large grants were also made from time to time to national organisations for their work in Aylesbury. In 1980, for example, the Abbeyfield (Aylesbury) housing association received £6,000 to assist in converting accommodation for elderly persons, and the British Red Cross £12,327 for their Aylesbury day centre, the trustees 'appreciating the services which the centre provided for old people'. Exceptionally, funding was provided for the salary of a temporary community worker for the Walton Court housing estate.

Numerous smaller grants were made to many individuals and groups for a great variety of purposes: hearing aids for partially deaf children (1979), a 'talking newspaper' for the blind (1980), special footwear and other aids, holidays and riding lessons for deprived or disabled children, equipment for young footballers and cricketers and help for youngsters planning expeditions under the Duke of Edinburgh's Award Scheme. Many playgroups and similar organisations were helped, often with sums of less than £100, in order to purchase toys and equipment such as climbing frames. The list could go on and on.

By June 1984 the new almshouses were almost ready for occupation and applications for tenancies and related matters were taking up much of the time of the monthly meetings. The occupants were to be accommodated free of charge, apart from a contribution towards the cost of heating and maintenance. Professional managers were engaged, whose charges became part of the regular annual administration costs, and after this the subject of the almshouses only occasionally recurs in the minutes. This approach was in contrast to the more 'hands-on' policy adopted by the trustees of Hickman's Charity, who had recently embarked on a programme of expanding their almshouses accommodation – converted as well as purpose-built – in the Old Town area of Aylesbury.

While the almshouses project was still dragging on, the trustees had decided, at the suggestion of Mr Pearce, that it would be a good idea to balance the Charity's portfolio of investments by the purchase out of accumulated income of some tenanted agricultural land locally if the opportunity offered. The result was the purchase in 1985 of some 75 acres of land fronting Tring Road and Broughton Lane, formerly part of Fowlers Farm, for £195,000, a price that reflected the potential development value of part of the property that was likely to be affected by the proposed Aylesbury southern bypass (a project so far unrealised). The Charity Commissioners raised no objection to the purchase, but they insisted that, as a permanent investment, it had to be financed out of the sale of an equivalent amount of the Charity's stocks and shares and not, as the trustees had envisaged, out of accumulated income.

As a direct result of the Commissioners' decision the trustees began looking urgently for 'some major projects which could be carried out for the benefit of the youth of the town in particular', with educational provision a priority, following the recent expenditure on almshouses. It was also noted that the limitation on the age of beneficiaries to under 25 had prevented some schemes being implemented. It was decided to seek the help of the county council's newly appointed chief education officer, Mr C.M. Garrett, who was invited to attend in May 1985 to discuss the matter. In response, Mr Garrett put forward three projects, two of which were approved, while a third was deferred for further consideration. Those approved were a grant of £100,000 for equipping a schools' technology (computer) centre for Aylesbury, with a further grant of £20,000 to cover staffing for one year only, and grants of £6,000 to purchase instruments for the existing Aylesbury Music Centre, a resource for the local schools, and between eight and nine thousand pounds to replace the grand piano at the High School.

In January 1985 a grant of £50,000 had been made towards the cost of the new Aylesbury Gallery in the county museum, which opened to the public in December. This was the first major grant of its kind. Designed to a high standard, the gallery was, for long, an important and popular part of the museum's repertoire.

Also in December 1985 a presentation took place to mark the retirement of Miss Margaret Dickins, senior partner in Parrott & Coales, who had acted as Clerk to both Harding's and Hickman's charities since 1940. She was succeeded by John Leggett of the same firm.

The year 1986 saw a major grant of £120,000 for equipping a new catering suite, for training purposes, at Aylesbury College. This had been the third of the chief education officer's proposals, deferred for further consideration. The new unit, now known as the William Harding Restaurant, was completed in October 1987 and has since become familiar to the many members of the public who enjoy the generally high standards of cuisine and service provided by the trainee staff at very moderate cost. Two years later a further sum of £49,000, for a 'computer suite' at the college, was paid on the strength of the grant made over five years previously.

The new schools' technology centre, to be known as the William Harding Technology Centre, was formally opened on 3 February 1987. In June 1988 an additional grant of over £21,000 was made to enable all the Aylesbury schools to be permanently linked to the Centre, as well as further grants designed to provide equipment for individual schools. Access to computers was thus made available to junior schools also.

Over the following five years expenditure on computer technology was such that the trustees found it expedient to make use of the services of an independent computer consultant, Mr Raymond Lawlor, a local teacher with a background in industry, to scrutinise bids for grants from individual schools and to advise and liaise on the re-use of redundant equipment to minimise waste.

Despite all this activity the amount of income unspent – reported in June 1987 to be £1.7 million, of which £1.3m. was still uncommitted – continued to grow. The trustees had on at least one occasion, in June 1986, expressed their frustration that the constraints of the Scheme made it difficult for them to spend income as it accrued and that Clause 42, which prohibited the funding of projects that were directly in relief of public funds, was often a deterrent to making grants for otherwise desirable objects.

Then in July 1987 the Charity Commissioners, who as recently as February 1984 had reminded the trustees that the Charity 'did not exist for the benefit of the inhabitants ... generally', threw them a potential lifeline by suggesting that the Scheme could be amended to embrace 'any charitable purpose for the general benefit of the inhabitants of the town of Aylesbury'. This proposal was thought to be 'very constructive', but there was to be a delay of over four years before it was embodied in a supplementary Scheme in November 1991, by which time the accumulated income was nearing £3 million. The trustees expressed themselves pleased to have the additional scope that the new Scheme conferred but 'anticipated that their main objects would remain to help the young and the elderly'.

Meanwhile, in 1988, a second capital project had been inaugurated by the acquisition of a small area of land in Mill Way, off Friarage Road, belonging to St Mary's Church of England School, as a site for almshouses at a cost of

40   *Walton Pond, Walton, by R.A.S. Carter. A winter scene showing the restored village pump in the foreground. Harding House is on the right.*

£73,733. The site had previously been rejected by Hickman's Charity, who were concerned about access to the town centre, but it was felt that the prospect of a new supermarket nearby and of a pedestrian bridge across the busy Friarage Road made the location acceptable. As part of the project some additional accommodation was provided at the existing site at St John's Road. The contract was eventually placed in January 1991 and the almshouses, now known as Duck End, were completed in 1992. Building and related costs were in the region of £250,000.

In July 1989 the impending introduction of the National Curriculum led to a fresh approach from the new chief education officer, Stephen Sharp, who saw it as the top priority for financial assistance for the immediate future. The new curriculum was, of course, primarily the responsibility of the LEA itself, but in a report to the trustees Mr Sharp urged that the best way for them to serve the children of Aylesbury was to start introducing the new curriculum in September instead of waiting until the 1990s. The trustees agreed, feeling that it was 'an opportunity for the Charity to do something of great significance for Aylesbury schools'. The upshot was an immediate allocation of over £314,000, of which £46,000 was later assigned to the six Aylesbury secondary schools so that each could purchase one piece of computer equipment; the rest was to be shared among the remaining schools. By the following May bids from schools totalling £210,000 had been approved. The total grant 'for National Curriculum development', paid in February 1993, came to £601,735.

Other matters which engaged the attention of the trustees in these years included the flood control scheme for Aylesbury, projected by the National Rivers Authority in 1989, which impinged on the Charity's estate at Broughton, sporadic negotiations with developers seeking to purchase options in anticipation of strategic planning decisions affecting the property, and the deteriorating state of 23 Walton Road, the founder's former home. The house, a listed building belonging to the county council, had previously been used by the social services department as an annexe to The Orchard, a former residential home for children with emotional problems, which was then occupied by squatters. The trustees contemplated purchasing the house but could not find an acceptable use for it and concluded that their aim should be to prod the county council into ensuring its preservation. This simple objective took a long time to achieve. In November 1990 the county council was reminded that the charity had donated, or agreed to donate, a total of nearly £800,000 for educational projects since 1987, and in April 1992 the trustees felt driven to take the drastic step of threatening to withhold all grants until something was done.

2. An Even Wider Mandate, 1991-2000

The new Scheme of November 1991 gave the trustees a much freer hand in disposing of the Charity's income and, although it is often difficult to be certain that a particular project would not have been eligible prior to its introduction, it was followed by a greatly increased volume and variety of giving. Coincidentally, the year 1992 also saw a big growth in the routine workload at the monthly meetings, arising from an increase in the number of applications for assistance, especially from students and young people. This phenomenon, the trustees noted, was 'illustrated dramatically' by the extent of the agenda for the October meeting which contained over 45 separate applications for new or revised grants – some 21 of them from individuals – taking up 16 closely typed pages of the minutes. Three reasons were suggested for the increase: greater local awareness of the Charity's existence, the current economic recession, and a lack of available funds for grants from the LEA. The response was to delegate decisions on the more straightforward applications to the chairman or another nominated trustee in association with the clerk, a system which seems to have worked well.

As we have seen, over the years many of these routine grants had, in any case, been the subject of standing orders. Recommended limits were also set, for example, for grants to sports clubs for additional equipment. Occasionally, as in this instance, the advice of the Charity Commissioners was sought before a standing order was made. In addition, clubs and societies applying for grants were expected to supply information about membership and financial resources. Finally, in 1995, somewhat late in the day, the important decision was taken that future grants to schools for information technology equipment would normally be limited to two-thirds of the estimated cost.

Further apparent evidence of financial hardship at this time is the number of persons applying for the annual distribution of £20 (soon to be increased to £25) made at Christmas 1991, amounting to 1,845, a total expense of £36,900. In September 1993 the trustees discussed the concerns expressed by the trustees of Hickman's Charity, who also provided an annual cash distribution, about the tendency among some applicants to regard it as a matter of right, subject to age and residence and not to need. As a result it was agreed in future to adopt an application form similar to the one devised by Hickman's and to allow only one gift to a married couple. After this there was a sharp drop in the number of applicants over the next few years.

Other than grants for education, the largest single grant made at this time was one of £100,000, approved in 1992, for equipping the splendid new art gallery planned for the county museum, which had been forced to close for urgent structural repairs in 1989. It was followed three years later by a further grant of £48,000 towards the now internationally famous Roald Dahl Children's Gallery. Both galleries were ready in time for the reopening of the museum in late 1995.

Sport, too, continued to share in the Charity's bounty. In 1994, after long consideration of the alternatives, a grant of £60,000 was made towards the cost of an all-weather sports pitch at a site off Turnfurlong, to serve three neighbouring schools, and a further grant of £10,000 was made to the Aylesbury Vale District Council in aid of a similar pitch off Meadowcroft. Also in 1994 a contribution of £50,000 was made for changing room facilities at the Stoke Mandeville stadium.

In March 1992 Mr Lawlor approved a further grant of more than £124,000 for the technology centre, but in his accompanying report he noted that, while primary and middle schools were making use of the facilities, other senior schools were not. The reasons adduced were the inconvenience of fitting in visits within school timetables and the wish to have facilities of their own. A re-launch was planned for September 1992. In November 1992 the trustees professed themselves unwilling to make further grants for the purchase of computers until details had been obtained of how surplus equipment from the technology centre was to be allocated and utilised. Conscious of the increasing cost of computers, they were not convinced that the education department had a definite policy to coordinate requirements and avoid duplication within the Aylesbury schools. As a result some bids were deferred. In November 1993 grants for information technology totalling nearly £355,000 were paid on behalf of 10 schools, of which £295,000 was distributed among the Grange (£116,716), the Grammar School (£88,459) and Mandeville and Quarrendon upper schools.

In late 1992 a third capital project was initiated when a suitable site for more almshouses was identified at Walton Road. Appropriately, it was located at Walton Lodge Lane (now William Harding Close) adjacent to the founder's former residence. It had previously formed part of the grounds of The Orchard children's home and was still in the ownership of the county council. Contracts were eventually exchanged in April 1995 but planning permission was conditional on an archaeological investigation. The trustees thus found themselves responsible for the cost, estimated at £32,000. The work was duly carried out by the county museum's archaeological unit, who uncovered prehistoric Bronze Age artefacts and other features of considerable importance for the early history of Walton.[4] Unfortunately, the detailed report still awaits publication. The almshouses, comprising 12 purpose-built two-bedroom flats in four linked blocks, were finally completed in 1996. They brought the total number of units, located on four separate sites, to thirty-five.

In September 1993 Mrs Miscampbell resigned and was replaced as county council representative by Mr D.C.T. (Crispian) Graves, currently serving as chairman of the county education committee. There had been three other new appointments since 1985. Mrs Freda Roberts, MBE, an energetic Yorkshirewoman with a long record of service in local government, was nominated by the Aylesbury Charter Trustees in 1988 in succession to A.A. Bayes. The Venerable John Morrison, archdeacon of Buckingham, a former vicar of Aylesbury, had replaced W.T. Philbey on the latter's death in 1989, becoming the second clergyman of this rank to hold office in the Charity's long history. The same year Mr B.M. Griffin, a farmer living at Bierton, had been co-opted in place of R.A. Wyatt, who had resigned after moving to the Isle of Wight.

In 1996 a grant of £165,000 was made to Aylesbury Grammar School, of which £120,000 was to complete conversion and refurbishing of the art suite, now to be known as the Design Centre, located in a recently acquired industrial unit within the adjoining Wynne-Jones Centre. The remainder was for art and ceramics equipment and for upgrading essential design technology equipment, as well as to fit out and equip a food technology area. No wonder that the school's historian, referring to its 18th-century benefactor, compared the Harding trustees' role to that of a latter-day Henry Phillips. These improvements were doubtless instrumental in assisting the school to attain technology college status the following year, a distinction held by only 150 schools in the UK.[5]

In 1997, after more than 10 years in existence, the future of the technology centre, now located at Quarrendon School, came into question when its continuing usefulness was queried in a discussion paper prepared by the county council's education department. Having spent more than £270,000 on it since it was first mooted in 1985, the trustees were reluctant to accept that the centre no longer had a useful role, even for children attending first schools, and offered to fund transport costs to and from the centre. It was soon clear, however, that the county council was experiencing a crisis of funding and was having to reorganise and 'downsize' its departments. Also threatened was the Queens Park Centre – where Youth Action still had its headquarters – whose premises were for a time in imminent danger of being sold by the council. Grants actually paid in the calendar year 1997 can be categorised as follows: tools, books, etc., for individual students, £13,107; cash grants to individual students, £20,390; travel grants for clubs and societies, £15,185; grants to youth clubs, £48,957; Aylesbury schools and educational establishments, £125,634; general grants and for relief in need, £118,307; alms to elderly poor (1,100 recipients), £30,250, making a total of £371,250.

The two single largest grants paid in this year were £48,000 for the Roald Dahl Gallery and £77,000, part of the grant for the new Design Centre in the Grammar School. Four other grants of £10,000 or above accounted between them for a further £60,000, the two largest being £20,000 to the Aylesbury Concert Band for instruments, music and uniforms, and £15,000 for furniture and fittings to the PACE Centre, an independent establishment for children with motor disorders, which had recently moved to a site adjacent to Haydon Abbey combined school. The proportion spent on education and schools this year (32 per cent) must surely have been considerably less than average for the decade.[6]

Among the major grants approved, but not paid out, in 1997 were a study support initiative in Aylesbury schools (first phase), £35,000; Broughton First School, library and computer equipment, £22,600; Sir Henry Floyd Grammar School, computer equipment, £40,000; Aylesbury High School, drama studio, £39,000; Walton Educational Trust, to furnish and equip William Harding House, £60,000. This last grant must have given the trustees special satisfaction. It enabled 23 Walton Road, the founder's old residence, now to be renamed in his honour, to be used as a branch of the Park School for children with learning difficulties. The restoration of the building itself, made possible by assistance from business sources in partnership with the county council, was completed during 1998. In the course of the works, timber framing dating from the mid-16th century was revealed behind the Georgian brick front – almost certainly part of William Harding's original dwelling.

In February 1998 a meeting was arranged with the county council's new director of education, David McGahey, who confirmed that, because of budget reductions, the £60,000 per annum needed to staff the technology centre would no longer be available. A more fundamental point was that technology in schools was changing as a result of new developments in communications. Arising out of this meeting, arrangements were made to ensure that equipment in the centre still in use would be distributed to Aylesbury first schools, the trustees having for some time been concerned that the less advantaged schools might be losing out. Another development was the proposed regular annual attendance of the director of education to review common concerns with the trustees.

In July 1998 Mr McGahey was again in attendance to announce the imminent launch of a new nationwide government initiative on the use of computers in schools, to be known as the National Grid for Learning. It was to be linked to the Internet, a new and crucial development since the 1980s. A grant of

£296,000 would, he said, give the Aylesbury schools a big advantage by enabling them to implement the scheme in the first year instead of having to spread it over four years. Once again the Charity was being asked to pay for the more speedy provision of a service which was being made available to all schools. It was envisaged that there would be links with the College of Further Education and the library service, and possibly with local business.

The 32 schools in Aylesbury town were, in fact, the first in the county to be networked for the new grid. By July 1999, when the director of education next put in an appearance, the grid was up and running and the trustees accepted 'that the National Grid for Learning had in effect replaced the Technology Centre which had originally been funded by the Charity so bricks and mortar had been replaced by electronic communication'. As an added bonus, the coordinators of the scheme took it on themselves to prepare the Charity's very own William Harding website. The trustees were duly appreciative but modestly declined to allow their individual photographs to be displayed on it.

Looking to the future, at the same meeting suggestions were put forward about areas for future submissions by the LEA in relation to local schools. They included tackling racial injustice, citizenship skills, Bucks achievement zones, environmental projects, social exclusion, music and 'support of innovative initiatives'. Some of these ideas were presumably fleshed out in the proposed 'strategic plan' submitted by Mr McGahey the following September, which met with approval, though the trustees were careful to insist that their overall discretion should not be curtailed.

The issues raised were largely a response to the introduction the previous year of official published 'league tables' grading the performance of individual schools throughout the country, which were also discussed with the director of education. At their March meeting the trustees had been concerned about the perceived poor performance of the Aylesbury primary schools which they found 'disappointing bearing in mind the considerable resources invested in Aylesbury Schools not only by the County but also by the Charity'. They recognised that there were underlying causes including areas of deprivation in the town, the existence of special needs and of children with English as a second language. An additional factor was the practice of parents choosing to send their children to schools outside their immediate catchment area in other parts of Aylesbury and surrounding villages, thereby distorting the general position.

These problems were, of course, far from being unique to Aylesbury. A concrete example of their effects had been supplied in July 1998 by Raymond Lawlor, the information technology consultant, reporting on one school where the number of children on the roll was less than half its capacity of 1,250; of these, 50 per cent fell within the category of Special Needs, of whom 20 per cent had English as a second language. To make matters worse, the computer equipment available was hopelessly out of date.

Other general points raised around this time were the questions of defining the town boundaries in the light of the general expansion of Aylesbury, and of the Charity's concern for special schools which were physically situated outside the Aylesbury area but were catering for significant numbers of Aylesbury children because appropriate schools did not exist within the town. A case in point was Furze Down School in Winslow. It was agreed that such schools should qualify for help from the Charity since, conversely, help had always been given to schools such as Aylesbury Grammar School, situated within the town, which had a high percentage of children from outside Aylesbury. This had long been the case, owing to the retention of selection in the county's schools.

In September 1999 the Charity Commissioners were once again querying the accumulation of surplus income, to which the trustees' response was that they had no specific policy to accumulate income, that major projects were under consideration, and that it was in any case unreasonable to look at the accounts on a year-by-year basis. They pointed out that there had in fact been an excess of expenditure over income the previous year. Despite the surplus, as a result of falling interest rates gross annual income had actually begun to decline the previous year and it continued to fall, from a peak of just over £700,000 in 1997, to £525,000 in 2000. What no one could have foreseen was that the millennium year would mark the end of an era of growth and stability in world markets, leaving the outlook for share capital generally much more uncertain.

Of potential importance for future planning was the clarification, obtained from the Charity Commissioners at this time, that the Charity's long-standing policy of not giving grants for building work was a decision of the trustees themselves, as were the restrictions on funding salaries and vehicles, and that none of these were prohibited by the Scheme. A further application to the Commissioners a few months later made it clear, however, that grants for medical equipment were definitely outside the Charity's remit.

One of the 'major projects' which the trustees had in mind at this time was a new purpose-built home for the Aylesbury Music Centre, an organisation which had been in existence since the mid-1980s, whose administrative headquarters were then located at Elmhurst First School and whose 900 pupils – members of 29 bands and orchestras – were having to practise out of hours, using the premises of Aylesbury High School under the direction of Mr Hugh Molloy. At their meeting in July 1999 the trustees had been informed by the director of education that a substantial grant from central government had unexpectedly become available, conditional on an equivalent contribution by the county council or some other local source.

Here was a different, and perhaps a more satisfactory, basis for funding than in the case of the two most recent joint ventures. The trustees' response was that they would be willing to commit significant funding to this 'exciting' project, but were concerned to ensure that the centre would reach out to all children and not just to those attending on Saturday mornings. Soon plans were in hand to build the new centre within the High School's grounds. When completed, in 2001, it had its own separate entrance from Walton Road. The Charity's contribution to the total cost, estimated at £662,000, was £200,000.

Among the other recipients of large grants in excess of £20,000 during 1999 and 2000 were schemes for providing employment for people with learning difficulties, channelled this time through the county council's social services department; the Jigsaw Theatre Company, for a disability awareness project; the church of the Good Shepherd, Southcourt, for refurbishing their hall; and Southcourt Baptist Church, to support community work in Southcourt and Walton. The largest single educational grant was one of £30,000, made in May 2000, to assist a bid for performing arts college status on the part of the Sir Henry Floyd Grammar School and a 'family' of seven other secondary, primary and special schools. It was part of a promised £200,000, to be paid over two years.

In July 2000 Mr Roblin gave notice of his intention to retire at the end of the year, after 30 years as a trustee and 19 as chairman. He was one of only two of those named in the 1978 Scheme still remaining in office, the other being Mrs Williams. Mr Griffin was elected chairman in his stead following a secret ballot. His place as a co-optative trustee was taken by Mr Michael Sheffield. The previous three years had seen other changes in the ranks. In October 1997 Mr W.J.Y. (Bill) Chapple had replaced Mr Graves as county council representative. The following January Mr Leslie Sheldon succeeded the Venerable John Morrison, who had resigned on becoming Archdeacon of Oxford, and in 1999 the double vacancy created by the death of Mr Robinson and the resignation of Mr Pearce was filled by means of another round of musical chairs, as a result of which Mrs Betty Foster, a newcomer, and Mrs Roberts became co-optative trustees, while Mr Chester Jones replaced Mrs Roberts as the nominee of the Aylesbury charter trustees.

At the December meeting it was agreed that, in recognition of Mr Roblin's services to the Charity, the new music centre should be given the name of the Roblin Hall (there already being a Harding Hall within the High School complex).

A few years earlier, in the midst of all the hectic activities of the 1990s, the trustees had found time to honour the Charity's founder by means of a plain and dignified commemorative plaque in slate in the parish church of St Mary's. It was a fitting tribute to the man who made it all possible, making good the neglect of the original trustees all those years before. It was dedicated at the annual civic service held on 13 October 1996. The inscription reads, 'In Memory of William Harding, 1643-1719, Yeoman of Walton, A great benefactor of Aylesbury.'

APPENDIX

Trustees of William Harding's Charity

This list was compiled mainly from the minute and account books, for the periods for which they survive. Other sources used include duplicate apprenticeship indentures (CBS CH/AG/3, 1850-95), annual returns to the Charity Commissioners (CBS AR124/83, 1908-42) and published local directories. Death in office, if known, is indicated by (d.) and resignation by (res.).

The Original Trustees Named
in the Founder's Will

William James . . . . (d.1754)
Noah Pitcher . . . . (d.1736?)
Thomas Watson . . . . (d.1736?)
Thomas Williams . . . . (d.1732)
Matthias Dagnall . . . . (d.1736)

Successor Trustees, to c.1776

Rev. John Dudley, D.D. 1732-45
Wilson Williams 1736-58
Matthias Dagnall, Jr . . . . 1736-73 (d.)
Benjamin Burroughs 1736-7
Arthur Hodskins 1737-8
Edward Price . . . . 1737-c.1774 (d.)
Thomas Sheen . . . . 1745-74 (d.)
John Wilkes 1754-c.1776
Archdale Williams . . . . 1758-66 (d.)
Thomas Towers . . . . 1766-73 (d.)

New Trustees Appointed by Chancery c.1776

Sir Francis Bernard, Bart. . . . . (d.1779)
William Minshull . . . . (d.1807)
Thomas Dagnall . . . . (d.1792)
Joseph Burnham . . . . (d.1799)
William Brooks . . . . (d.1780?)

Successor Trustees, to 1897

Rev. William Stockins . . . . . . [1794]-1827 (d.)
John Parker . . . . [1794]-1811 (d.)

Joseph Brooks . . . . [1794]-1798 (d.)
William Rickford (senior) . . . . 1798-1803 (d.)
Robert Dell . . . . 1799-1804 (d.)
Joseph Pitches . . . . 1803-8 (d.)
Peter Kennedy, M.D. . . . . 1805-7 (d.)
James Neale . . . . 1807-18 (res.)
William Rickford . . . . 1808-54 (d.)
Woodfield B. Eagles . . . . 1808-52 (d.)
Z.D. Hunt . . . . 1812-20 (d.)
Robert Dell 1819-33
John Churchill . . . . 1821-48 (res.)
Thomas Dell 1827-35
John Dell 1833-52
Thomas Fell 1835-65
Z.D. Hunt 1848-74
Moses Lovett . . . . 1852-[68]
Francis Hayward . . . . 1854-56 (res.)
Robert Dell . . . . 1856-[58]
Thomas Dell . . . . [1860]-63
Richard Rose . . . . [1860]-[81]
H.A. P. Cooper . . . . 1864-[88]
E.R. Baines 1867-78
Acton Tindal 1879-80
James Crouch . . . . 1869-[88]
Henry Watson 1875-88
Edward Terry . . . . 1881-1903 (d.)
Charles Henry Watson . . . . [1889]-[92]
Charles Hooper, M.D. . . . . . . 1883- 1905 (d.)
Charles E. Cobb . . . . 1890-1902 (res.)
G.A. Lepper . . . . 1895-1901 (d.)
W.B. Eagles . . . . 1892-[1912]

Trustees 1897-1955

From 1897 onwards, under the powers of the 1894 Local Government Act, the number of trustees was enlarged to include three representative trustees appointed by the Aylesbury Urban District Council, which was succeeded in 1917 by the Aylesbury Borough Council. Representative trustees were appointed for the life of the appointing council, but were eligible for reappointment and could also be (and often were) co-opted as permanent trustees before completing their terms. In this and following lists, only first appointments of representative trustees are indicated (where known).

Trustees 1956-76

Under the Charity Commission's new Scheme of January 1956 the Charity was to consist of nine trustees, two representative and seven co-optative. One of the representative trustees was to be appointed by Buckinghamshire County Council (BCC) and the other by Aylesbury Borough Council (ABC). County council representatives were to hold office until the appointment of a successor, which might be made at any time after the next ordinary day of retirement of county councillors after the appointment. Borough council representatives were to hold office for terms of three years, co-optative trustees for five years. The seven existing trustees, namely Rose, Palmer, Harris, Howard, Ivatts, Brown and Holland, were deemed to be the first seven co-optative trustees and were entitled to hold office for life.

Trustees 1978-2000

Under the Scheme introduced in October 1978 two 'nominative' trustees, appointed by Bucks Council and the Aylesbury Charter Trustees respectively, serve for four years, while seven co-optative trustees are appointed for terms of five years. Existing trustees were continued in office for periods ranging from two to five years.

Notes

Abbreviations:

BAS. . . . . . . Buckinghamshire Archaeological Society
BRS. . . . . . . Buckinghamshire Record Society
BSR. . . . . . . Buckinghamshire Sessions Records
CBS. . . . . . . Centre for Buckinghamshire Studies
        (formerly Buckinghamshire Record Office)
DNB . . . . . . Dictionary of National Biography
PRO . . . . . . Public Record Office
        (now the National Archives, Kew)
VCH . . . . . . Victoria History of the Counties
        of England: Buckinghamshire

Chapter One – Founder's Kin

1 MS volume in the Charity's possession. Unless stated, this list is the source of the information about property transactions etc. given in chapters 1-3.
2 M. Spufford (ed.), *The World of Rural Dissenters 1525-1725* (1995), pp.412-14.
3 A.C. Chibnall (ed.), *The Certificate of Musters for Buckinghamshire in 1522* (BRS, 1973).
4 CBS D/X 617/2, court roll, 1548.
5 Birmingham Central Library, Hampton (Pakington) MSS 503010; there is a microfilm copy in CBS.
6 *Ibid.*
7 Hereford and Worcester Record Office, 705:380, BA 2309/61 (v), 1560; 705:349, BA 5117/1 (xiv), 1569; 709:349, BA 3835/8 (i), *c.*1602. British Library, Dept of Manuscripts, Cotton, roll 1/14, 1627.
8 Bierton parish register, transcript in CBS. W.H. Rylands (ed.), 'Heralds' Visitation of Bucks in 1634', Harleian Soc., 1909, p.12.;VCH vol. ii, p.363; Robert Gibbs, *A History of Aylesbury* (1885), p.119.
9 H.A. Hanley, '"A Singular Commodity": The First Century of Bedford's Charity, Aylesbury,

1494-1597' in *Records of Buckinghamshire*, vol. 35 (1995 for 1993), pp.54-65.
10 CBS D/X 485, photocopy of 'parliamentary' survey of Walton, *c.*1650, f. 6; Hanley, *op.cit.*, p.58. VCH, vol. ii, p.343.
11 CBS D/X 1086, deed, 1571. Julian Cornwall, 'An Elizabethan Census', in *Records of Buckinghamshire*, vol.16 for 1959, pp.258-73.
12 CBS D/A/Wf/16/191.
13 CBS D97/3, 1604. This deed is included in H.R. Moulton's published sale catalogue for 1930.
14 CBS D/LE/17/2
15 John Wilson (ed.), *Buckinghamshire Contributions for Ireland, 1642 and Richard Grenville's Military Accounts 1642-1645* (BRS, 1983), p.83.
16 BAS Library Wyatt MSS, transcripts of PRO SP 28/150, Walton (E222-27).
17 CBS D/X 485.
18 E.K. Chambers, *Sir Henry Lee* (1936), p.254.
19 CBS D/X 1086, deed, 1571; VCH, vol. iii, 13.
20 G. Eland, *Papers From an Iron Chest* (1937), pp.44-5.

21 CBS D97/3; see also p.12

22 CBS D/LE/1/313.

23 Hanley, *op.cit.*

24 Wilson, *op.cit.*, pp.85-6.

25 CBS D97/3; D/X492.

26 George Lipscomb, *The History and Antiquities of the County of Buckingham* (4 vols, 1847), vol. ii, p.449.

27 PRO PROB 11/300.

28 Hartwell parish register in CBS.

29 BAS Library Gurney notebooks, GU/NB XIX, p.79v.; GU/F34. CBS D/LE/1/71. CBS catalogue of Lee MSS, passim.

30 VCH, vol. iii, p.363; CBS D/LE/17/2; John Bruce (ed.), *The Verney Papers* (Camden Soc., 1852), p.284.

31 BAS Library GU/XIX, p.80 (abstract of will; for further details of its contents see pp.16-17); C.G. Bonsey and J.G. Jenkins (eds), *Ship Money Papers and Richard Grenville's Note-Book* (BRS, 1965), pp.74-5.

32 VCH, vol. iv, p.532.

33 Bonsey and Jenkins, *op.cit.*, pp.74-5.

34 This paragraph and the previous one are based on Bonsey and Jenkins.

35 Joseph Foster, *Alumni Oxonienses, 1500-1714* (1968); his age at matriculation is given as eighteen.

36 Wilson, *op.cit.*, pp.85-6.

37 CBS D/LE/1/209. BAS Library GU/NB XIX, pp.80-1.

38 CBS D/LE/17/3; W5 (will of Thomas Jennings). Lipscomb, vol. ii, p.449.

39 CBS D138/22/3; D/LE/17/8; D/A/We/44/117 (will of Michael Jennings).

Chapter Two – William Harding (c.1643-1719)

1 PRO PROB 3/19/212.

2 CBS D/LE/17/3.

3 CBS D97/3.

4 CBS D/A/V/8, f. 22v., 23.

5 John Broad (ed.), *Buckinghamshire Dissent and Parish Life, 1669-1712* (BRS 1993), p.28.

6 CBS D/A/V/8/f. 22.

7 CBS D138/22/3 (1665); D/LE/17/9.

8 BAS Library GU/NB VIII, f. 230. CBS W5.

9 CBS D/LE/1/313; D/LE/17/9.

10 PRO C/5/610/127-8.

11 I.K. Ben Amos, *Adolescence and Youth in Early Modern England* (1994), p.40.

12 Ann Kussmaul, *The Autobiography of Joseph Mayett of Quainton (1783-1839)*, (BRS 1986) and her *Servants in Husbandry in Early Modern*

England (1981); CBS PR169/13/2/9; see also H. Hanley, 'Population Mobility in Buckinghamshire 1578-1583' in *Local Population Studies*, No 15, Autumn 1975, pp.33-9.

13 Anne Laurence, *Women in England, 1500-1760* (1994), p.36.

14 Parish registers and mother's will.

15 CBS MS Archd pprs Bucks b24 (Aylesbury Bishop's Transcripts, 1670); M31/D1254, Lee v. Edmunds, microfiche copy of case in the court of Arches, 1682; PR11/13/29/30-32 (parish apprenticeship papers); PR 11/12 (overseers' accts). *Bucks Sessions Records*, vol. i, p.257 and vol. iii, p.253.

16 BSR, vol. iii, p.20.

17 W.R. Mead, *Aylesbury Grammar School 1598-1998* (1998), p.10. Broad, *op.cit.*, p.xlii; Romney Sedgwick (ed.), *The History of Parliament: The House of Commons, 1715-1754* (1970), p.197.

18 This and the following paragraph are based on Jean Davis, *The Case of the Pretended Marriage* (1976).

19 Rylands, Heralds' Visitation, p.221. VCH, vol. iii, p.195.

20 CBS D97/3 (deed 1678, incomplete).

21 CBS D/PC/241/1.

22 BSR, vol. i, pp.343, 347, 362 and vol. ii, p.60.

23 CBS D/A/We/44/117. CBS Typed transcript of Stoke Mandeville Bishop's Transcripts of parish register in Office library.

24 CBS D/A/Wf/48/75.

25 CBS Ms Wills Peculiar 26/1/8.

26 CBS Ms Wills Peculiar 3/12 (A close stool is a commode).

27 CBS D/X 276/14; D97/3 (1706); see also PR16/25/1Q, account book of Bierton Feoffees Charity.

28 Broad, *op.cit.*, p.6; Michael Reed, *Buckinghamshire Probate Inventories, 1661-1714*, (BRS, 1988), pp.155-6.

29 CBS D97/3 (1713).

30 CBS D97/3; this deed is not included in the 1739 list of deeds.

Chapter Three – The Endowment

1 Probate copy in the possession of the trustees. There is also a transcript in the trustees' account and minute book, 1719-40, which is the principal source for this period.

2 Hartwell parish register.

3 Threshing accounts in Charity account and minute book.

4 George Lipscomb, *The History and Antiquities of the County of Buckingham* (4 vols, 1847), vol. ii., p.64.

5 H. Hanley, *The Prebendal House, Aylesbury* (1986), pp.36-8.

6 CBS PR11/13/29/30-32.

7 International Genealogical Index (IGI), microfiche edition, sub James. MS pedigree of Cockman by Mrs V. Pether in CBS library.

8 CBS D/LE/7/25, copy will of Mary Cockman; PR11/13/29/33 (apprenticeship indenture, 1713).

9 Arnold H.J. Baines, *The Signatories of the Orthodox Confession of 1679* (1960), p.13 (biographical note on Matthias Dagnall). Hanley, *op.cit.*, p.37. CBS D/X/1212 (private accounts of Sir Thomas Lee, 1736-49).

10 BSR, vol iii, pp.xxi-xxii and vol. vii, p.vii. CBS CH3/L/9. Robert Gibbs, *A History of Aylesbury* (1885), p.35.

11 BSR, vols i-vii, passim.

12 BSR, vol. i, pp.418, 458 and vol. ii, p.263.

13 Beatrice Saxon Snell (ed.), *The Minute Book of the Monthly Meeting of the Society of Friends for the Upperside of Buckinghamshire, 1669-1690* (BRS 1937), p.128.

14 PRO PROB 3/19/2/2. The accounts suggest that the total may be an underestimate.

15 BSR, vol. ii, p.356.

16 Oxfordshire Record Office Mss DD Par Banbury c.2; Mss Arch. Papers Oxon b.56, f.241. International Genealogical Index (microfiche edition), under Gurman/Jarman.

17 BSR, vol. vi, p.85; her name follows that of Anne Pettipher, also of Aylesbury, who makes a mark.

18 CBS D/X 1212, Jan. 1737. Printed in J.D. Hunt, *The Oxford Book of Garden Verse* (O.U.P., 1993); see also Roy Strong, *The Artist and the Garden* (2000), p.230.

19 BSR, vol. vii, pp.100, 116.

20 DNB. Two of his sons later sat as M.P.s for Aylesbury.

21 DNB. Francis North (1704-90), 7th Baron North; he was previously (1729-34) 3rd Baron Guilford. He was created 1st Earl of Guilford in 1752.

22 Gibbs, *op.cit.*, p.35; Venn, *Alumni Cantabrigienses*. CBS Q/PB/2 (MS poll book).

23 Gibbs, *op.cit.*, pp.606-7; Joyce Donald, *Long Crendon*, (1971), Part 1, pp.30-1; see also BSR, vol. VIII, p.37, with reference to a payment made to Burroughs in January 1732 for supplying water to the gaol.

24 Gibbs, *op.cit.*, pp.36, 392; CBS, typed index to Bucks Sun Fire policies to 1731; CBS D/BASM/5, catalogue of manorial records; copy calendar of Gutteridge-Lee MSS; CH12/E/2, survey of Bedford's Charity estate.

25 Gibbs, *op.cit.*, p.35. MS volume in the possession of the trustees of Bedford's Charity.

Chapter Four – Apprenticeship and the poor law

1 Joan Lane, *Apprenticeship in England, 1600-1914* (1996), p.1.

2 L.J. Ashford, *The History of the Borough of High Wycombe* (1960), pp.41-2.

3 K.D.M. Snell, *Annals of the Labouring Poor, Social Change and Agrarian England, 1660-1900* (1985).

4 BSR, vol. ii, p.170; John Broad and Richard Hoyle, *Bernwood* (1997), pp.102-3.

5 Snell, *op.cit.*, pp.278-9.

6 For an 18th-century example see Lane, *op.cit.*, p.249

7 M. Dorothy George, *London Life in the Eighteenth Century* (1962), p.224.

8 BSR, vol. v, p.40; introductions to vols v and vii.

9 *Bucks Charities Reports, 1832-33*; Lane, *op.cit.*, p.92.

10 BSR, vol. v, p.195. Lane, *op.cit.*, pp.90-1.

11 Lane, *op.cit.*, p.90; *Bucks Charities Reports, 1832-33*; CBS CH23/L/1.

12 *Bucks Charities Reports, 1832-33*, pp.900-1; John Broad (ed.), *Buckinghamshire Dissent and Parish Life, 1669-1712* (BRS 1993), p.187.

13 CBS PR11/13/29/1-39; PR11/14/7, 8, 13; BSR vol. ii, p.144; VCH, vol. ii, p.80.

14 CBS PR11/12/3. See also reference to Brill above.

15 Only post-1700 apprenticeships checked.

16 Nos 14, 26, 36, 39. Papermaking, being a 'new' trade, was not covered by the 1563 Act.

17 M. Dorothy George, *op.cit.*, pp.230-1.

18 G.F.R. Spenceley, 'The Origins of the English Pillow Lace Industry' in *Agricultural History Review*, vol. 21, part ii (1973), pp.81-93.

19 Ashford, *op.cit.*, pp 150-3; CBS PR11/12/3; VCH vol. ii, pp.78, 80.

20 Peter Clark and Lyn Murfin, *The History of Maidstone*, (1996), p.93; BSR, vol. v, p.92; CBS Q/SO/10.

21 CBS PR11/1/6.

22 John Broad, 'Parish Economies of Welfare' in *The Historical Journal*, 42, 4 (1999), pp.985-1006.

23 CBS CH3/L/2/9.

24 CBS PR11/13/29/42 (1803). Other post-1720 indentures in the series are not parish apprenticeships and one (no 40) is a Harding's indenture, the earliest original example found. Spot checks in the post-1756 overseers accounts proved negative.

Chapter Five – The Charity in Action

1 K.D.M. Snell, *Annals of the Labouring Poor ... 1660-1900* (1985), p.293.

2 Keith Wrightson, *Earthly Necessities* (2000), p.312.

3 H. Hanley, *Hickmans Charity: A Tercentenary History* (2000).

4 W.A. Pemberton, 'Some Notes on the Court of the Archdeaconry of Buckingham in the Eighteenth and Early Nineteenth Centuries', in *Records of Buckinghamshire*, vol. xxii (1980), pp.19-32.

5 Copy MS index to Sun Fire insurance records, 1714-31, in CBS Local Studies library.

6 *Bucks Sessions Records*, vol. iii, pp.275, 305. I am grateful to Barbara Willis for information on the Neale family.

7 See p.71.

8 Guy Crouch, 'The Building of County Hall' in *Records of Buckinghamshire*, vol. xii (1927), supplement, pp.i-xiv. See also N. Pevsner and E. Williamson, *The Buildings of England: Buckinghamshire* (1994) pp.153-4.

9 CBS D/A/We/66/186.

10 John Camp, *Aylesbury and the Ivatts, 1723-1973* (1973).

11 Information on Freeman, Brownson and Jennings (see also following paragraph), taken from London livery company records in the Guildhall Library, was kindly supplied by Mr John R. Millburn. For miscellaneous extracts from livery company records relating to Aylesbury apprentices, 1650-1744, including three involving Harding's (1732, 1738 and 1744), see *Bucks Ancestor*, vol. 10, no 2 (June 2001), pp.52-3.

12 Edward Legg, *The Clock & Watchmakers of Buckinghamshire*, (Bradwell Abbey Field Centre, 1976, booklet), p.26. A clock made by Neale was owned by George Bernard Shaw (*ibid*).

13 I.K. Ben Amos, *Adolescence and Youth in Early Modern England* (1994), pp.81, 92.

14 CBS D/X 1212/3 (Lee papers); Ms Wills Pec 26/3/31 (will of Susannah Nurton).

15 Joan Lane, *Apprenticeship in England, 1600-1914* (1996), p.121

16 W.G. Briggs, 'Records of an Apprenticeship Charity 1685-1753', in *Derbyshire Archaeological and Natural History Society Journal*, vol. lxiii (1953), pp.43-61.

17 This and the following paragraph are based on Ben Amos, *op.cit.*

18 Ben Amos, *op.cit.* p.130.

19 CBS PR11/13/80.

20 CBS PR169/13/2/8; *Bucks Charities Reports, 1832-33*, p.553.

21 John Skinner, 'A Demographic Crisis in Aylesbury 1742', in *Bulletin of the Society For the Social History of Medicine*, vol. 30.3 (June-December 1982), pp.44-6; CBS CH3/AM/1.

Chapter Six – Wilkes and Chancery

1 For biographical information on Wilkes in this and following paragraphs see H. Hanley, *The Prebendal House, Aylesbury* (1986), pp.40-3; Robert Gibbs, *A History of Aylesbury* (1885), chapter xxiv; Peter D.G. Thomas, *John Wilkes: A Friend to Liberty* (1996).

2 CBS D/X 463 (MS transcript of Wilkes-Dell correspondence), no. 23.

3 *Ibid*, nos.28, 45.

4 *Ibid*, no. 52.

5 See also Alan Dell, 'A Political Agent at Work in Eighteenth-Century Aylesbury' in *Records of Buckinghamshire*, vol. 30 (1988), pp.117-22.

6 Richard W. Davis, *Political Change and Continuity 1760-1885: A Buckinghamshire Study* (1972), p.21; Gibbs, *op.cit.*, p.223. Bribery on this scale was ended by the Aylesbury Election Act of 1804, which made it prohibitive by extending the boundaries of the parliamentary borough.

7 PRO C12/1027/2.

8 CBS Q/RPl/2/3/23.

9 CBS PR11/13/29/41 (Robert Bates); BSR, vol. v, p.40. Note in Aylesbury burial register, 1738.

10 Gibbs, *op.cit.*, p.232-3.

11 Thomas, *op.cit.*, p.114. Lloyd-Hart, *op.cit.* pp.51, 74-5.

12 PRO C12/368/4; C33/439,447; C12/232/1. Aylesbury burial register.

13 PRO C12/232/1; Hanley, *op.cit.*, pp.43-5; E. Stephens, *The Clerks of the Counties* (1961). Gibbs, *op.cit.*, p.36.

14 John Chenevix Trench and Pauline Fenley, 'The County Museum Buildings, Church Street, Aylesbury' in *Records of Buckinghamshire*, vol. 33 (1993 for 1991), p.23; W.A. Pemberton, 'Some Notes on the Court of the Archdeaconry of Buckingham ...', (1980); CBS D/BASM (catalogue of manorial records), *sub* Aylesbury; D114/94/1 (sale particulars, 1806).

15 CBS IR/1, IR/1A. See also chapter 8.

Chapter Seven – Rural Distress

1 VCH, vol. ii, p.86.

2 W.R. Mead, *Aylesbury Grammar School 1598-1998* (1998), pp.17-19; Robert Gibbs, *A History of Aylesbury* (1885), p.36; *Universal British Directory*, 1792, under Aylesbury (Parker, Brooks).

3 CBS PR11/13/29/40; CH23/AG/3 (duplicate indentures); Ian F.W. Beckett (ed.), *The Buckinghamshire Posse Comitatus 1798* (BRS, 1985), p.68.

4 *Bucks Charities Reports, 1832-33*, pp.593-5. PRO C12/232/1.

5 *Ibid*, p.595.

6 PRO C12/232/1; *Bucks Charities Reports, 1832-33*, pp.564-8.

7 *Bucks Charities Reports, 1832-33*, p.595.

8 K.D.M. Snell, *Annals of the Labouring Poor ... 1660-1900* (1985), p.257; Peter Clark, *British Clubs and Societies, 1580-1800* (2000), p.433.

9 Snell, *op.cit.*, pp.234-7. This trend must, however, owe something to an Act of 1768 which shortened the term of service of all apprentices by three years, to end for males at age twenty-one. (Joan Lane, *Apprenticeship in England, 1600-1914* (1996), p.5)

10 I.K. Ben Amos, *Adolescence and Youth in Early Modern England* (1994), pp.123-30.

11 E.P.Thompson, *The Making of the English Working Class* (1963), pp.576-7, 593.

12 L. Schwarz, *London in the Age of Industrialisation, 1700-1850* (1992), pp.231-40.

13 Presumably refers to elliptical carriage springs, a recent, major improvement to coach travel.

14 *Universal British Directory*, 1792, under Aylesbury (Pitches); Gibbs, *op.cit.*, p.250.

15 Alan Dell, *William Rickford, 1768-1854* (1986), p.2.

16 Gibbs, *op.cit.*, p.282.

17 Dell, *op.cit.*, p.2; R.W. Davis, *Political Change and Continuity* (1972), chapter 3.

18 CBS QS/Rd, MS return of charitable donations, 1812.

19 T.W. Faulkner, *Abstract of Returns of Charitable Donations for Poor Persons in the County of Bucks* (1820). There is a copy in CBS.

20 Gibbs, *op.cit.*, pp.624-5; CBS E/LB/11/1, log book of St John's School.

21 Davis, *op.cit.*, chapterss 3 and 4.

22 *Bucks Charities Reports, 1832-33*, pp.593-5. (The Bierton property is erroneously stated to be in the borough of Aylesbury.)

23 *Ibid*, p.603.

24 CBS CH23/AG/2.

25 CBS CH23/AG/5.

26 CBS CH23/FA/1-2, bank pass books, 1841-62; the account books are still in the possession of William Harding's trustees.

Chapter Eight – The Story of Elm Farm

1 M.E. Turner, 'The Cost of Parliamentary Enclosure in Buckinghamshire' (PhD thesis, University of Sheffield, 1973), pp.262-3, 275, 355.

2 CBS IR/9.

3 CBS IR/21A, Walton enclosure award and map.

4 CBS Q/RPl/2/1-53, land tax duplicate returns for Walton.

5 Gibbs, *op.cit.*, pp.384-5. *Bucks Charities Reports, 1832-33*, p.595.

6 CBS CH23/E/6. The parish rate books list Perrin as separate occupier of the old farmhouse in 1843 (PR11/11/55Q). Confusingly, Bryant's one-inch county map of 1825 shows a 'Walton Field Farm', but no farmstead in the appropriate position.

7 See also J.K. Fowler, *Recollections of Old Country Life* (1894), pp.145-9.

8 CBS CH23/E/8.

9 CBS CH23/E/4/5.

10 CBS PR11/11/74Q; CH23/E/7.

11 E.T. Mackrill, *The Aylesbury Charities* (1889).

12 CBS AR 124/83/box 2564, MS annual return to Charity Commissioners for 1935.

13 CBS AR35/2002, box 10, sale particulars, 1895; CH23/AG/7/1.

14 This and following paragraph are based on a draft minute book, 1897-1912, in the trustees' possession.

Chapter Nine – New Departures

1 Robert Gibbs, *A History of Aylesbury* (1885), p.49; Alan Dell, *William Rickford, 1768-1854* (1986), pp.18, 42. Other biographical details in following paragraphs are taken from Aylesbury directories.

2 Printed prospectus in CBS Local Studies Library.

3 Useful statistical information on the town's economy in this period can be found in David Thorpe, *Buckinghamshire in 1851* (BAS, 2002). See also his 'Aylesbury and High Wycombe in 1881' in *Records of Buckinghamshire*, vol. 41 (2001), pp.217-31.

4 The following analysis is based on the minute book, collated with the register of apprentices, which does not give occupations.

5 Buckinghamshire Family History Society (1998).

6 I am most grateful to Dr David Thorpe for supplying these statistics.

7 Accounts. *General Digest of Endowed Charities, Buckinghamshire* (1868).

8 Typed extracts, 1856-60, from missing minute book, in the trustees' possession.

9 W.R. Mead, *Aylesbury Grammar School 1598-1998* (1998), p.41.

10 DNB; Gibbs, *op.cit.*, p.643.

11 Gibbs, *op.cit.*, pp.624, 628-31; Ralph C. Hazell and others, *Hazells in Aylesbury 1867-1967* (1968), p.23. The workforce included many female employees, mostly employed in the bindery and as office staff.

12 CBS CH23/AG/4.

13 A copy is among the records in the trustees' possession. The Charity Commissioners' copies of annual returns for Bucks charities are in CBS (accession AR124/83), but those for Aylesbury prior to 1908 cannot now be traced.

14 Thorpe, 'Aylesbury and High Wycombe in 1881' in *Records of Buckinghamshire*, vol. 41 (2001), p.228.

15 Mead, *op.cit.*, p.44; VCH vol. iii, p.18. See also chapter 8.

Chapter Ten – The Town Hall Connection

1 Ralph C. Hazell and others, *Hazells in Aylesbury 1867-1967: A Scrapbook to commemorate the first 100 years at the Printing Works* (1968), p.4.

2 Ralph C. Hazell, *op.cit.*, p.23 and preface. The figures for Hazell's include many female workers employed in the bindery and in secretarial work.

3 Charles Arnold-Baker, *The Companion to British History* (1996); no source cited.

4 CBS (AR 124/83), Annual returns to the Charity Commissioners.

Chapter Eleven – The End of Apprenticeship

1 W.R. Mead, *Aylesbury Grammar School 1598-1998* (1998), pp.118-19.

2 *The Bucks Herald*, 19 May 1977.

Chapter Twelve – In the Major League

1 Figures in this and the following paragraph are taken from L. Herbert and M. Eastwood (eds.), *Guide to the Major Trusts* (1989).

2 Mr Pearce's acuteness in matters of local landownership was later to bring rich financial rewards to his home parish. See A. Dell and R. Pearce, *Stoke Mandeville* (1992), pp.4-5.

3 W.R. Mead, *Aylesbury Grammar School 1598-1998* (1998), p.120. AGS received a further grant for computers in 1993.

4 *Records of Buckinghamshire*, vol. 36 (1994), p.179.

5 Mead, *op.cit.*, pp.132-4.

6 Trustees' summary annual report for the year 1997. According to the Charity Commission's register of charities, the Charity's gross income for the same period was £700,376; total expenditure was £476,225.

Select Bibliography

(See also the notes to individual chapters)

Manuscripts

Held at Parrott & Coales, Solicitors, Clerks to the Trustees:
Minutes of meetings of the trustees for apprenticing children, 1720-40, 1794-
1852, 1930 to date; draft minutes, 1897-1912.
Accounts (including estate accounts, etc.), 1719-40, 1844 to date.
Registers of apprentices and their masters/mistresses, 1906-71.
Other miscellaneous papers, C20.

**In Centre for Buckinghamshire Studies (formerly Buckinghamshire
Record Office)**
CH 23. Deposited records of William Harding's Charity, comprising register
of apprentices, 1826-62; counterpart apprenticeship indentures, 1850-95
(52 bundles); estate papers, various, including draft and counterpart leases,
1838-1907; vouchers, 1859-89 (28 bundles); bank pass books, 1841-70; other
miscellaneous items, C19-C20.
Accession AR 124/83. Annual returns of accounts of Bucks charities to the
Charity Commissioners transferred from the Public Record Office. Boxes
4486, 2564, 4716 relate to William Harding's Charity, 1901-40.
PR11. Aylesbury parish records.
IR 20. Walton enclosure award and map, 1799-1800.

Published Works

General
Ben Amos, I. K., *Adolescence and Youth in Early Modern England* (1944)
Broad, John, 'Parish Economies of Welfare' in *The Historical Journal* vol. 42, 4
(1999)
George, M. Dorothy, *London Life in the Eighteenth century* (1962)
Kussmaul, Ann, *Servants in Husbandry* (1981)
Lane, Joan, *Apprenticeship in England, 1600-1914* (1996)
Laurence, Anne, *Women in England, 1500-1760* (1994)

Snell, K.D.M., *Annals of the Labouring Poor, Social Change and Agrarian England, 1660-1900* (1985)

Thomas, Peter D.G., *John Wilkes: A Friend to Liberty* (1996)

Local

Ashford, L.J., *The History of the Borough of High Wycombe* (1960)

Baines, Arnold H.J., *The Signatories of the Orthodox Confession of 1679* (booklet, 1960)

Broad, John (ed.), *Buckinghamshire Dissent and Parish Life 1669-1712* (Bucks Rec. Soc., 1993)

Buckinghamshire Sessions Records 1678-1733, vols i-viii, ed. William Le Hardy (Aylesbury, 1933-58, 1980, and n.d.)

Davis, R.W., *Political Change and Continuity 1760-1885: A Buckinghamshire Study* (1972)

Dell, Alan, *William Rickford, M.P. (1768-1854)* (Aylesbury, 1986)

Gibbs, Robert, *A History of Aylesbury* (Aylesbury, 1885)

Hanley, Hugh, *Thomas Hickman's Charity, Aylesbury: A Tercentenary History 1698-1998* (2000)

Hanley, Hugh, *The Prebendal, Aylesbury: A History* (1986)

Hanley, Hugh and Hunt Julian, *Aylesbury, A Pictorial History* (Phillimore, 1993)

Kussmaul, Ann, *The Autobiography of Joseph Mayett of Quainton (1783-1839)*, (Bucks Rec. Soc., 1986)

Lloyd Hart, V.E., *John Wilkes and the Foundling Hospital at Aylesbury 1759-1768* (1983)

Mackrill, Edward T., *The Aylesbury Charities* (Aylesbury, 1889)

Mead, W.R., *Aylesbury Grammar School 1598-1998: A Commemorative Volume* (1998)

Reed, Michael, *The Buckinghamshire Landscape* (1979)

Reports of the Commissioners for Enquiring Concerning Charities: Buckinghamshire (1832-33) (1 vol.)

Index

Compiled by Susan Vaughan

Page numbers in **bold** refer to illustrations. Places are in Buckinghamshire unless indicated otherwise. The following abbreviations have been used in this index: b. – born; d. – died; fl. – floruit; m. – married; **PL.** – Plate.